CO-BWX-754

EPONA

Book 1 Highlands Series

Ubuntu South Africa.

3 UMFANA PUBLISHERS

Copyright © by 3 Umfana Publishers

First Published 2019

All rights reserved

The characters and events portrayed in this book are fictitious. Any similarity to real persons, living or dead, is coincidental and not intended by the author.

No part of this book may be reproduced, or stored in a retrieval system, or transmitted in any form or by any means, electronic, mechanical, photocopying, recording, or otherwise, without express written permission of the publisher.

Cover design by: Bookcoverology

3Umfana Publishers
https://michelledaltonauthor.com/3-umfana-publishing/

To those who have lost their lives in the rampant violence terrorizing all South Africans.

Prologue

"Death is certain, life is not."

Sadie Munro found herself staring blindly at the small mausoleum; her family's final home. Her mom's words echoed through the empty hallways of her pain. Barely half a year before she'd had a family, a life filled with promise, laughter, and man who she thought had loved her.

Sadie fidgeted with the black wool cap covering her bright auburn tresses, then adjusted the large sunglasses hiding her face and blood shot eyes. She resisted the urge to rub her left leg despite the cutting pain. Selwyn, her father's best friend and their family solicitor, had brought her to the graveyard, the one located on a hill overlooking the lush green countryside of KwaZulu Natal, South Africa. It sat just outside her hometown of Pietermaritzburg.

"You need to say goodbye," he'd insisted.

But standing here looking at their tomb was like facing her judge and jury. It was her fault, if she hadn't…. This should have been her final resting place, not that of her beloved family.

Her eyes travelled over the names on the bronze, emblazoned epitaph.

Here lies
Stewart James Munro
Lindsay Levy Munro
Stephen James Munro

Sadie Victoria Munro
Beloved family, dearest friends.
Sadie reached out with her index finger and ran it across her name. The world was not supposed to know she'd survived. It read like a poorly written tragedy.

"It's safer that way," Selwyn whispered.

A shudder rippled over her skin. She shook her head as she refrained from clasping her hands over her ears. Silent voices from her nightmares begged and pleaded as flames crackled and horses screeched.

It's all in my mind, she reminded herself.

"Are you sure about this?" Selwyn asked laying a gloved hand on her back for comfort.

A head shorter than her five feet nine, he carried himself with dignity. Today, out of respect, he wore his Kippah.

He'd stood by her through it all. The hospital, the legal works, the rehabilitation, and … the funerals.

"Yes. I have nothing left here."

"I haven't heard from them since I called to let them know." He reminded her. "How do you know he'll accept you after he'd so easily turned his back on your father; his only son?"

Sadie looked at Selwyn. A guarded look edged his soft brown eyes, as though he knew something she didn't. But all that was overshadowed by the pain of their shared loss. It had carved the deep grooves into his forehead and left sharp grey lines around his lips.

She was responsible for so much pain.

If he knew the truth, he wouldn't be standing here supporting her, trying to fill the void of father and protector.

If he knew, he'd hate her as much as she hated herself.

"I have no choice, with Ob-Obaje." She swallowed the lump in her throat. "Still out there somewhere…like you said, it's safer this way," Sadie said as she lay her hand on the cold granite one last time.

She looked up at the stone-faced angel who sat protectively atop the grave of her family. Grief gnawed at the soft mucous membranes at the back of her throat.

It took all her will not to throw herself at the small mausoleum. Plead to the heavens to turn back time. She would give her life in return for theirs. Why had Death taken them when his sickle was meant for her neck?

Selwyn stepped forward and wrapped an arm around her shoulders.

"It wasn't your fault."

You don't know the whole truth.

Sadie pulled her jacket taut across her shoulders. Winter teased with signs of an early spring; green veld and pretty blossoms, but no warmth.

"My flight leaves in five hours. We must go."

She touched the stone one last time, turned, and limped back to the car. She wouldn't look back.

Chapter 1

"Oh, no, no, no, nooo! *Bliksem!*" Sadie wailed at her phone as she gripped the large thin steering wheel of her rental SUV.

Why hadn't she thought to charge the damn thing on the plane? She'd never been one for devices and social media, so it never dawned on her to plug the stupid thing in! The rectangular piece of technology flashed an empty red battery in the corner of its screen. Sadie tried to imprint the last of the directions to Munro Manor in her mind before the phone died. She pulled over to the shoulder of the narrow road, which was more dirt than tar, and stared at the electronic map before the device went blank.

She'd managed to rent the last car in the lot. Fergus's cars stood at the very far end of the tarred parking area outside Inverness airport, and while his shipping container, make-shift office screamed, *Dodge City*, Sadie had no other choice. Every other form of transport had already been rented or was on its way to some big auction in the very town she'd just driven through – Lairg.

The old Japanese sedan, which smelled like aged cheese and something Sadie tried not to imagine, had no place for her to plug in her phones charger.

"Damn it all to hell!" She slapped the dashboard.

"Okay, deep breath Sadie, you can do this.*"

It wasn't far to go. She was to continue straight for a few more kilometers, then turn right onto some nameless path, which should lead her straight to the gates of Munro Manor, her grandparents' estate. The only problem was the overpriced rental's blasted odometer no longer worked. Oh well, she'd have to judge the distance and make sure she didn't miss the turn-off.

Sadie scanned her surroundings. The scenery was spectacular. Thick forests of tall pines and other trees she didn't recognize, reminded her of the tales of long ago. The ones filled with adventure and the mischievous magical beings a person read of in epic tales.

Where there was no wood, the hills and valleys were awash with purple flowers. On the distant horizon, peaking over the tops of the pointed Christmas trees, the black smudge of a mountain range with snow-white tips loomed over the valley below. The sky was clear, and the sun shone warmly through the window, but the air carried a sharp chill that bit at her skin.

Sadie frowned at the dead device then turned her attention back onto the road. Her eyes burned, her vision blurred from more than fifteen hours of travel and three hours stopover in London before catching the small plane to Inverness.

Bitter irritation churned in her stomach as she pushed her foot down harder on the petrol pedal and slipped the gear into first. Her left foot slipped off the clutch and caused the sedan to spin its treads as she bolted down the narrow road. Her injured leg hadn't quite grasped the art of driving yet.

She leaned forward, hoping to make sure she wouldn't miss the turn to Munro Estate, when a blue blur flashed across the road and bolted into the forest on her right. Caught off guard, Sadie swerved and brought the car to a skidding halt.

Was that a ...?

No, impossible!

She was far more exhausted than she felt.

Sadie rubbed her eyes and rolled her window all the way down before she brought the car back onto the road. She entered a sharp bend, then peered into her review mirror and exhaled. Nothing. She was seeing things.

Her eyes caught a flash of something ahead. She turned her attention back to the road as a black Range Rover came hurtling toward her.

"Bliksem!"

She slammed her foot down on the brakes for a third time, pulled hard to the left. Something in the front wheels snapped with an almighty clang rendering the steering useless. Sadie found herself and the car bumping down the side of a ravine at lightning speed.

Her mouth opened but the scream jammed in her throat.

The car landed in the ditch with a hard thwack! A tooth-grating whine was followed by a deafening clunk. Her head bounced off her hands gripping the top of the steering wheel sending a thundering jolt down her neck and into her back.

Chapter 2

"Dear God, are you okay?" a deep voice called
from the hill above.

Sadie rubbed her forehead and neck with trembling
hands. The sound of grating gravel and crunching grass
told her the person was heading her way. Sadie stuck her
head out the window. The sun shone directly in her sight,
blinding her.

"I-I'm okay!" Her throat ached as she spoke. Her
fear induced muscles refused to relax.

Sadie's heart thumped against her chest bone.

A tall man came to stand beside the car. Shock and
confusion swam in a pair of dark bronze eyes. Thick dark
brows arched above them. They complemented sharp, even
features covered with neatly trimmed facial hair hugging
his lips, cheeks, and chin. Chocolate colored hair curled
past the collar of his brown suede jacket. Combined with
his white cotton shirt and jeans, he looked nothing like the
locals. Not that she'd seen many, but none of them dressed
like a mid-town yuppie.

"Are you okay?" He reached for the door handle.

The man sounded more British than Scottish.

It took a split second for Sadie to unlock the door,
fling it open, nearly slamming it into the tall man. She
clambered out, taking care not to let her left pant leg ride
up.

"Yes, I'll be fine, thank you." She took care placing
the open car door between him and herself before she
looked up.

Standing, she realized just how tall he was. At least
a head more than her.

"I'm sorry. I wasn't paying attention to the road,
and that bend can be treacherous on the best of days. Were
you heading to the Munros?"

Sadie considered him before she made up her mind
as to what she would say. "Um – Yes, Malcolm Munro. Do

you know him? Is that where you came from?" She hoped
he'd have a phone, so she could call her grandmother.

"Yes, I know him, and no, I was coming from my
estate. Our properties share this road. It's the only one that
leads to Lairg from here. My place is a little further on.
Saorsa land borders on Munro land. You here about
tomorrow's auction?"

His mesmerizing gaze swirled in amber, like dark,
raw honey.

"No um yes…um." She didn't like telling strangers
her business. "Look, do you have a phone?"

He nodded. "Yes, but I should probably drive you
there. It's the least I can do…."

He motioned with his hand to her broken-down
jalopy before he turned his gaze back on her.

"Have we met before?"

Sadie's frazzled instinct was not to trust him.

"I doubt it. Look I need to get a move on." She
made to get back into the wreck of a car.

Damn it all, she wouldn't get this piece of scrap out
of the ditch.

"You'll be going nowhere in that. Come on. It was
my fault you ended up in this hole. I'll take you to Munro
and get this…," he pointed to the car, "towed."

She had no other choice. There was no way she
would make it all the way to her grandparents' house on
foot, not with her leg, and certainly not with her luggage.
She had nowhere to go and no car to take her to nowhere.

'*Are you sure he'll accept you?*' Selwyn's warning
ran ice cold fingers down her spine.

"Blane. Blane Buchan."

The man held out his hand, pulling her from her
worried thoughts.

Sadie started at the sudden movement, then looked
him squarely in the eyes deciding it might be a good idea if
he knew she was related to Malcolm Munro. Less chance
of him trying anything untoward with her.

She clapped her hand into his and squeezed – just
as her father had taught her.

Blane's hand was twice the size of hers, and for a moment, his touch sent a spark of excitement up her arm and down her spine, igniting a fluttering through her stomach.

Sadie shook off the sensation. "Sadie Munro. My bag is in the back."

With that she pulled her hand from his and ducked back into the car to grab her backpack and keys.

"You're a Munro?"

Sadie heard the confusion in his voice as she reached across the seats for her bag.

She stood up and closed the door, "Yes." Was her short reply making it clear she would give him no more than that?

#

Blane stepped onto the road with her suitcase in his hand and turned to make sure she was managing. It was a steep incline and she seemed to move with difficulty. She climbed with effort, and it was not because of the slippery hill.

He'd recognized a familiarity in the woman's face, but her accent had thrown him. He was a little rattled when she'd introduced herself as a Munro, especially after what he'd heard in town. Perhaps she was a distant relative? No, she looked too much like the old laird to be too far removed from the bloodline.

"You need some help?" he called to her.

Her head snapped up and her eyes, greener than the moss-covered pebbles on the shore of the loch, cut straight through him.

"No. I'll be all right, thank you."

Oh, she was a Munro all right. As stubborn as Malcolm Munro, if not more so. Blane swallowed his curiosity and refrained from asking her where she fit in the Munro's family tree. Her curt answer earlier had made it clear she was not comfortable divulging any information about herself.

According to the gossip of the townsfolk, Munro's son and his entire family had been murdered. There'd been no mention of anyone surviving the heinous crime.

The tall, fire-haired beauty stepped onto the road, drawing his attention. Coherent thought fled his mind, including the reason he'd been speeding down the road earlier. Blane realized he was staring when she landed a piercing glare on him.

"Um… thirsty?" he asked.

Sadie nodded.

He found it hard to look away when the tip of her tongue ran along her pink lips. Blane opened the back door of the rover to load her suitcase and pull a bottle of chilled water from the small fridge he'd had installed.

"Thank you."

She took the bottle and leaned against his car as she drank.

Blane allowed his eyes to wander. She had ivory skin and long elegant fingers, which clasped the bottle as her lips hugged the rim. The image ran an electric thrill through his body.

She had a few freckles, sprinkled like an afterthought, over her nose and cheeks, and a faint scar, which receded into her hairline.

He averted his gaze when she screwed on the top and glanced at him. He saw, from the corner of his eye, her lips tighten and her cheeks pale as she leaned forward to rub her left leg.

"Are you sure you're okay?" He reached out to put a hand on her shoulder and pulled it back when she jumped away.

She looked up at him, her pallor hinting a soft pink.

"Sorry." He held both hands up in surrender to make sure she knew he meant no harm.

"It's been a long day." She handed him the empty bottle.

Their eyes met for a fleeting moment. It was hard not to notice how her pupils enlarged and the edges of her nostrils flared ever so slightly. A physical reaction he knew his own body mimicked as he stood pinned to the spot.

Sadie gave him a weak smile, then walked around to the passenger door.

Something inside Blane shifted.

The way her bold green eyes had pinned him where he'd stood beside the car, made him feel as though the Earth had momentarily frozen on its axis.

An old quote from Carl Jung, one Blane had last read in school, came to mind.

'*The meeting of two personalities is like the contact of two chemical substances: if there is any reaction, both are transformed.*'

Chapter 3

Once settled in the car and on their way to Munro estate, Sadie found her voice. "Where were you rushing off to?"

"Bloody hell, I forgot!"

Sadie watched as Blane grabbed for his phone in the back pocket of his pants, tapped the screen a few times with his thumb, all the while dividing his attention between the road and the screen, then brought the device to his ear.

"Could you please pull over?" Sadie asked and pointed to the phone in his hand. "Don't you have a handsfree?"

Blane gave her an impatient smile as he pulled to a slow stop and brought the phone to his ear.

"Mac, any trace? No, um meet me down at Glenmuir rock. Yes, I just had a small… detour to make. The chip still not working? Shite!" He placed the phone between his legs on the seat.

Sadie frowned. "Lost something?"

"A horse. An Andalusian Blue Roan as it turns out. The damnable beast has the blood of Hades riding in her veins, but I suppose it's to be expected after what the poor thing's been put through," he explained keeping his eyes glued to the road.

"What do you mean?" Sadie shifted in her seat and clenched her hands together.

"I happened on her a month back, when I was down in the Lake District. I found her fettered to a pole in a muddy encampment owned by a sodding drunken arse…"

Blane took a deep breath. "Pardon my language, but it angers me to think people can abuse creatures and get away with it. She was starved, her neck bloodied from pulling at the rope binding it. All it took was a bottle of cheap rum and a few hundred quid to make her mine. I hired a trainer to heal her, then bring her up here to Saorsa. But the poor thing spooked when they brought her out from the horse box and ran for the hills."

Well the man had a small heart.

"And the trainer?" She found herself asking when really, she was done with horses.

Blane huffed. "Well, he'd been paid and refused to have anything more to do with her. Said she was more trouble than she was worth."

Her finger nails cut in to her palms at Blane's words. She'd known trainers such as the one he mentioned. Only after prestige and money. He probably inflicted more harm than healing, Sadie suspected. Her stomach flipped. Was the blue flash she'd seen earlier the Roan? No, she didn't care, she couldn't, wouldn't, not ever again. Besides, all she'd seen was a blur. It was probably nothing.

Sadie pushed away the memories the man's sad equine tale stirred and focused instead on the trees and surrounding moors as they drove. She didn't want to remember, but neither could she ignore the smoldering embers of her greatest love — horses.

She'd inherited her father's gift with horses, but hers was far more potent. Her mother's nickname for her was Epona, after the Celtic Goddess of horses. The locals back home had their own name for her — *nomuntu ugwulumazuokhuluma namahashi* — the one who can speak to horses. They said she had the spirit of the horse inside of her. She could tame the wildest of the equines with only her voice, and a soft touch. Trainers from far and wide had come to *Leigheas Stud,* with their problem animals and always left satisfied.

But that was the past.

Pain lanced through her bludgeoned heart.

The ache of loss must have shown.

"Sure, you're alright? You're white as snow."

Sadie nodded. "Probably best to keep your eyes on the road. Like I said, it was a long flight." She didn't mean to sound as cold as she just had, but she also did not need some strange man's concern.

"From where?" he asked as he turned on to a smaller road.

"South Africa." She kept her gaze glued to the scenery beyond the front window.

"Oh."

Silence settled as a weird energy, like the rippling frazzle of static electricity riding one's skin, formed between them. The hair on the back of her neck rose, and her stomach bounced around like a ping pong ball. Nausea washed over her. There were too many odd feelings flooding her body at once.

Sadie tried hard not to care; not about the jalopy, the strange Englishman, nor his lost steed, but soon gave in. "You know, the more you chase after her the harder she'll run."

Blane said nothing but shot an inquisitive glance her way.

Sadie swallowed. "I grew up on a stud farm."

This man would lose the mare in these vast moors, and if they weren't careful, they'd drive it to injury or death. Idiots. They needed to track her. Gently follow the trail she'd left. She'd stop running soon enough. But no, it wasn't her problem. Horses were her past. Horses were the reason she'd lost everything.

#

A stud farm? Was she a granddaughter after all? There was definitely something out of place about this woman.

"So, what should I do?" He glanced across to her.

"You should hire a better trainer." A tone of absolute forlornness rode her words.

What was it with this woman? One moment she's concerned and giving advice and the next, all tight lipped and cold.

Blane maneuvered the car up and over the winding country road toward the Munro gates. He glanced at her and caught a glimpse of a broken darkness in her jade green eyes before he turned his attention back to the road.

He'd had some dealings with old man Munro. The old laird had given him much advice when he'd first bought Saorsa and they sat on the Town Council together. Malcolm Munro could be a right boorish fool and a force to be reckoned with, but he was a good man and a strong laird

– or had been until a few months back, when news of his son's death had reached them.

Malcolm and his elegant wife had aged a hundred years on that day, and the old Laird had been bedridden for weeks after. The entire Lairg had held their breath thinking it would be his end. But he'd survived, although he was a mere shell of the grumpy stubborn old boar he'd once been.

Was Sadie their granddaughter? The likeness was too close to discount it.

He swallowed the urge to ask, and instead dared another glance. The woman was tall, her features elegant, her posture regal. Why not tell him then? Then again what did it matter to him?

She was quite the beauty, but for the shadow hanging over her like a foreboding storm. Was it possible one of the grandchildren had survived?

It was strange to think of such blatant violence occurring in a country supposedly healing from its past, but then he didn't know much of the political situation there, and rarely believed half the news reports. He had firsthand experience of how underhanded and twisted journalists had become. Did Malcolm or his wife know Sadie had survived? Or was he right off the mark?

#

Sadie stared out of the window. Her eyes followed the land around her as it flattened out, then rolled up and dove down, rolled back up and rounded into a hill or sprouted into a dense forest.

It was hypnotizing and soon her thoughts began to play hopscotch. Memories jumped from the here back to the humid green countryside of Pietermaritzburg; to her time spent alone in a hospital room with only her solicitor as a visitor, back to… A bump in the road jolted the car and brought Sadie back to the now.

Why hadn't her Nan tried to make contact? Did they know? Or did they despise her for surviving and not their son? But Nan would never do that? Why then, and what was Selwyn hiding from her?

Ropes of fear tightened around her heart and pushed her diaphragm up into her throat. The air in the car became heavy. Her finger found the button and pushed down to open the window. She leaned forward and allowed the crisp breeze to pelt her face and suffuse her lungs with fresh Highland oxygen.

God, the beauty that surrounded them was magnificent! She'd loved the highland tales her Nana had so often regaled her and her brother, with his happy face bounced into her vision and tugged at the already taut chords entangling her heart.

The entrance to Munro Manor caught her attention. Two stone pillars stood guard, each brandishing a large black iron gate. On them, a large crest proclaimed this to be the lands of Munro. Butterflies fluttered in her stomach then proceeded to morph into a stampede of wildebeest.

The road continued to cut through the forest of pines, which intermittently gave way to open land, bedecked in purple flowers and shrubbery. The sharp smell of crushed pine needles rushed up Sadie's nose and her eyes watered. Everything about the place was so alive. The air so clean. The colors so vibrant. Even in the shaded areas, deep inside the forest where the sun's golden fingers fought to reach through the thick canopy, one could clearly make out the purples and whites of wildflowers.

Sadie scrunched her eyes and leaned further forward. It must be the shadows playing tricks. She could have sworn she'd seen… Was that Blane's mare? And who was sitting astride the majestic equine? Agh, she really was exhausted.

Nan's tales of magical 'wee folk' came back to her. Her tall stories of small people with wings and funny faces lurking and cavorting in the dense foliage brought a smile to Sadie's face.

"Are these purple flowers, Heather?"

"Yes, you've come at the best time of year. They cover the moors and crags, and anywhere their roots find soil." Blane explained.

The forest gave way a last time to the estate itself.

The car slowed as they drove up a hill. They reached the top and edged over the crest.

Sadie gasped at the grandeur spread out before her. A lake as large as a small ocean lay in the valley below. Its surface reflected the bowled blue heavens above. Sadie wondered if she stared long enough, might she see angels walking on its crystalline surface?

This was nothing like home.

A large, red stone mansion sat perched on its shores, surrounded by gardens, manicured to perfection. Bright green lawns were precision cut, well thought out flower beds hugging their edges. There was peace here, an ancient quiet that drifted like the soft mist over the water and through the trees, reaching out to embrace her mangled soul.

"That's Loch Shin," Blane pointed.

A range of emotions washed over Sadie as the car brought her closer to her grandparents' home. Her fingers ached as she dug them into the sides of the leather car seat.

Tyres crunched their way down the drive and came to stop at the front entrance of the grand dwelling, its stone a funny ochre shade, as though it had stood out in the rain too long and rusted. It was beyond anything Sadie could have imagined.

A powerful sense of home blossomed inside of Sadie. A knowing, so profound, burned the center of her fractured soul; she belonged here. Sadie allowed it to rise to the surface and mask her fears. The sensation comforted her and gave her the courage to open the car door.

She looked up as she stepped out. So many windows all dark and cold. They mirrored a sadness Sadie suspected might have taken residence when her father had turned his back on his birthright. That was a lifetime ago, and now, here she was, his daughter, his only remaining blood, standing on the very soil he'd shunned.

Sadie prayed she'd be allowed to call it home.

She limped toward the bottom step then faltered. *What if....* No, she was here now and there was no turning back.

She glanced back at Blane, his eyes so dark and so bright at the same time. Sadie swore they were the gateway to the universe.

"Well, thank you." She hesitated, her gaze dropping to her feet.

"Would you like me to wait?"

Sadie didn't answer immediately but nodded after a moment. Her mind and heart were drowning in uncertainty.

The cumbersome front door pulled open. From it, two black barking balls of fur came bounding toward Sadie.

The smaller of the two, skidded right into her. The larger cocker spaniel sat and stared up at her with large knowing eyes. Sadie knelt onto her good knee and rubbed their ears.

"Hello, you must be Prionnsa. Nan told us all about you." She turned to the small pup. "I haven't heard of you, but you look like you can be a handful."

Sadie took a deep breath and stood. Her efforts strained by the ache in her bad leg. She turned her face up. Staring back at her from the front door was the ashen face of her grandmother. Months of un-cried tears forced their way up Sadie's gullet, but refused to break their banks.

"Sadie?"

The broken voice of the old woman, grief and disbelief so evident on her beautiful aged face, tore what was left of Sadie's heart from her chest.

Her Nan had always looked the picture of perfection. Agnus Munro, aged better than most women, but standing there in the arch of the front door, the loss of her son and his family was carved into her very bones.

"Oh, my dear sweet lass. Yer alive!" Her sharp violet gaze bled into relief.

Her hands clasped over her mouth, the way someone would if they stood face-to-face with a ghost.

"Yes, Nan."

"Dear God lass! We were told you were dead!"

The older woman rushed down the steps and threw her arms around Sadie.

Her grandmother's tears soaked her shoulder. Sadie wrapped her arms around her Nan and breathed in the familiar scent of the Four-Seven-Eleven perfume. Memories of all the times Nan had visited, rushed back; the laughter and the joy. There were memories of Nan teaching Grace, their domestic worker, Mom, and herself how to make a 'decent' shortbread. The gifts from a faraway land, a place Sadie never expected to see on her own. The pain of remembering when life was good, and whole, snaked its way around her broken heart and squeezed.

Was this home?

Chapter 4

Movement drew Sadie's attention to the top of stairs. Her body stiffened as she looked up to see a man with a full head of gray hair, stubborn auburn streaks noticeable here and there, and a pair of eyes as cold as an arctic ocean, which were flooded in disbelief. But it was his face which caused her heart to stutter; the perfect likeness of her father, except that one side seemed to sag a little.

The lines of life had etched their way across his skin and bone.

Was this how Dad would've have aged had his life not been stolen? Regret scorched her throat and burned its way into her belly before gripping guilt's hand and settling in her center.

Sadie watched, intrigued as he focused that frozen glare on Blane.

"Thank you for bringing her."

Blane nodded then turned to Sadie who still clung to her grandmother.

"Will you be all right then?"

"Of course, she'll be all right, yer fool." Malcolm stepped onto the landing, outside the door, leaning heavily on his cane.

Sadie shot the old man a withering stare. This was not a good start. She looked back over her shoulder to Blane, who seemed unaffected by Malcolm's crude retort.

"Yes, thank you. Good luck with your, er... horse."

Blane nodded and walked to the back of his car to remove her luggage. He brought it to where she and her grandmother stood as her grandfather huffed and disappeared inside.

"Thank you, Mr. Buchan. Just ignore Malcolm This is a great shock to oor systems," Agnus Munro apologized.

"It's a pleasure, and dare I say, it's good to see some of his old feisty self, returned." Blane smiled.

Nervous flutters echoed across Sadie's chest and the tension of the day squeezed her stomach in to a tight knot. But it was Blane's smile which caused Sadie's knees to wobble. "Th-thank you again, Mr. Buchan."

"It was my pleasure. I'll call as soon as I have news on your car."

"Your car? How did you come to meet Mr. Buchan, lass?" Nan's voice quavered.

"It's a long story. One I'll share later." Sadie, interjected before Blane could answer.

"Well then, good day to you both." He lifted a hand before turning on his heel and walking back to his car.

Sadie sighed as Agnus curled her arm around her waist. She felt, rather than saw her grandmother smile, like a child who'd just eaten sugar.

As they watched Blane drive away Sadie dared to ask the question which had been burning a hole in her heart all these months.

"Why did you think I was dead, Nan? Is that why you never came?" Sadie pulled away and looked down at her Grandmother's face, which still wore a shocked grey pallor.

"Yer grandsire got a phone call. All he heard was that everyone had perished in some heinous attack. He dropped the phone and fell ill from the shock before he could hear out the full explanation of what had happened or even who had called with the news. I tried to call, but... We had no clue who else to contact… your phones… they were all… and the papers confirmed our worst fears, dear. It read that all of you were dead, killed by some…"

Of course, all Sadie belongings were destroyed in the fire that day.

"But why'd ye not call us then? Why leave it until now?" Nan cocked her head.

Sadie shrugged. How could she explain it was because she feared Nan would hate her for having survived when her father had not? Worse still, until today, she'd not had the guts to face her, not with the truth of what happened that day carefully tucked away in the deepest recesses of her very being. Truth was, she was afraid of being judge by her only family left on earth.

Nan's frown deepened when she avoided the question and asked one of her own instead.

"Did you only get the one call from Selwyn?"

"Was it Selwyn who called? Oh, aye. We heard no more after that. Only what we read in the papers Mrs. MacNelly, from the post office, found on her computer. Why would he not tell us you lived?" Nan's voice choked. So many questions, so few answers.

A cramp shot up Sadie's leg, reminding her of her exhaustion. Now was not the time to try and make sense of her grandparents' absence at the funeral or Selwyn's lie. Instead, she simply smiled and gave her grandmother one last hug.

"Later, okay Nan? I am here now. I… am I..."

"Yes lass, oh yes, ye are most welcome. This is your home now. Come on, let's get you settled and then you can meet your grandsire."

Nan clasped her hand tightly as they turned toward the door.

Sadie's stomach knotted at the mention of coming face-to-face with her grandfather, the man who'd pushed her father away when he'd dared to love her mother.

"Mr. Foggart," her grandmother called as she took Sadie's hand in her own.

A middle-aged man dressed in a neat, modern suit stepped through the door and onto the landing.

"Please, could you bring Ms. Munro's bags up to the Victorian room and call Mrs. Perkins on your way? I'd like her and Annie to do the bed up and get the bathroom supplied, thank you."

The man simply nodded, descended the stairs, and took Sadie's large suitcase and backpack before vanishing through the front door. Sadie wanted to protest, but Nan waved it off and lead her up the stairs and into the great house.

"This is not Leigheas Studdery, lass. Here I make sure there is work for the people in our small town. I know it's hard for you to see another do what ye can, but if ye didn't, they'd be sitting without a job, ye ken?"

Once inside, Sadie took a moment to admire her surroundings. She'd read of houses such as these, but never had she seen one, or thought she'd ever live in one either. The ceiling domed high above their heads where they stood in the spacious entrance hall. A rich red carpet, with a gold and black embroidered pattern, ran straight from the door to the staircase where a magnificently carved balustrade wound its way up to the second and third floors. Large paintings of stags and hounds, men in kilts, and men on horseback hung beside portraits of beautiful woman in centuries-old dresses. Sadie took these to be her ancestors, although, she was sure she'd stepped inside a museum.

On the first-floor landing was a bold, imposing stained-glass window. Its black and white panes came together and formed the picture of an eagle perched on a twisted branch with the words, 'Dread God' scrawled above it, and more odd language scrawled beneath. Probably Gaelic, Sadie decided. The declaration was as imposing as the one on the front gates.

Sadie stumbled forward. Her nan caught her as she tripped over the two cocker spaniels, which had not left Sadie's side and now stood pressed to her calves.

"Prionnsa, Donn! Mind oot the wey ye mangy mongrels." Nan's drawls sharpened as her voice took on its no-nonsense tone.

"Looks like you have two new fans," Agnus added then smiled.

The stairs were an effort, but once in her room, Sadie let go of the deep sigh she held since arriving. Nan pulled open the old cupboard and dresser drawers to air before Sadie's clothes were unpacked.

"Mrs. Perkins and Annie will be up shortly to freshen the room." Agnus drew open heavy velvet drapes and leaned into a large window that creaked and groaned before it gave to and swung open.

"We'll be in the library, dear. You meet us there. I'll have Annie bring some tea and a light snack." She tucked an errant strand behind her granddaughter's ear. "You must be exhausted." Then pulled Sadie back into her arms. "Oh, thanks to the heavens who had spared ye."

"Come on you two." Agnus called to the dogs. They didn't move. Prionnsa had glued himself to the foot of Sadie's bed, and Donn sat beside the bed on the floor, still too small to jump up.

"Leave them, Nan. They'll be okay."

#

Malcolm stared out his favorite window of the study. His heart beat like a Bodhran and his sight blurred with feelings he could not, dared not, name.

She looked so much like her father, except for her eyes. Those were her mother's.

Bitter memories of the fair-haired, green-eyed lass who had taken his son from him all those years ago surfaced. If she hadn't tempted Stewart with her fluttering lashes and promises of far off lands, he'd still be here today. He'd still be alive. If only Stewart hadn't been so hungry for adventure, fallen in love with the savage beauty of Africa, had just quieted down and listened to him, he'd still be alive!

He and Agnus had had so many arguments in the beginning. But with the birth of their first grandchild, a girl, the same one who'd risen from the dead and appeared at his front door this very day, Agnus had put down her foot. From then on, Agnus had visited twice a year — without him. It was hard to swallow one's pride; to admit you were wrong.

Footsteps behind him drew him out of his miserable thoughts and he turned to find his wife standing in the doorway. God, she was still a beauty.

"Oh Malcolm!" She strode up to him and wrapped him in her arms.

Agnus was his everything. She was as beautiful as the day he'd first laid eyes on her at the Edinburgh Military Tattoo. She'd stood there beside her parents in the prettiest blue frock, her nut-brown hair hanging loosely over her shoulders, her eyes bright as the morning star. Fifty years together was more than a lifetime. Half of them, filled with so much pain and regret.

"Can you believe it?" She leaned back, her violet eyes glistened with joyful tears.

Malcolm didn't answer. He didn't know what to say. Yes, he was relieved, happy, bordering on ecstatic but...

Agnus frowned then stepped back.

"Malcolm, you won't ruin this with yer stubborn ways, do ye hear me? Her mother is dead and buried." Her accent thickened with anger. "Dear God, the time for forgiveness is at hand. We've been given a gift, a chance at redemption, and still yer heart bleeds green and your stubborn mind is dead-set?" She turned her back on him.

Malcolm stepped toward his wife and placed his hand on her shoulders. It shook, his fingers curled as he forced the affected limb to tighten its grip. "She looks so much like him."

"Aye."

"Her eyes..." he began.

"Are Lindsay's, aye." She turned to face him. "She has so much of them both in her Malcolm. Please don't push her away."

Malcolm wanted to promise he would behave, but it would be hard to wash away half a lifetime of hurt, and near impossible to hide the anger and jealousy he harbored against his granddaughter's parents. Munro Manor was meant to be Stewart's. Instead, his son had run off with that woman and thrown his inheritance in Malcolm's face.

Granddaughter... He rolled the word over in his mind. He had never allowed himself to think of his runaway son's bairns as his grandchildren. Agnus was the one who would fly over to visit, bringing back albums of photographs. Pictures he'd never had the courage to view. Now, here his son's eldest was under his roof, their only heir, his blood.

She had survived and come here... home... to them.

Chapter 5

"Weel then, Ms. Munro. The bed is made, fresh towels an' soap are in the bathroom. There's a laundry basket beside the basin. I'll collect the washin evera mornin." Mrs. Perkins, the housekeeper, instructed.

"Please call me Sadie?"

The housekeeper pursed her lips and nodded stiffly.

"And honestly, if you could just show me where everything is, I could do it myself Mrs...."

"No such thing! Tis me job thank ye verra much."

Sadie smiled and stepped out of the older woman's way.

She judged the housekeeper to be around her mother's age. She had soft brown eyes and dark hair, run through with gray streaks here and there, tied up in a neat bun at the nape of her neck. Her dress was well worn, clean, and she had a colorful strawberry embroidered apron over it. Her nails were short, but neat and Sadie noticed, like her mother, Mrs. Perkins preferred orthotics.

Sadie waited for Mrs. Perkins to leave before she rinsed her face and freshened up, then made her way cautiously down the staircase, followed closely by the two dogs. The steps were broad, but her body was weak with exhaustion and her bad leg throbbed from overuse.

She hesitated when Mr. Foggart waited in the foyer to take her to the library, which was situated to the far left of the front entrance. She wasn't used to being surrounded by people who served other people all the time. Sure, they'd employed workers on the farm, but nothing like this.

Sadie didn't see her grandparents, standing arm in arm looking out the window at the loch. Instead, her attention was drawn to the vast shelves lined with hundreds, if not thousands, of books. Her eyes drank in the lush, multi colored spines. Some were bold and bright, and others wrinkled and cracked from use and time.

Who, she wondered, read all these books?

"Ah, there you are. All settled in?" Agnus motioned with a hand. "Come in my dear. Come and meet your Grandsire."

Sadie swallowed the anxiety pushing her diaphragm into her empty stomach and sending a wave of nausea washing over her.

Agnus walked up to Sadie, slipped an arm through hers, and lead her to Malcolm. She'd never thought of him as her grandfather. In her mind, he was Malcolm. The man who disliked her mother and who her father rarely spoke of. The old man's silvery blue eyes stared at her. They reminded Sadie of a spooked horse. His forehead wrinkled, and the corner of his mouth turned down.

Just like Dad.

There was a slight drop to the one side of his face. She hadn't imagined it when he'd stood at the front door on her arrival. It was slight, but it was there.

They stood a few moments in silence each recognizing the ghosts of the past in the other.

Malcolm vanquished the tension when he stuck out his hand to greet her. "Malcolm Munro. It's good ye came," then nervously tucked his hand back into his pocket.

Sadie, too shocked by his gesture, didn't reciprocate.

"Ahem, weel then, I take it the pair of ye have much catching up tae do. I have sheep tae tend for the morrow's auction."

"Make sure ye take Ghillie with ye," Agnus mentioned cautiously.

Malcolm frowned, then slapped his thighs, and called to his dogs. "Cummon ye wee fluff balls."

The two spaniels didn't move. Prionnsa raised his head and groaned, flashing sad brown eyes at his master.

"Och, stay behind then ye lazy gud fer nothins." he grumbled before knocking the end of his cane on the carpet and heading off.

Sadie stood frozen to the spot.

"Och, don't take the old fool to heart, my dear. I think he's just a little shaken, as are you? Well, that and his most loyal subjects," Agnus nodded toward the dogs, "have just abandoned him." She winked as a grin tugged at the corners of her mouth.

Sadie turned toward her grandmother. "He has so much of Dad in him. It… it hurts to look at him."

"Aye."

Nan patted her shoulder and nodded before leading Sadie to a corner of the large room.

Four high-backed chairs stood around a beautifully carved wooden table all facing a majestic stone fireplace.

"Come sit, dearie. I can see yer tired." Nan pointed to the table. On it sat a tray with tea and sandwiches.

Sadie nodded, and she flopped into the comfortable chair as her grandmother poured them each a steaming cup of Oolong. It was something they both loved.

"Here, you must be hungry?" Nan offered a plate with small wedged sandwiches on it.

Sadie shook her head.

"You look more like Stewart than you know. It hurts for him…us, to gaze at your pretty face too, my dear. That and your grandsire's regrets have finally come home to roost." Nan sipped her tea and turned her gaze out onto the Loch. "Gorgeous, is she not?" She nodded a head toward the large body of water.

Sadie followed her gaze and the pair stared out over the water. There was a certain serenity watching water, one which Sadie was coming to love more the longer she looked at it.

"I never did tell you."

"Tell me what, Nan?"

"That you share the gift." Her nan's voice wobbled ever so slightly.

"Gift?" Sadie turned from looking out over the loch to her nan.

"That special way you have with the animals. It's plain as day in the way the dogs turned ta ye. But yer grandsire buried his, a long time ago. Had to. In our day, it was not wise to share one's gifts with the world. And he was heir to the manor. There was no room for anything else. Yer Da never told you it was part of the reason he left?"

Sadie shook her head, "Why are you telling me this?"

"Oh," her nan sighed and wiped the corners of her mouth with a napkin before continuing, "So you could better understand the crabbit ole fool I suppose."

Sadie sipped her tea then said, "He told me never to be ashamed of it… my gift. I only ever thought it was because of mom… and so did she."

She watched Agnus for a reaction, but her grandmother was well versed in keeping a straight face while contemplating the best way to navigate difficult waters.

"Och, it's so long ago now and when I think back to it, so unnecessary too. But it was a number of reasons. One thing you will learn about your grandsire is that he is the definition of stubbornness. He also has a rigid view of how things should work; rigid and outdated." Agnus sipped her tea. "He found it so hard to accept your father's ideas and notions. The two were like the same ends of a magnet, always pushing away from one another." Agnus took another mouthful of tea and set her cup down on the table.

Sadie watched as memories slid past the old woman's gaze.

"Would they have ever made peace?"

Agnus shook her head.

"Yer father was close to giving in, letting go and moving forward, or so I thought when last I'd visited."

Sadie settled into a comfortable silence, turning her attention once again to the still surface of the waters beyond the window, as they finished their tea.

"Well then, I guess I should show you around. It's easy to get lost in this drafty old house," Nan said as she placed her cup and saucer back on to the tray and stood.

Sadie placed her cup on the tray, then stood. It took a moment for her to gain her balance, causing a frown to crease her grandmother's forehead.

"I'm tired, Nan. No need to worry." She assured, but couldn't look her nan in the eye for fear she might see the truth of how broken she truly was.

#

Damn the horse, damn the woman, and damn his wayward thoughts!

Blane poured a stiff whiskey from the crystal decanter on the table in his study. The mare was gone, nowhere to be found; the useless horse-tracking software had failed, dismally. But that, he thought, was the least of his issues. What bothered him was why he was unable to get Munro's green-eyed, flame-haired, granddaughter out of his head.

Blane downed his drink and sucked in air through his clenched teeth to sharpen the aftertaste. The cool air ignited the amber liquid, which burned all the way down his throat and into his stomach. He stared out the window, the setting sun reminding him of her hair; a sanguine gold.

The memory of her pulling away when he'd innocently reached out to steady her, poked at his pride. Had he come across so brutish? He was certain it was more than that. The dark sorrow in her gaze spoke volumes.

He poured another whiskey, took a sip, and recalled an article he'd seen in the papers not too long ago. Something about it niggled him. It had reported on the local Laird's son's demise. Strangely, the article had not mentioned any survivors. They must have gotten it wrong then.

Blane downed his second drink and sat behind his desk making sure to bring the decanter filled with whiskey along. His errant thoughts returned once again to the memory of Sadie Munro and her moss green gaze. Her pale pink lips…. For a moment, he allowed himself to wonder what they would taste like. He doubted he'd ever find out. He was certain that she hadn't liked him one bit.

Her fair skin wore a smattering of speckles. He'd never appreciated freckles before. The types of women he'd found attractive looked nothing like Sadie Munro, nor were they strong willed, in an unselfish sort of way. But that was then, back when he sat at the wheel of the Buchan family fortune. Back when his life had no meaning, and everyday revolved around what he wore, or drove, or where he ate, and who hung on his arm.

Things had changed since then. He had changed.

So, what was it about the woman that called to him like a flame called to a moth?

It wasn't simply her physical beauty that had tampered with his concentration all day. There was something else about her, something blatantly different, which had stoked the fires in his cool, bored soul.

Blane had a habit of surrounding himself with 'distressed princesses,' as his mother had put it. She'd often lectured him on his innate need to save stray puppies, birds with broken wings, bankrupt businesses, and prissy women with head problems.

Though he'd always been able to turn a bad business around, the same could never be said for the poor damsels.

That was why he'd bought this bankrupt estate and fled from London, his superficial, cut-throat business life, and Cybil. Blane released a heavy sigh then downed the last of his whiskey. That was as narrow escape as he'd ever had.

His mother's words trickled through his thoughts.

'Blane, darling. You don't always have to be the savior on a white stallion. Some people need to learn to sink or swim, or they'll always cling to you for support. And women who need saving all the time are emotional vampires. They will suck the life from you.'

But this was not the case with Sadie Munro. She was strong, in a broken sort of way.

Blane poured a last dram and pondered the morning's excitement. Was it her fierce desire to prove a point? He was unused to women who didn't need him. Or was it the darkness which hugged her like a soft woolen blanket, that attracted him?

Either way, Sadie Munro was an enigma, one he now realized he'd not easily solve.

Chapter 6

The soft, red duvet whooshed as Sadie sat down on the large four poster bed. The stress and anxiety of a long journey began to seep from her bones. Slowly the muscles in her back and neck relaxed.

She and Nan had spent most of the afternoon chatting, then enjoyed a light dinner, without Malcolm, in Nan's Solarium. Not once had either of them allowed the conversation to lean toward that day or why her grandparents hadn't attended the funeral?

Sadie was grateful for that. She'd had questions, but she'd neither the strength to ask nor to hear the answers. Perhaps some things were better left alone?

Sadie thought back to the tour through the large house. The kitchen, scullery, laundry, dining room, ballroom, three sitting rooms, and a room made entirely out of glass, which her nan called the solarium.

She sighed at the thought of how long it would take to clean a house this size. Back home, they'd employed workers in the house and stables, but her mother had not allowed her children to become complacent. Each of them had their own duties; keeping their bedrooms clean, dishes, laundry, not to mention working the farm and the stables. She smiled when she remembered her mother's words. 'A little elbow grease never hurt anyone.'

The few friends she'd had, had scoffed at her for not leaving home after school. But none of them had ever understood that Leigheas was more than her parents' home. It had been her sanctuary, the one place in the world she knew she belonged.

Sadie promptly pushed the memory away. It hurt to remember.

Instead, she shifted her thoughts toward her grandfather. It had been an emotional afternoon, meeting Malcolm James Stewart Munro. The old man had come across brusque and hesitant. They both reminded the other of what they'd lost. Would they warm toward one another in time?

And as thoughts do, her mind flowed from her grandfather to the strange, yet kind, Blane Buchan. How odd to meet a man who came across both tender and strong at the same time. Most guys, where she came from, were abrasive in their manner, and few enjoyed the company of women who claimed their independence.

She wondered what his story was. Was he really an Englishman with a heart of gold? A man who went around saving abused horses and stranded woman, after he'd driven them off the road of course.

A small ember warmed a long-forgotten corner of her heart when she remembered how he'd offered to stay and wait while she'd made her way to the front door, as though he'd sensed the uncertainty of the situation. Also, his offer to have her jalopy towed. She should contact him first thing in the morning about that.

Sadie pulled off her jacket and draped it over the foot of the bed, then flopped onto her back and savored the feel of the soft bedding beneath her stiff, aching flesh. Eyes closed, she let go and allowed every muscle in her anxiety-drenched body to slacken. A tidal wave of emotion washed over her. Something warm and wet rolled down her cheek. She touched a finger to it. A single tear and no more. Her shattered soul would not allow her absolution. No crying. No release — the guilty were not allowed forgiveness.

Taking a few deep breaths, she sat up and looked around. The lamp in the corner threw a soft, warm light across the large bedroom. To her left, a large window was draped with thick gold and red brocaded curtains, hanging from black steel rods with intricately shaped leaves on either end. At the foot of the large bed stood a comfortable couch covered in a similar red fabric as the curtains. Across from the bed was a grand fireplace, smaller than the one in the library, but as efficient at warming the room with its belly full of red-hot coals.

A door to the right of the large fireplace led to the bathroom. Sadie sniffed her jumper, then wrinkled her nose. Eeew! A long hot shower was what she needed. A shiver rode her skin from head to toe. Time to undress. Time to reveal her brokenness.

She reached to pull the boot from her damaged limb. She turned her head away. She wouldn't look at it, doubted she ever could. She rolled up her pants leg and removed the fake appendage, avoiding looking directly at that too.

A fresh wave of nausea roiled in her belly like squirming worms in a jar as the faux limb exposed what was left of her leg. If she couldn't stomach the sight of her stump, nobody could.

That's why he ran. That's why you will grow old alone. Her heart reminded her of the morning Darren, her ex-boyfriend and first real love, had stared at her leg. Disgust had spread across his face before he turned, without so much as a word, and walked out of her hospital room for good.

The smooth bottom of the surgically rounded stump ached for her to rub it, but Sadie couldn't. The mere thought of touching it threatened to push the meager contents of her stomach up through her throat and out her mouth. The doctors had decided the damage to her shattered lower leg was too extensive to reconstruct, and so they had amputated it just below her knee.

A soft knock on her bedroom door caused Sadie to start. Damn it all, she'd forgotten to lock the door!

Before she could answer, Agnus opened it up and stepped in.

"So sorry to bother you, my dear. But I forgot...." Her grandmother's eyes fell on the fake limb and then slowly dragged their way up to her bare stump.

Sadie waited for the horror to register on her grandmother's face before she turned and ran screaming from the room. Instead, Agnus closed the door and came to sit beside her. Her violet eyes burned with love as she took Sadie's hands into her own.

"We'll get through this together lass. I can't imagine the pain you've had to bear, but neither do I expect you to keep it to yerself. I can't... I won't force you to speak, but I am here when yer ready," and she pulled Sadie into her warm embrace.

If ever there was a time to cry it was now. Her grandmother's love and acceptance were the last thing she had expected and nothing she deserved.

Agnus let go. "Do you need help in the bath?"

Sadie shook her head. "Bath? I'll be fine." She saw the uncertainty in her grandmother's eyes. "I promise. If I need you I will call."

Agnus nodded, stood, and placed a kiss on her forehead. "Well then, I am sure yer exhausted. I hope you sleep well. Ye've had a long day, so sleep in on the morrow. I came to make certain the grate was placed well in front of the fire and the rug pulled away." She smiled and after making sure all was to her liking, she left.

Chapter 7

Agnus kept a tight-fisted grip on the pain and the panic running rampant within her heart as she made her way down the hall to her bedroom. Thank God, Malcolm was still downstairs. She shut the door and sank to the floor.

Oh, dear God above. What had happened to her family? Not once had she thought her granddaughter had suffered any injuries. Was that why it had taken six long months before she appeared here on their doorstep? She'd wanted so badly to explain their absence at the funeral; that at the time all she could think of was to remain by her ailing husband's sick bed, fearing she might lose him also. The urge to ask why Sadie had not called sooner had about burned a hole in her tongue. But her gut told her the answers would come in good time. Though she'd never expected this.

She'd tried to make sense of why no one knew Sadie had survived? Was there something else Sadie wasn't telling them? Slowly Agnus rose and walked over to her vanity. She wiped away any streaks her tears had left. A thought struck her. There was no way the girl would cope alone in that bathroom.

#

Sadie gathered what she needed and with some effort, hopped to the bathroom, which was modern, with a Victorian flare. The floor was covered in wood and the walls a golden creme color. The claw foot bath with its matching bronze taps complemented the décor. On the far side, another fireplace. Sadie shook her head. She had never ever seen a bathroom with a fireplace in it. She hated getting cold when bathing and the cozy fire was perfect. A loo sat in the far corner beside a large window with sandblasted panes.

Sadie judged the edges of the bath.

Crap!

It was definitely not built to accommodate her disability. As if by luck, Agnus voice came through the door. Sadie jumped, dropping her towels, cosmetics, and pajamas.

"Sadie, lass..."

She walked in holding a plastic stool and rubber mats in her hands. Sadie reached forward and grabbed the edge of the vanity for balance.

"I suspected the bathroom was not... well," she shrugged. "We'll sort it out first thing on the morrow." She held up her hand when Sadie made to argue. "It will be no trouble, my dear. Here, this should work for now." She walked over to the bath and placed a rubber mat inside and another on the floor with a foot stool on top. Then she bent down and collected the toiletries, towel, and clothes Sadie had dropped.

"Thanks, Nan." The absence of questions was as welcome as the practical help.

"Right then, here's a bell too. You ring it. I will wait in the bedroom and help you when you are ready to get in and out. The sound will travel better than your voice and I will leave a hot pot of chamomile tea beside your bed." Agnus squeezed her granddaughter's hand and left the bathroom.

#

Nan had been a lot of help. Though it was humbling to accept, Sadie knew it would have been an impossible task otherwise. It was harder still, to see the pain in Nan's eyes when she took in the full extent of Sadie's injuries. It hadn't only been her leg which had been marred in the attack.

After wriggling into her pajamas, Sadie pushed herself back, so her bum came to rest almost in the center of the large bed. Nan had pulled back the covers.

A dull itch annoyed toes that were no longer there. It irked her that the missing limb had the power to ghost her. More times than not she was sure it had all been a bad dream. She often felt the muscles of her amputated foot and calf stretch and ache; it was as real as the bed she sat in. But it was the pain that haunted her the most; the intense memory of her bones bursting open with every fall of the machete.

Sadie shuddered and willed the dark memory from her mind.

The occupational therapist had tried to convince her it would help to tie the bottom of the loose pant leg over her stump, to relieve the sensation of that annoying missing foot. Sadie refused. To do that would mean she accepted her damaged, broken self, the her that was no longer whole, strong, or able to ride.

Sadie reached for the steaming cup Nan had left on the table beside her bed. The chamomile tea's delicate flower essence seeped into her exhausted, aching muscles. It warmed her stomach and appeased her nerves. Balancing the pretty porcelain cup and saucer in her hand, she returned it to the table and switched off the light.

She wiggled down the mattress and pulled the covers up to her chin, careful of Prionnsa laying at her foot. Donn was snuggled into a fur ball on the floor beside her bed. The warm comfort of the cotton linen, and the fact she'd made it all this way on her own, filled her heart with a peace she hadn't known in a very long time. Her eyes followed the shadows cast by the warm glow of the fading coals in the furnace as they danced along the elaborate cornices of the ceiling. Before long she drifted off.

The roll of distant drums followed by a whinny tugged at her consciousness. Sadie sat up, ears pitched. Nothing… except the sound of the wind as it whispered through the trees. Was she dreaming? Prionnsa groaned, but Donn remained asleep on the floor.

Shaking her head at herself she lay back, tucked the soft thick bed-covers around her and snuggled into her pillow. Her lids grew heavy once more as she sailed away on the small pea-leaf boat to the land of Nod. This time, however, the sailing wasn't so smooth.

Screams of terror echoed through the air, and angry red flames licked the heavens. The bruised and bloodied faces of her family swam above her head. Their ghoulish pleas for release tore at her soul.

Sadie tried to run, to call for help, but she couldn't move.
The Devil's laughter echoed all around her.
Billowing black clouds of smoke morphed in to a foreboding figure lumbering toward her.
Wild, wide eyes pinned her down. A machete gripped in his claw, rose above his head. Her mouth opened. No sound came out. Her muscles ceased. The long, sharp, cane cutting blade sliced through the air on its way down....

Sadie awoke to a scream... her scream.

Sweat drenched bedclothes clung to her skin, the covers twisted around her body.

She dared not move. Where was she? This wasn't her bedroom. This wasn't her...

Prionnsa sat beside her head whining sorrowfully and Donn groaned where she stood on the floor, front paws leaning against the bed.

Memories rushed back and though her heart still thumped a panicked tattoo, her mind took hold of her current surroundings. She was no longer in Africa, and no longer in immediate danger. She was in Scotland, with her family.

She was safe... for now.

Prionnsa positioned himself on her lap, his big eyes searched hers.

"It's okay, boy." She shifted the furry lump off her, untangled the sheets, then sat up swinging her leg over the side of the bed.

Sadie reached for the tea cup, downed the last ice-cold sip, pushed her tangled, sweat-soaked tresses off her face and sighed deeply.

Would the dreams ever go away?

No, they were her penance, her debt to pay. If it weren't for her and her dead-set stubbornness... if she'd just for once listened to her father... perhaps....

An unexpected fuzzy sensation permeated her fear. It numbed her anxiety and washed away her regrets. Sadie closed her eyes.

Impossible!

It simply could not be. But her ears and a low moan from the dogs confirmed what she refused to acknowledge, the sound of hooves on damp soil.

It had been so long since she'd felt the presence of a horse. Could it be their neighbor's lost mare?

She was certain her grandparents owned no horses.

Was the Roan close by? Could she sense Sadie? Sadie stood, balanced on one leg, then hopped around the bed and over to the large bay window. She pulled the curtain away and peered out.

The crescent moon blanketed the area in her heavenly glow, it was bright enough to make out shadows and movements. It stroked the mirrored surface of the loch and the tips of the tall pines with soft silver fingertips. The view was breath taking.

Sadie fought with the window lever. The lock was jammed, so she pressed her nose against the glass and focused. She squinted into the darkness to see if she could spot the source of the galloping.

Nothing stirred.

Even the wind had gone to sleep.

"Must be my imagination," she whispered, trying to ignore her disappointment.

That part of her life was over. No more training and no more horses. She turned, leaving the curtains open to allow the sickle-shaped goddess a glimpse of her and hopped back to her bed.

Chapter 8

"Good morning my dear. Did you sleep well?"
Sadie peeled open her eyes to find her grandmother
standing, tray in hand, beside her bed.
"Morning Nan." She sat up, rubbed her hands
across her face, yawned, and then stretched.
"Here let me…" Sadie threw back the covers to
reach for the tray.
"Och no, sit back lass and enjoy."
Agnus placed the tray in the center of the bed and
sat down beside her. Her grandmother's eyes were bleak
with worry.
"Did I wake you?" Sadie knew Agnus must have
heard her call out for her parents and brother last night. The
house was vast, but it would not have dulled her nightmare
ridden screams.
Agnus stroked Sadie's cheek. "No, you know I am
a bit of a night owl. I was up reading when I heard you stir.
The moon was bright for a wee sliver." Agnus glanced
toward the open curtain.
"Yes, it was beautiful, and the lake was magic."
Sadie paused a moment. She had to know if it was her
mind playing tricks….
"What is it, lass?"
"Did… did you hear *it* last night?"
"Hear *it*? Do you mean the pines? Aye, I know. It
was like the first time I came to visit you." Agnus paused,
and Sadie watched as her grandmother swallowed her pain.
"The sounds at night were so verra different from here."
Sadie nodded. No need to mention something she
had clearly dreamed up. A low groan drew her attention
down to the floor beside her bed where Donn sat staring up
at her longingly. Prionnsa ever the well-mannered prince,
sat regally at the foot of her bed.
"Good morning girl." Sadie leaned over to pat the
spaniel on her head.

Agnus stood up. "Well, eat up now. Mr. Drummond and his lads will be here at noon to sort out the bathroom. I'll be in the solarium tending my orchids when you're done. I'd like to take you for a walk through the garden today, if you're up to it?"

"I'd love that, Nan," Sadie smiled as the old lady slipped out.

She peered at her wristwatch on the table beside her bed.

Good heavens, it was nine o'clock. Nan had let her sleep in.

A soft savory aroma tugged at her nose and reminded her of the tray Nan had brought in. Sadie smiled as her stomach gurgled in response.

Breakfast!

Sadie pulled the tray onto her lap and lifted the cloche.

Nan had remembered. Poached eggs and salmon, smothered in hollandaise sauce and fresh asparagus, her favorite. Yes, it was good to be… home. Home, safe and loved once more.

You don't deserve it.

The reminder stole her hunger and filled it with a berg of frozen guilt. Sadie looked down at the perfectly prepared plate of food. She knew if she didn't eat, Nan would worry. With some effort, she managed a bite, or two, then spotted Donn still sitting beside her bed. With care she divided the leftover breakfast onto her small toast plate handing Prionnsa one and Donn the other.

Sadie swung her leg over the edge of the bed and without looking at it, pulled the left pajama pants leg over her stump.

Prionnsa remained at the foot of the bed. Donn, the sweet happy pup, hadn't stopped licking the now sparkling breakfast plate Sadie had placed on the floor for her.

"Enjoy that, did you, gorgeous? It's thanks for the company last night." She stood and hopped toward the bathroom.

After a quick wash at the basin, she sat down to put on her prosthesis, then dressed. Jeans were her favorite; they were one of the few pairs of pants which sat neatly over her faux leg. A billabong t-shirt, jumper and trainers finished her simple yet comfortable ensemble. She tidied up and pulled her Bedding straight.

Nan had said she'd be in the solarium.

The passage outside her bedroom was long and wide, its walls adorned with more portraits of people she didn't know, and rugs. She smiled to herself. She had never seen a house where rugs were hung on a wall. The intricate carvings on the ceiling told of hours of delicate, painstaking work by many skilled hands. Goodness, but this house reminded her more of a work of art than a home.

A door down the far end to Sadie's left caught her eye. She couldn't say why, but something about it called to her. Without thinking, Sadie walked up to it.

Its wood panels were thick and dramatic, held together by large black iron bolts and filigree pewter, which enveloped the black iron handle and lock. It looked identical to every other door in the house. Yet something was different about this one. Different and alluring.

Sadie's palms began to sweat, and her blood rushed through her body, the sound echoing like the Augrabies Waterfalls in her ears. Why?

She put her hand on the lever and pushed down.

Prionnsa groaned.

"What's the matter boy? Have Nan and Malcolm got a skeleton hidden inside?"

It wasn't locked but had obviously not been used for a long time. The handle proved a bit sticky, as though it did not want to let her in. Sadie pushed. It moved an inch or so. Its hinges whined in warning and disuse, just as they did in those old scary movies where nothing good was to be found on the other side of a creaky old door.

She stepped back then leaned hard into the door and gave it a thorough shove using her shoulder as a ram. It flew open and Sadie stumbled across the threshold.

She was sucked back in time. Dust motes fluttered around like old moths. The bed was made, but not used; the curtains hung closed and limp. With only a sliver of overcast morning light to guide her, Sadie's gaze caught sight of the bedroom wall.

Her dad as a teenager, her dad as a plump little toddler, her dad on his first day of school. Dad. Dad. Dad. Trophies for rugby, horse riding, and other achievements stood dust-ridden on a shelf in the opposite corner. Panic washed over Sadie as the room burst into flames and the desperate screams of her father echoed in her ears.

Prionnsa jumped up against her legs, forcing her to stumble backward and out of the room, breaking the trance of horrid memories gripping her. The door followed, slamming shut as though to sternly confirm the dog's advice.

Sadie limp-trotted to the staircase. She leaned against the balustrade, panting as she wiped the sweat from her brow. What was she thinking snooping around like that? She couldn't face her grandmother like this.

Back in her bathroom she rinsed her face then caught her reflection in the mirror. Her green eyes shone like the morning star. Her dad had always said. What she saw in them now was not joy or love or even the zest for life, which had once bubbled like a boiling cauldron within her. Instead, she saw fear, regret, and heartbreak.

Sadie straightened, dried her hands, sucked in a deep breath, and released it. She blinked away the past and went to meet her grandmother.

\#

It was overcast outside, but the solarium seemed to find a way to drink in the sun's heat through the clouds. The warm environment kissed Sadie's cheeks and she decided that this room, besides the library, was her favorite.

Sadie turned her attention from the glass roof, back to the spectrum of nature's colors in all their exotic beauty.

"Your orchids look a thousand times more beautiful than the photo's you brought us." She made her way toward her grandmother.

Agnus nodded and smiled as she continued to primp and preen the exotic plants.

"Yes, my dear. Next to my roses, these are the blooms I most appreciate." Nan smiled proudly.

A sound at the door drew their attention.

"Ahem, weel you two, I'll be on me way then." Malcolm shuffled from foot to foot as he stood in all his tweed glory, just beyond the door.

"Yes, well off with you then, and good luck." Agnus came to stand beside Sadie who gave her grandfather a small wave of her hand.

There was something different in the old man's eyes today. She wasn't sure what, but it diminished the grave look he'd worn when she'd first met him.

"Yes, see you later then." With that, he turned and walked off, cane in hand.

"Who is that with him? And where's he going that he needs luck?" Sadie stepped back to peer through the glass panel. She watched as Malcolm slipped behind the driver's seat, another man, tall as sapling pine in the passenger seat beside him, before speeding away in the off-white and muddied English four-by-four.

"Is he allowed to drive?" the last question came out more of a whisper as she wondered if Malcolm was indeed recovered enough to handle the large vehicle.

"Och, ye can try to tell him otherwise. Poor Ghillie often slips from the front seat white as a sheet. Your grandsire goes nowhere without him," Nan explained. "It's the Lairg sheep auction today. Oh, forgive me, child, I didn't think… would you like to go?"

Sadie shook her head. The further away she was from crowds the better. She followed Agnus back to the long counter where all the orchids were kept and touched the edge of a bright blue bloom with the tip of her finger.

"Will your neighbor be there?" she asked not looking at Agnus.

"Oh, Mr. Buchan? Yes, I suppose he will. Why?"
Nan's eyes twinkled.

"I need to discuss the return of the rental car with
him. He mentioned he would have it towed. Has his family
been here as long as you... ours?" Sadie looked over to
where her grandmother stood.

Agnus smiled. "No. That land has been laying there
doing nothing since old man Ross passed, oh, some ten odd
years ago."

Sadie walked around the bench to where her nan
stood fidgeting with a plant and sat down on the tall chair
beside her.

"Didn't he have any children, this Mr. Ross?" Sadie
asked.

"Oh, yes, he had a whole brood of bairns. But none
who were willing tae move back from the big cities and
leave their fancy lives behind." Agnus darted her a look,
then carefully removed a withering flower from one of her
beloved plants.

"Mr. Buchan is a Scot by birth, but raised in
Sassain... England, my dear." She added for Sadie. "He
bought the land just over two years ago. Talk around toon
is..."

Sadie smiled. She loved it when her Nan let her
accent slip. To her, the Scots lilt always sounded so warm
and homely. Her father had worked very hard at not
sounding Scots. By the time Sadie was a teenager, he
sounded like an English-speaking Natal boy, but for his
hair. Ginger was as rare to the region as a White Rhino was
to the wild.

A sharp pain jabbed at the inside of her chest, her
mind flickered back to the room upstairs. Sadie pulled
away from the memory and back to the conversation with
her grandmother, who stood staring at her.

"Lass, it's all right tae think on them every so
often." Agnus' eyes were warm and filled with so much
love, but when Sadie looked closely, she could make out
the heartbreak framing them.

Nan returned to her flowers and the conversation as though nothing was out of place.

"Like I said, the talk about toon is that our Mr. Buchan is a very wealthy man who lost his love for the fast pace of city life."

"Oh, so … what does he know about sheep then?"

"Och, not so verra much. He spent a wee bit o time bothering yer grandsire for assistance, and then managed to snag a decent manager who kens sheep. It's a good thing he came. His ambitions have breathed new life into Lairg. Oh, the sheep farming was doing okay, but the town and its people need more than that. Besides, the farmers are a dying breed, and this fancy man from London kens how to attract the younger generation. He's working on something called Eco-farming. He wants Edinburgh University to come up here and do research on how farmers and the natural environment can co-exist." She smiled then turned and fiddled with some implements on a table behind her. "Since Mr. Buchan took up the reigns on the town council and hired staff to man his property, things have been moving along quite fine."

Agnus sprayed her orchids with water then stood back and admired her plants. "Time for some tea?"

Sadie nodded.

"While he seems to have the Midas touch when it comes to business I've heard it does not extend to his luck with the lassies," Agnus dropped the comment before making her way to the door to summon whoever it was she summoned to bring the tea.

"He's a player." Sadie scoffed as she followed her Nan.

"Och no, but as the gossips around these parts have it, he left a fiancé back in London."

"So, he's engaged?" Sadie surprised herself, not expecting the pang of regret at the news?

"Och, no, they say he left her two weeks a'fore they were to wed."

Sadie wanted to ask why but swallowed her curiosity. It had nothing to do with her. She didn't want to care. Besides, no man would ever come near her. He'd turn and run just as Darren had the moment he saw her brokenness. The fact Blane had dumped his fiancé at the alter two weeks before the wedding spoke volumes. But, why act so chivalrous after he'd run her off the road? Why move to Lairg?

Ugh, whatever.

Men!

Sadie doubted she'd ever understand them.

They sat down at a table in the far corner of the solarium. Sadie turned her face up. She closed her eyes and enjoyed the warmth hugging her while Agnus poured their tea.

"There's a town meet tomorrow night to discuss some plans Mr. Buchan has in mind for our wee community's growth. As your grandsire is a Laird and sits on the council, we'll have to go. It will do you good to get out, and I'd like to introduce you to some of our friends?"

Sadie lowered her head, her sight a little fuzzy before she focused on Nan, who handed her a cup of tea. She sipped, then sighed. "I don't think that's a good idea."

Agnus sipped her own tea and smiled. It was a smile that told Sadie this wasn't a request. The same one that had made her dad squirm so often.

"Och, my dear dinnae fash noo."

The deep accent enforced the message that Sadie had no choice.

"Nan, I am no good in crowds and…"

"And you will be just fine, lass. You can't stay cooped up here like Rapunzel in her tower."

Sadie realized she would not get out of this. "Okay, but I'm not the social butterfly you remember." Sadie sipped her tea, careful not to spill as her grip trembled.

Since the attack, she avoided crowds as much as she could, another plus point to living in the Scottish Highlands. She'd just have to make sure she remained in the shadows unseen from the public eye and cameras.

Especially the cameras!

"Wonderful. It's nothing fancy, I'm sure you have a decent pair of slacks and … shoes?"

"Yes," Sadie grimaced, but Nan appeared not to notice.

It was good to be here. Safely tucked away from the world. And while Sadie felt uneasy about meeting the town, it was the sense that everything was too good to be true, which caused her soul to fret and her instincts to shudder with apprehension.

Chapter 9

"Still no sign of the mare?" Blane called to his farm
manager as he walked toward his car.

Kenneth Mackenzie, whose face reminded Blane of
a well-worn leather shoe, shook his head.

"Naw sorra Mr. Buchan. That beastie could be half
way ta Ben More by noo, that's if tha brownies aven't ad
her fur dinner," his raspy chuckle clear evidence of too
many cigarettes.

Blane shook his head. Mac was a great farm
manager, and he had an odd sense of humor. This was not a
situation Blane felt warranted humor. He hated that a
scared, hurt animal was lost in the woods to starve and die
alone. What was worse, it happened on his watch. It was
more his fault than anyone else's. His heart ached. His only
intention with the mare, ever, was to heal her, and give her
a large paddock to roam in for the rest of her days.

Blane huffed, and rubbed his fingers through his
beard as he tried to clear his head. There was nothing they
could do for the poor animal anymore. Best to get on with
things.

"Och by the way and if ye dinna mind me asking,
did ye manage tae get the Munro lass's rental sorted wi ole
Fergus?"

Blane tapped his jacket pocket. "Yes. That tip about
threatening to tell his wife of his betting habits down at the
pub did the trick. Thank you, Mac."

Mac shook his head. "Aye that's braw then, Mr.
Buchan. I'll see ye doon at the auction." He winked as he
turned and walked away.

Blane got in behind the wheel of his Rover. He
wondered if Sadie would attend the auction. A warm
sensation stirred in his chest at the thought of seeing her.
She'd be a ray of light in the dank commotion his day was
heading toward.

He peered up at the heavy, grey clouds through the
front windscreen. It was destined to be a long, muddy day.
The sky had just offloaded gallons of water and everything

was soaked. Thankfully the sheep had been herded to the showgrounds just outside of town earlier that week.

Blane started the engine and sighed when his phone rang. Cybil's name flashed on the screen. He was loath to answer it. His fingers wrapped around the hand-stitched leather of the steering wheel and squeezed.

Cybil, it seemed, had neither accepted the end of their relationship, nor the fact he'd resigned as head of the company.

He would call his younger brother, Michael. She needed a distraction and Michael, who'd been running things since he'd left on his sabbatical, always had a soft spot for Cybil. Now he thought on it, they'd make the perfect London couple.

He'd known the moment he'd proposed that he would live to regret it. But in his defense, it was in the thralls of passion. An alcohol fueled lust would tamper with any sane man's common logic. If anything, Cybil was a tigress in the bedroom. Her skills on how to please, were unlike anything he'd ever enjoyed. But he'd soon tired of it, and her nagging, not to mention her constant demands. She was as shallow as the puddle which had collected overnight at his front door.

An SMS, popped up on his phone's screen – *We need to chat, Darling!*

An odd sensation wrapped itself around his chest as though someone had strapped a ratchet tie around his ribs and was pulling it taut. He'd not felt it since before he'd left London, and the money driven rat race. Would she never understand that he was done with her?

A sharp jab stabbed at his temple.

It must be all the stress of his first sheep auction and the town meet tomorrow night. He had a lot riding on the townspeople accepting his proposal, but first there were sheep to sell.

He clicked the gear into drive and took off. He pressed the accelerator a little too hard, causing his tyres to kick up some mud as he drove off. The annoying sensation faded as he allowed his mind to entertain thoughts of the woman with fiery hair and emerald eyes.

Chapter 10

It was late afternoon by the time Malcolm arrived home from the auction. He made his way from the garage to the back door of the house, kicking his wellies off before entering. Mr. Foggart stood at the ready with his loafers.

"Thank you." Malcolm nodded and sat on the wooden chair in the scullery to slip on his shoes.

"Tea will be served shortly in the library, sir."

"Good. I'm chilled tae me bone."

Once shod and his outside coat dropped in the laundry for Mrs. Perkins to wash, Malcolm made his way to his library and the promise of a warm fire crackling away in the hearth.

He found Agnus in one of her favorite spots on the cushioned bay window sill, book in hand. Even at her age she still managed to sit curled up like a teenager. The sight of her caused his heart to sigh. Every time.

"Where's the lass?" he asked as he flopped down into his chair, then sat up straight and leaned forward. "Where are my dogs?" He searched the area around his feet.

"Out there, all three of them." Agnus said without looking up from her book.

Malcolm frowned then stood, grunting his frustration as he stomped over to the window to find his granddaughter sitting on the bench facing the loch. At her feet were his two cocker-spaniels. A comforting sensation, like drizzled honey on fresh hot toast, filled his heart. The sight of his granddaughter sitting where her father used to, with *his* dogs at her feet, was a blessing he didn't deserve.

"Isn't it time they came in? There's a chill in the air," he barked.

He didn't mean to sound so gruff, but he had no idea how to show he cared.

"They haven't left her side all day. Ah, the tea."

Agnus slipped off her seat and walked over to the table where one of the young maids, Annie, set down the tray.

"You can leave. I'll pour, thank you Annie." The young girl nodded and left.

Malcolm reveled in awe as he kept his gaze glued to his granddaughter.

"Here you go." Agnus pushed two hot mugs into his hands.

"What's this noo, woman?"

"Why don't you go and enjoy a nice cup of tea with your granddaughter. Take an extra scarf if yer that worrit about the chill, aye. Who knows, your pups might decide to follow you home." She winked, then walked over to a chair by the table, and sat down to her steaming cup of Oolong.

\#

Sadie looked up when the dogs stirred, to find her grandfather standing, two steaming mugs in hand, beside the bench, a look of confusion and uncertainty on his wrinkly old face.

"Yer Nan doesn't alloo her pretty tea cups oot doors."

His hands shook ever so slightly as he handed her a mug.

Sadie smiled and nodded. "Thank you."

The droop on the one side of his face wasn't as pronounced as it been the day before. She watched from the rim of her mug as Malcolm shuffled and fidgeted where he stood. It was obvious he didn't know how to act in her presence. The feeling was somewhat mutual.

"How was the auction?"

"Och verra gud. This year's flock went wi the first crack o the hammer." His eyes fell to her feet where his two spaniels lay.

Sadie nodded and sipped her tea, not missing her grandfather's hesitant glance at his pups.

"Well I think he's missed you," she said to the dogs and watched from the corner of her eye as Malcolm's left eyebrow arched. "Off you go, we'll play catch again tomorrow." And with that, the two spaniels jumped and huddled around Malcolm's ankles.

Malcolm merely tipped his hat at Sadie and left.

Oh, well, it's a start.

So much of him reminded her of her father, especially his brusque manner and inability to express his feelings. Dad and Mom had often fought about how he simply couldn't acknowledge when he was wrong, or upset, or say I love you of his own volition.

Sadie now began to understand why. The Munros, it seemed, refused to acknowledge their ability to feel too deeply. Mom had said that often, and mentioned Sadie taking after her dad. What her mom didn't know, or understand, was that they felt so deeply it hurt too much to share it with the world.

She took a deep sip from her mug and pushed any memories of the past back into the dark room she had constructed for them. The smoky oolong infused with every fiber of her chilled body.

There would never be forgiveness, or apologies, or goodbyes; not for the likes of her.

Sadie watched Malcolm wander toward to the house, two lopping spaniels at his heels. Her aching heart hurt a little less and warmed a fraction more. The old man had made some effort to connect with her. It was a good start.

Like herself, Sadie knew Malcolm carried a lot of guilt. Perhaps that would be the one thing they did have in common? She turned back to face the setting sun.

A soft orange glow had broken through a gap in the blanketed sky as it dipped behind the distant peaks on the far side of the loch. Red, and indigo stained the dull grey of the early evening sky. It reminded Sadie of the sunsets on the farm back home.

Her thoughts drifted and shifted as fear ridden memories began to override the glorious descent of the afternoon sun.

The dimming sanguine beams of the setting sun morphed from one of beauty to the fire ridden horizon of not too long ago. The intensity of the illusion brought her to her knees.

Burning horse flesh, and singed wood, invaded her nostrils. Screaming animals. Frantic pleading from the grooms and staff. Crackling timber pierced the peaceful dusk air. The shrill of death scraped against the inside of her ears. Her heart bashed at her ribs and dark spots filled her vision.

As suddenly as the memories flooded her mind, a warm sensation reached in and wrapped itself around her fractured soul. It was followed shortly by a distant whinny, and stomping of hooves, which pulled her back to the present.

Sadie released the breath she'd clung onto and sucked in another. Her fingers dug into the grass and soil. The cool breeze off the loch washed away the memory of death and pain. She stood with effort.

A soft whinny echoed through the forest. Sadie shifted her weight to look back toward the pine trees that bordered the garden. It was darker now, but she was certain she wasn't seeing things.

At the edge of the grove, she could just make out the shape of the mare, the Blue Roan, camouflaged by the shadows. Sadie squinted. The form faded into the dark. No, it must be another illusion. Her heart still ached for her horses and her body longed to sit astride one.

The roan was long gone, dead at best. It was her longing that played tricks with her eyes. Sadie bit back the hurt.

Anger and hurt filled her heart and she spun around, desperate to get back to her room, away from the forest and what it might hold.

"Ooph!" Her body hit solid muscle and ricocheted backward. A large, strong hand curled around her upper arm and stopped her from tripping over her false foot.

Chapter 11

Blane parked on the far side of the gravel horseshoe drive at the front entrance of Munro Manor. From here, he could see all the way down the water facing side of the manor house where Sadie sat watching the ebb and flow of the Loch Shin.

He pushed the gear lever into park and cut the ignition.

He had a standing appointment with Malcolm, but seeing Sadie upon his arrival, he decided he'd handle the issue of her rental car beforehand, that, and it was a good excuse to get to know her better. He'd made a point of finding Malcolm at the auction today and hoped his disappointment hadn't been too obvious when he was told she'd remained at home.

Blane slipped his mobile phone into his shirt pocket when Sadie slid off the bench and on to her hands and knees. His heart jolted as he watched her head loll forward. Blane jumped from his car and ran to her aide. But before he reached her, she'd righted herself and come to stand, somewhat wobbly, and stared toward the forest which edged the northern side of the garden.

He'd not intended to startle her, nor had he expected them to meet so abruptly, but Sadie's reaction surprised Blane none the less.

The sparkle in her eyes morphed into pure fear. Their moss green deepened to a foreboding juniper.

Once he was certain she'd regained her balance, he let go and stepped back. "I'm sorry. I didn't mean to alarm you."

"What are you doing here?" She wrapped her long arms around herself and took step back.

"You weren't at the auction." Was all he could manage. His brain still trying to grasp what he'd just witnessed.

"Ja, I wasn't up to it after the long flight and all." Her answer was short, but the tone in her voice confirmed

what Blane thought. There was so much more to Sadie
Munro than met the eye.

"I came to tell you we've given up searching for the
horse, and I gave Fergus back his piece of scrap." He
reached into his back pocket, pulled out a neatly rolled wad
of cash and handed it to her. "Here's your money."

Her cheeks returned to a healthy glow with a touch
of honey.

"Thank you. It really wasn't necessary. I could have
taken care of it." She reached out a hand and took the wad
of notes from Blane as she asked, "How did you manage a
refund? It was a rental."

"Fergus is easily persuaded when motivated
sufficiently, and I have a suspicion it would have let you
down whether we'd had our run in or not. No man worth
his salt should ever borrow, and especially not rent out, a
piece of scrap like that to a person."

He watched as she tucked the money into her
pocket. He tried for a smile and hoped it softened the
tension between them.

"True." The corners of her mouth turned up into a
dazzling grin, crinkling the freckles on her nose. This
woman had a beauty few owned. It glowed from the inside
out like a halo.

Her long tresses cascaded over her shoulders in a
waterfall of honey, auburn, and autumn. Blane ignored the
urge to reach out and brush his fingers through them.

She straightened, her gaze almost level with his,
then surprised him by asking, "Why'd you give up on her?"

Her words, like a fist to his belly, left him dumb
struck for a moment.

"We didn't. My manager, Mac, was up till all hours
of the morning. There's no sign of her. Any track she might
have left was washed away by the rain. She's nowhere to
be found near Saorsa, Munro, or Lairg for that fact."

He watched as Sadie turned her head back to the
forest.

"Oh."

Something about her tone inflamed his feelings of failure and guilt.

He smoothed a hand over his head and into his nape where a hair band held his shoulder length dark curls together.

"I thought I'd have seen you at the auction today?"

Their eyes met again and the air between them quickened. An ethereal bolt of lightning struck him on the crown of his head and ran the length of his body. It scorched every cell he owned on its way down, then exited via his toes.

Sadie's eyes grew wide and the pink of her lips deepened to a hungry scarlet. Blane stepped forward, his instinct pleading for him to reach out and cup her cheek in his hand. He burned to feel her soft skin touch his.

But she answered by taking a step back. Her arms wrapped once again around her chest as she turned slightly away from him. What was it about this woman? She came across as self-assured and independent one moment, but when one got too close, she shied away like a skittish...

mare.

An awkward silence stirred in the air between them and Blane watched again as she peered toward the woods.

"Tell me more about the mare. You said you'd found her in dismal conditions."

Blane allowed his gaze to follow hers and for a split second he swore he saw... "Is that..."

"What?" Her green gaze skewered him.

"Nothing, it's just... the shadows, they play games with your eyes in those woods."

He turned his gaze from the forest to the loch. The sun winked a last time from beyond the horizon before dipping them in a charcoal dusk. The water lay as flat as an ironed sheet. The nocturnal inhabitants chittered and rustled as they awoke and began to forage beneath the fallen leaves of the trees. A soft mist, like a bride's French laced veil, draped itself over the loch. This truly was God's country.

"The mare? Her conditions were appalling. Underfed, tethered day and night to a pole in the middle of a muddy paddock, rife with hoof rot and mange." He tore his gaze from the still waters to her stormy gaze. "It was touch and go by the time I got her to a decent vet. According to a neighbor, who I made sure knew she was as bad as the drunk because she never reported him, the owner used the poor mare for target practice with beer cans. When he was well drunk, he would line up the empty cans and hit them with his golf club to see how many would strike her."

Blane paused.

Sadie's skin had paled.

"Sorry, I didn't mean to upset you."

"Don't stop. I want to know." Her voice was a mere whisper.

"The short and long of it is, we saved her body, but I doubt any one person could have ever saved her soul."

The moment the last word fell from his mouth he knew he'd stepped on a land mine. He should have known better. She'd survived a horrendous attack according to the internet articles he'd researched last night. Why had he told her about the bloody mare? Why did he find it so easy to open up to her?

Without another word, Sadie turned and walked off. Not a word. Not even a last glance.

It took a few long strides to catch up with her. She walked fast but with a lopsided gait.

Irritation prickled his nerves. He'd apologized.

"Slow down, Sadie. I just want to-"

Sadie stopped, turned, and lifted her chin in a way which reminded him of a Queen sitting astride her brood mare. "Want to what Mr. Buchan? You came all this way to return my money, thank you. Now what? To tell me of a horse so damaged she probably couldn't be saved in any case?"

"But you asked about her..."

"So, I did. And thank you for answering."

Blane felt the rush of frustration slap his cheek when she turned and continued to walk away.

"Will you just stop for one second?"

Sadie skidded to a halt on the gravel at the side of the Manor and pulled her hands through her long fiery tresses. "Look, I'm sorry. I- I feel bad for the horse and for you."

Her words said one thing, but the storm in her eyes another.

Blane scrutinized the woman with hair like fire and eyes like crown jewels. Her tone had softened again.

"Shall I walk you back to the house?" he offered.

"No, thank you. I said I'd be okay. You don't have to…" she started to protest.

Blane put up his hands in mock surrender. "I'm also here to discuss some business with Malcolm before tomorrow night's town meet."

He watched as Sadie's cheeks turned the same shade of pink as the roses in her grandmother's garden just behind her. While his intention was not to embarrass her, he found himself battling to bridle the desire her flushed skin stoked within him.

"Yes, of course…," her voice a mere whisper before she spun around and walked off into the house leaving Blane stunned, and left to make his own way to the front entrance.

#

Her heart galloped like a wild horse.

Never had she felt so confused, scared, and angry all at once. Who did this man think he was? Going out of his way to help her. What did he want from her? Why did his presence stir feelings in her she'd safely stowed beneath a glacier of ice? How dare he revive such emotions!

Sadie plodded through the front entrance and up the steps. She did not stop to wipe the mud from her boots. She didn't stop till she stood huffing by the window in her bedroom. She needed air.

With a shaking hand, she tugged at the brass lever. It wouldn't open. She leaned into it with all her weight until it squealed, groaned, and finally popped. It flew open and bounced on its old copper hinges.

How had Nan opened it so easily the other day?

Cool evening air rushed in and washed over her. The smell of fresh pine, damp soil, and woody scent with a hint of icy loch water invaded her nostrils. Slowly her anger cooled, and her angst dissipated.

Her mind found order and she could breathe in without her throat constricting. What in the world had come over her? Why had she snapped at Blane like that?

She knew why.

Some silly part of her had liked the way he looked at her, had thrilled at the electricity, which had crackled like white fire between them in the garden. Another part of her forbade her to get too close. If he ever found out the truth about her injuries….

She shoved her hand into her pocket and pulled out a wad of notes.

Beneath that odd English persona and handsome muscle, she had also seen a man with a kind heart.

Ugh!

Sadie sat down on the bench beneath the window sill. She didn't deserve kindness, nor did she have the strength to deal with her demons and this... man with his dark eyes and softly-bearded face and…

Could getting to know him better heal some of the hurt, the pain, glue together some of the cracks in her fractured spirit?

'*The short and long of it is, we saved her body but, I doubt any one person could have ever saved her soul.*'

His words sliced down the center of her shattered heart.

No, she knew there was no saving to be had when a soul was damaged beyond repair. She also knew she'd never survive rejection like she had with Darren again, so best to maintain a distance. It was safer for all involved. And if it meant she'd have to act cold, and somewhat bitchy, then so be it.

She sighed and let her gaze wander over the beauty beyond her window. Evening shadows rose from beneath the rocks and shrubs, covering the garden below. They snaked up the thick trunks of the tall pine trees and inch-by-inch, they covered the world in a blanket of night. Like bluebells blossoming at dawn, tiny twinkling diamonds appeared one by one across the bruised heavens.

Here in the Northern Hemisphere, the stars sat differently in the sky, but they shone as bright and bold as they had back home.

No, this was home now. As if to confirm her sentiments, a barn owl hooted from the branch of a nearby pine and startled Sadie before flapping large wings and taking off on his nocturnal hunt. Her gaze followed the bird as it swooped down and flew into the forest. Movement just beyond the owl, caught Sadie's eye.

It was the Roan! From up here the view into a clearing was clear enough, even in the dusky light. She had not imagined it earlier; the horse was alive. She should let Blane know. Sadie jumped up from her seat, then froze mid-air.

How was she going to convince the man his horse was still alive when she acted the way she had? Not only that, he had spooked the poor thing once before and chances were, he would do it again. He obviously had good intentions, but lacked experience with horses, especially those of the damaged variety.

She turned back to the open window, her eyes easily finding the dark form of the equine, though the last shafts of indigo and black drowned out all the shadows and the mare. Her legs ached to sit in a saddle. As though to contradict her, a bolt of pain shot down her thigh and into her non-existent foot.

She'd never ride again.

"But what, my dear, are we going to do about you?" she whispered into the night.

Chapter 12

Malcolm wiped his cheeks dry with his handkerchief before dabbing at his tears which had fallen on the clear film covers protecting the photos.

Agnus' hand on his shoulder startled him, and he turned to see his beloved wife looking down where he sat with the albums of her visits to South Africa.

She sat on the arm rest. "May I?" She pointed to the open photobook on his lap.

Agnus had turned to a photo of Stewart with brown muck running off his head and over his face.

"Lindsay had had enough of him traipsing with his muddy feet through the house. After he'd gone and stomped manure into her good rug she'd decided there was only one way to sort him oot. She waited, standing on a chair hiding behind a pillar on their verandah one afternoon before lunch, armed with a bucket of the freshest horse poop. When he didn't remove his wellies at the foot o the stairs, she upended the bucket of runny muck. It was Sadie who'd had the sense tae wait wi a camera."

They both rolled with laughter at the sight of their son's face, shocked, and covered in horse shite. Malcolm hadn't laughed so hard in years.

"Did he learn his lesson then?" Malcolm stroked the image with his index finger.

"Oh aye, he sure did."

"Oh and look heer." She turned the page. "This was a solar oven Stephen designed for one of the competitions his school entered him in," Agnus pointed.

Malcolm looked down at the photo of a fair-haired boy with bright blue eyes, chest puffed out like a cock o' the roost, beside what looked like a box covered in tin foil.

"He was her spittin image," Malcolm whispered.

"Aye and such a bright spark…"

They looked toward each other. Their pain rolled down their cheeks. Malcolm closed the album and placed it on the floor then pulled Agnus onto his lap and wrapped his arms around her.

They wept until there were no tears left.

"Forgive me."

"Och, husband, it wasn't yer fault. T'was nobody's but the murderer himself's fault."

"Aye, but if I'd nae been such a dolt we'd have had more o them before…."

Agnus tightened her grip around his shoulders.

"Shh now. What's done is done, and there'll no be a thing tae change it. We have her noo and that tis more than either of us could ever wish fur."

Chapter 13

Fingers of soft autumn sun tickled Sadie's face. She had fallen asleep on the bay window's bench after waking from yet another nightmare in the early morning hours. Prionnsa lay atop her lap with Donn draped over her legs like a black fur rug. The dogs rarely left her side, and they'd been a great comfort when she awoke screaming, again.

She kissed the greying black fur of the old spaniel before stretching her arms above her head and yawned. It promised to be a bright, beautiful day, but she was exhausted and only wanted to crawl back into bed.

No such luck, though. She'd heard the mare in the forest again in the wee hours of the morning. Today, she was determined to find the horse and lure her out of hiding. There may be no hope for her, but perhaps with a little faith, the mare stood a chance.

She would venture a little further along the shore to get closer to the far end of the forest. If her patience and her luck paid off, she could catch another glimpse of the Roan or even get a little closer without scaring her off.

A soft knock pulled Sadie from her thoughts. Mrs. Perkins entered, and Sadie promptly tucked her damaged limb under her other leg as if she were sitting cross-legged.

"Gud morning tae ye lass. Sleep well?" The housekeeper smiled as she headed toward the bathroom.

"No washing?" She came back out frowning.

"No, thank you, Mrs. Perkins. I know how the washer works."

The woman tsk'd, then fidgeted with the fireplace. "But ye ken how to tread half the highland in tae the hoos with ye?"

Sadie felt her cheeks warm. "Sorry Mrs. Perkins I promise to clean it up right away."

Mrs. Perkins held up her hand. "Nae need. Annie already has. I hear ye will be at the meet tonight?"

Ugh, the damned town meet.

"Yes, Nan wants to introduce me to her friends."

The housekeeper stopped prodding at the cooling coals and turned to face Sadie. Her brown eyes squinted as she rested her hands on her hips. "Aye, I reckon she'd be wanting tae chur wi ye. Sorra, I mean brag," Mrs. Perkins corrected when Sadie frowned.

Oh, great. That was all Sadie needed.

As if sensing her apprehension, Mrs. Perkins cocked her head to one side. "Och lass dinnae fash yer self. It's no every day the old girl has her family aboot her, aye."

Sadie found herself having to listen carefully when Mrs. Perkins spoke, her accent was so thick, but she caught the gist of it, and smiled at her use of 'old girl.' Her nan kept a formal appearance with her staff when other people were around, but in truth, she was very relaxed and shared a strong friendship with her housekeeper.

Mrs. Perkins left with a staunch warning that Sadie would please stop doing the washing and messing up her 'system'.

Sadie patted the two dogs. "Off with you both now, go outside and do what it is you do. After breakfast, we'll go for a nice long walk, okay." Donn flew off the seat and barked as she dashed out after Mrs. Perkins. Prionnsa, ever the prince, looked up at Sadie and groaned.

Sadie smiled. "She'll grow up and calm down soon enough."

She gave him one last pat before heaving him off her lap and onto the floor.

Sadie hopped to her wardrobe and opened the door. She needed to sort through her meager closet and find something respectable, but not too fancy to wear for tonight. Gran had offered to take her shopping in Inverness, but Sadie declined. She didn't see the need for a closet filled with clothes. Semi-formal. The worst kind of dress-code. One never knew what was too much or too little. *Ugh.*

\#

"Enjoy your walk," Agnus said as Sadie excused herself from the breakfast table. She'd managed a small poached egg and some toast at Agnus's insistence.

"Yup, thanks."

She left her grandmother and Malcolm to finish their morning coffee; the only time her nan ever drank the stuff, and headed out the back door, dogs in tow.

"Now you two, don't you dare go running off after her, do you hear me?" Sadie commanded.

"Running after who?" asked Ghillie as Sadie strode past his workshop.

Sadie couldn't remember the man's name, but everyone called him Ghillie, so she did also. Her eyes took in the tall broad-shouldered man. His prowess with all things technical reminded her of her brother Stephen. Then she pushed the thought of her beautiful sibling down deep and locked the door.

"Oh, hi Ghillie. Didn't see you standing there."

"Where is it yer off tae this mornin?"

"Just a walk."

"Aye, just a walk, is it? Not goin' tae luk fur what's making strange ructions in the wood?"

A shiver ran the length of her spine. *What did he mean?*

"We heard her too. Like she's calling tae somebody," he said simply and returned to his work.

Sadie stood a moment, gobsmacked. She wanted to ask him what he meant and why he hadn't mentioned it to Malcolm, or Blane for that matter, but thought better of it. The one thing she had noticed, in the few short days she'd been here, was that highland folk often spoke in weird terms — ones she battled to grasp.

Sadie made her way toward the woods, skirting the edge of the pines until she reached the sandy shores of the loch. It was nothing like the beaches back in South Africa. Here the sand was a little darker and strewn intermittently with smooth pebbles and washed up pieces of wood. Some stones were the color of night, sprinkled with a thousand stars shimmering across their wet surface. Others were a dirty white, and others still the same ochre of the manor's brick walls.

Sadie remained close to the trees and away from the water as she walked farther from the house. The sun was out. There wasn't a cloud in the blue ceiling above her, but it was still chilly. A slight breeze pushed her from behind and Sadie found herself pulling her jacket a little tighter around her shoulders.

The sudden rustle of brush had the dogs skid to a halt and pitch their ears.

"Don't you bark, Donn. Prionnsa, sit." Sadie whispered her command then peered into the dark pockets of forest.

A subtle warmth stirred in her solar plexus then cooled. Nothing. The dogs lost interest and trotted ahead.

Sadie didn't move. She had felt the mare. She remained standing, not moving a muscle as she stared into the dim light cast by the tall trees, allowing time for her eyes to acclimatize. The familiar warmth returned. The roan was close by.

Was she wasting her time? Was this just wishful thinking? She closed her eyes and tried to reach out with her inner senses; a second sight she had always owned, something one couldn't explain. It existed within her.

She reached from deep within and prodded the ethereal surrounds in search of the horse.

A cold sticky sensation filled her mind. It was fear. A fear she knew all too well herself, and longing, a need to be wanted, to be touched and stroked and loved.

Sadie stood until her leg protested with a sharp jab, pulling her from her strange meditation.

The sensation faded, and darkness settled in the pit of her stomach. Regret and guilt clouded her internal senses, and the connection slipped from her grasp. Anger replaced the warmth and Sadie seethed at the realization she may never be able to rekindle the flame that fed her gift ever again.

"Prionnsa, Donn, come," she called.

Frustrated, she turned and headed back to the house. She was wasting her time. What would she do if the mare were still here? She wasn't even sure she could help the poor animal, let alone ride it. Sadie kicked at a pebble with her faux foot. That felt good.

She walked to the edge of the water, picked up a handful of pebbles and threw them at the loch as she screamed. "Why?"

That felt even better than kicking something. Needing desperately to give into her emotions, she fell to her knees. The reflection of a crazed, green eyed, fiery haired woman, stared back. The muscles in her throat spasmed and tears burned like acid in her eyes, but that was all they did. Tease her with a fake promise of release and nothing more.

Un-cried tears and heartbreak threatened to suffocate her. With effort, she drew in a deep breath. It cut like razor blades all the way down her throat and into her chest before she forced it back out and shouted at the reflection.

"Why did you take them from me? I hate you! I will never forgive you! It's all your fault!"

Chapter 14

The Munro's 1960's Rolls Royce pulled to a stop in the large gravel parking lot across the road from the Lairg Town Hall. Mrs. Perkins had mentioned earlier in the evening, that the black polished antique was only used when Malcolm entered the town in his capacity as Laird.

The lot sported a few mis-placed street lamps, casting their dimmed orange light everywhere else but where one needed them to. Sadie slid out of the back seat and inhaled deeply.

Nerves prickled just below her skin and her stomach churned. She looked up. The air hung heavy with dark clouds. A chilly breeze swept up off the loch and toyed with the loose tresses of her hair.

A shiver ran down her neck and arms. She straightened, pulling the thick black wool coat nan loaned her, tight around her shoulders, then adjusted her black trousers. She'd matched them with a white blouse and the Munro tartan sash Agnus had proudly draped over her left shoulder. An old round brooch with a large orange jewel, pinned the tartan to her blouse. Nan had called it a cairngorm, and said it was her's now.

Sadie watched as the townspeople huddled around the entrance to the grey building across the road while she waited for Agnus and Malcolm to get out of the car. Most were old, like her grandparents, but there were a few young families with babies and toddlers.

"Ready, dear?" Nan asked.

Sadie forced a smiled.

Agnus was dressed in one of her more formal skirt suits, a beautiful blue knitted jacket with a sash made of the Munro tartan, and a matching skirt. The color brought Nan's eyes to life. Malcolm, though aged, looked dashing and quite the part in his kilt regalia.

"Weel coom on then or we'll be late." Malcolm held his arm out for his wife.

Agnus nodded and slipped her arm through Malcolm's as they headed off to the hall.

They wound their way between other parked cars. Sadie made sure not to stumble on the loose gravel when Blane walked up. Dressed in dark beige pants, which sat just right, a deep blue cotton shirt with sleeves rolled up to the elbow, and boots. He too, had a tartan sash pinned to his left shoulder. Its colors and pattern differed from the one Sadie and her grandparents wore.

Where theirs was a bold red interlaced with green and black, Blane's was a variation of light and dark green with thinner red, yellow, and black stripes breaking the cloth into squares. Pinning it to his shirt was a brooch shaped in the head of a woman. His dark chocolate hair was tied neatly in the nape of his neck. It suited his bearded face. Sadie couldn't help but notice how his presence drew the attention of every female within a five-hundred-meter radius, or that it had her insides fluttering about like a kaleidoscope of butterflies.

"Good evening Ms. Munro, Sir, Madam." He offered Sadie his arm.

Blane looked straight at her and smiled. While his eyes still managed to remind her of warm honey and chocolate, something about him was different. His entire body vibrated with tension. Perhaps it was the town meeting. Nan had told all her all about the exciting idea he had presented to Malcolm and now had to sell to the towns people.

"I won't bite," Blane, delivered a grin, which sent Sadie's heart into uncontrollable cartwheels inside her chest.

She cursed her body for reacting the way it did. She looked back and caught her nan's questioning glance.

Hesitantly she slipped her hand through his arm the same way she'd seen her grandmother do with Malcolm and allowed Blane to accompany her to the meet.

#

Sadie's fingers wrapped themselves around his forearm. Tingles shot up his biceps and tumbled down his spine. For some odd reason the sensation made him think of falling stars. Even through his shirt he knew her skin to be soft as silk and her touch warm and delicate as a feather riding the breeze.

Attraction pooled in the pit of his stomach, heavy and hot.

The effect this woman had on him was bordering on dangerous.

The reminder of a surprise arrival that afternoon at Saorsa pulled his thoughts from the encouraging sensations the tall red head stirred within him and toward what, or rather who, was waiting at home for him. Damn the Gods and their black humor! With any luck, his problem would be sorted out by the morning and would never bother him again.

But until then, it was best to keep his attraction for Sadie hidden.

They crossed the road and walked up to the front entrance.

"Aah, Mr. Buchan. I see you've brought a … friend?" A barrel bellied, red nosed man with a bald patch on the crown of his head greeted them.

"Och Mr. Ferguson, this is my granddaughter, Sadie."

Blane gave Agnus a grateful nod then to Sadie, "See you inside?" and walked off.

"Oh, dear me," blushed the potbellied man.

"Sadie, this is Mr. Ferguson. He is the local butcher and sits on the Lairg council," Agnus introduced the older man and Sadie nodded.

"Pleased to meet you, Sir." Sadie gave the man a hearty handshake.

From there, she was introduced to a dozen other faces ranging from her parents' age to what Sadie believed belonged in a museum.

"Och, lassie, yer the spittin image o yer da!" said one old crone. Her perfectly hair sprayed curls sparkled with a fresh coat of purple dye, and her eyes twinkled with a mischief Sadie couldn't believe belonged to one that old.

"She'll be the belle o tha' ball come winter," the cheeky dame grinned as she patted arthritic fingers on Sadie's cheeks, then turned to Agnus. "Tis a blessing, this one is." She patted Agnus' shoulder before hobbling off into the hall.

Sadie turned to Agnus who avoided her questioning glance.

Winter? Ball? Oh, heavens! How could she have forgotten?

Agnus had once shown them photos of the Munro Winter ball held every year at Munro Manor.

Fear coiled around her chest and squeezed. There was no way she could be seen in a ball gown, and all those people? Sadie clutched at her chest. It was hard to breathe.

Agnus came to stand beside Sadie. "Deep breath, lass. Nothing tae get yerself in a tizzy about noo. Besides, this is a good practice run tae get you back into society?"

Sadie straightened up and inhaled deeply before following her grandmother into the hall.

"Come now, it's time to find a seat, then after, we'll have some supper. The Ladies League for Lairg have prepared a wonderful buffet."

Agnus guided Sadie by the elbow to the rows of white plastic chairs facing the stage.

The hall itself was brightly lit with bold, ugly, white florescent tubes, which flattered no one. It was no warmer inside than it was outside, and Sadie rubbed her hands together, wishing she could have dressed like the other women: jeans, warm jackets, woolen socks. But she was the Laird of Munro's granddaughter, and as his heir, a certain amount of uncomfortable civility was expected.

Sadie sat in the front row beside her grandmother. Just below the wooden stage was a long table and behind it, sat the council, two of which were women. One was a greying, staunchly-built matron with a large, full bosom. The other was a pale, white-haired biddy, who looked as though she'd been borrowed from a forgotten shelf in the library and dusted off especially for this evening.

The matron's hawk-eyed gaze landed on Agnus and Sadie. Her dark eyes squinted with a malevolent focus.

"I don't think she likes us," Sadie whispered.

"Och dinnae worry boot Mrs. Learie. That old crone hasn't blessed this world with a smile since the day her mam pulled her teat away from her."

Sadie promptly covered her mouth trying hard to stifle a giggle. "Nan, you're wicked."

"So I've been told. Hence the blazing glare of death and laldie," Agnus winked.

"Come again, Nan?" Sadie had no idea what that last word meant.

"Condemnation, dearie. I meant condemnation." She motioned toward the table with a nod as the meeting was brought to order.

Sadie focused on her grandfather. Malcom brought the meeting to order then introduced the members and read the agenda.

Mrs. Learie was the first to address the problem of young loiterers. "Oot side the Sheep Heide Inn. It isnae verra gud for tourism to ave these foul mouthed sloppy dreised hethens and their flashy phones hanging around all times o the night in the main street."

To emphasize her point, she stopped talking and stared down every face in her audience as though to dare them to contradict her before continuing.

"I suggest a curfew." She turned to Malcolm, eyebrow raised, fists on fleshy hips, and waited.

A wave of shocked murmurs ran through the hall.

Nan's voice drifted over to her. "Oh dear, it seems our mistress o the watch is up to high doh tonight."

Sadie nodded taking her nan to mean the plump lady was all riled up and ready for action.

She stifled another giggle when she noticed how Mr. Ferguson's face had turned a shallow purple as he flustered and blubbered, "Dinnae be daft woman. This isnae the British occupation! Ye canae enforce curfew unless-"

Sadie watched as Mrs. Learie simply raised her hand and waved the blubbery butcher to silence, not once breaking her stand down stare with Malcolm.

Malcolm returned her cold hard glare with one of his own.

"Mr. Ferguson is correct Madam. Ye cannot enforce a curfew."

Sadie, once again buried her face in her hands, masking her own snickering as Mrs. Learie's cheeks blew up like a puffer fish. The town meet was turning out to be far more entertaining than she'd thought.

"Wh-what? Weel, we'll see aboot that Malcolm Munro. Gone are the days the Laird can lay doon the law…"

Malcolm smacked a flat hand on the table and everyone except Mrs. Learie and Nan jumped. "This isna aboot me woman! This is aboot the toon. Noo, the council along with the toon will vote. Besides, oor problem isnae the manky scunners hanging aboot the Inn. It's the fact we have no tourists for them tae chase awa!"

"Weel then, let's vote!" Mrs. Learie declared as she planted fisted hands on ample hips and tapped her foot.

Mr. Ferguson stood. "All in favor of a curfew raise ye hands then."

The vibrating whispers died down and the hall fell in to a cold silence.

'Will ye tell me nae one of ye fools stand by me tae fix up this toon?" Mrs. Learie's voice rose in pitch and volume.

Only the crickets replied.

"All those against?" Mr. Ferguson's voice echoed off the frozen stone walls.

A sound of rushing water filled the air as jacketed arms rose above heads leaving no doubt as to how the town felt about Mrs. Learie's proposal. Sadie was sure that if the puce coloring Mrs. Learie's face darkened any more, she'd blow a gasket.

"Right then," Malcolm's voice broke the triumphant silence. "Onto oor next bit o business then. Mr.

Buchan." He looked toward Blane as he waved a hand toward the town folk.

Blane stood, first nodding to Malcolm. "Thank you, Sir. Good evening good people of Lairg," He then turned to face Mrs. Learie who still stood glaring at all and sundry. "Madam?"

"Sit doon, Ann." Malcolm used a voice that gave Sadie the chills.

It was the same voice her father had used when he meant business. Mrs. Learie's mouth clamped shut and she sat down folding her arms across her bulging bosoms.

"Thank you," Blane nodded to Mrs. Learie, then turned to address the town folk.

Sadie, and everyone else's attention was instantly drawn to Blane. Not because his general appearance was pleasing, but, because of the power, or no, rather a strength and charisma, which seemed to exude from him like the light in a bulb, as he stepped out from behind the table.

"I have a proposal I think would appease those of you worried about both the future of our young folk, as well as Lairg."

Sadie shifted in her seat. The cold of the hall gnawed at her damaged limb. Toes she no longer had ached and cramped. She wished she could rub them.

Instead, she took a deep breath and smiled when Blane's eyes came to rest on her as he described his plans to invite the Department of Agriculture from Edinburgh University.

Why was he looking at her? His dark gaze made her uncomfortable and from the corner of her eyes she noticed a few heads turn her way.

Blane continued, "I propose we apply to tender to the University of Edinburgh's agricultural department. One, if awarded, it would see the university set up their research and practical departments here in Lairg. What this means for Lairg is an influx of persons, money, and job opportunities."

Blane set out his ideas in a manner which included every person in Lairg, and in so doing, spread the responsibility and accountability across the people of the town. Sadie looked around. There wasn't a face without a smile. Except for Mrs. Learie, of course. In a single half hour, Blane had managed to glue together a crumbling community with hope, sensibility, and excellent entrepreneurship.

"What it would entail, and what it would mean for the town of Lairg, is more than any of us could hope for," he finished and a round of enthusiastic applause ensued.

Above the din Sadie heard a carrying whisper. Obviously, it was meant to be heard.

"Weel seems oor fair bach has his eyes on Himself's granddaughter," followed by a giggle and, an equally pitched rejoinder.

"He's no bachelor dearie. Word is he's a taken man and his soon-to-be Mrs. Buchan as arrived at Saorsa this afternoon. My Fred who works wi auld Mac told me all aboot the helicopter landin there wi some English Lady in its bellie."

A gasp. "Flying? Weel then, tis true. The man is made o gold."

Agnus slid her hand into Sadie's and gave it a squeeze. "Small towns like these all have their blather mouths, dearie. Best not to pay them any heed."

Sadie sat frozen in her seat. What did they mean engaged? Was this simply gossip as Nan had pointed out? Nan had mentioned he'd broken off his engagement…was it back on? And why did she even care?

After the meeting concluded, it was dinner time. Plate in hand, Sadie followed her grandparents to a table. The lamb stew, mashed potatoes, and gravy (So. Much. Gravy.) called to Sadie's empty belly.

They sat down and Nan smiled at her as Malcom tucked in to his meal like a starved boar.

"Weel then, this must be the prodigal son's daughter returned?" The high-pitched voice belonged to Mrs. Learie.

Sadie's fork froze midair. She looked across the table at Malcolm. Thunder and lightning danced across his blue eyes. Before he had a chance to tear into the wicked woman though, Nan shifted in her chair to look up at the plump matron whose chest heaved with vengeance.

"Mrs. Learie, I would love to introduce you to our Sadie." She patted Sadie on the shoulders.

"Sadie, Mrs. Learie. Lairg's very own busy body, scunner, and self-appointed mistress of the local black watch. Also, its only member. By the way, the vote ended this evening." Agnus turned around and continued to eat.

"Weel, I never!" Mrs. Learie stomped her heel and marched off to another table.

"What's her problem?" Sadie asked, before slipping a fork full of meaty goodness into her mouth.

"Mrs. Learie suffers from a bit of a bossy pants complex. If she had it her way, wee'd all be wakin' up tae a trumpet call at four in the morning, afore having to dress in grey starched uniforms, an' marched off to a hard labor camp. Fun would be a crime, and happiness a sin," Nan explained and took another mouthful of food.

"Did something happen to make her so unhappy?"

"No. Some people are just born that way, lass. They are blind tae all the love and happiness aroond them, and hate anyone who has what she thinks she doesn't."

"And what's that?" Sadie asked again then slipped a fork full of potato, gravy and meat in to her mouth – so good!

"Och, Mrs. Learie is a Munro by birth. Her father and yer great grandsire were brothers. She believes she is owed the status that comes with the name." Nan answered.

"You're cousins?" Sadie gulped as she looked across to her grandfather.

"Hrmph!" Malcolm grunted with a mouth full of mashed potato.

"Malcolm! Mind yer manners. We dinna need tae see ye chewed up tatties!" Then to Sadie, "She has always maintained she was entitled to Munro lands. Of course, she was given what her birthright had her entitled to, but it has never been enough. She saw her chance greaten when

Stew… yer father left, but… we were blessed with you,"
Nan finished.

"And what was she entitled to?"

"Och, back then it was a dowry. One which her
useless husband, an Irishman no less, drank and gambled
awa," Malcolm added.

Well that made sense. A woman scorned, penniless,
and embarrassed.

Sadie ate more of the warm stew. It smelled of love,
everything highland, and made her mouth water. It was
good. The warm saltiness was layered with a hint of
rosemary and garlic. It slid down her throat and filled her
roiling belly with comfort.

Sadie couldn't help but smile at the deliciousness
she was experiencing. It reminded her of her mother's
poitjie – a well-known South African stew, which was
cooked in an iron pot over a large fire.

An ache drifted across her chest. It wasn't good to
be reminded of things she'd never experience again, or of
people she'd never hold in her arms. She pushed away her
plate.

Sadie leaned back into her chair and allowed her
thoughts to drift from her pain, to the forest and the mare.
Should she try to find the horse again tomorrow?

Two elderly gentlemen, and one young man with
limp blond hair, came to stand at their table.

"Gud evenin Sir, Madam, lass."

Sadie appreciated the broad accent, which rolled
over every 'r'like thunder across the Savannah.

"May we please 'ave a moment wi Himself?" the
older of the three inquired.

Malcolm waved a hand to the chairs on the opposite
side of the table. "Please sit."

"Come," Nan rose. "Let's go get some tea. I know
of more townsfolk who are aching to meet you."

Sadie tried to smile. *More townsfolk to meet?*

After what felt like the entire female and aged male
populace of Lairg had shook her hand, pinched her cheek,

and patted her back, Sadie managed to sneak off and find a quiet corner in which to stand and enjoy her tea.

Nan stood by the dessert table and chatted happily to a woman from her bridge club. A small gathering of farm hands caught Sadie's attention.

A fine framed middle-aged man with a mustache that curled up over his cheeks said, "Aye, me Francis said he'd heard that mare o Mr. Buchan's, calling all through the west end o the woods last night."

"Mac said there's no a trace of track. Sure, it wasna the wee folks luring him awa?" a potbellied woman replied, and everyone burst out laughing.

So, she wasn't the only one to hear the mare. Should she tell Blane?

Sadie's thoughts were abruptly interrupted when Mrs. Learie's sly, squeaky voice slipped over her shoulder like an unpleasant winter's chill.

"Weel I wonder what Mr. Buchan's fiancée would make of tae smiles shared between the two of yew?"

Sadie kept her expression blank and turned to face the icy scowl of the town's bullheaded wench.

"Yee'd never be gud enough, even if he was a free agent. Mixed blood and all." Mrs. Learie smirked.

Every cell in Sadie's body burned to ask the fat snickering cow if she spoke from experience. But instead, Sadie smiled, placed her cup down on the table beside her, and walked out of the hall.

Chapter 15

Fury, and the need to smack something real hard, roiled and poked at Sadie's better judgement. Fresh air and space were what she needed, or she'd not be responsible for unleashing Hell's judgement on Mrs. Learie!

The chill in the air soothed her burning rage. It was a beautiful, late summer's night. Sadie shoved her hands into her jacket pocket. Compared to Natal, this was nothing like the summers she'd grown up in. It was more like early winter than late summer. But beautiful none the less.

Sadie crossed the road and stood on a patch of grass at the edge of the loch. A faded wood, knee high fence acted as a barrier between her and the dark, lapping waters. The ranting of teenagers up the road, loitering out the front of the pub, echoed into the night.

Sadie drank in the semi-peaceful, autumn night air, and allowed the dark to envelop the loneliness within her. The voices grew louder, drawing Sadie's attention. One, a tall, skinny guy, whose dark unwashed hair shone like an oil slick beneath the glow of the street light, continuously glanced in her direction. His thin lips pulled into a tight snarl, drawing the hair on Sadie's neck to attention.

With her eyes glued to the small rowdy crowd, she knelt, picked up a rock, then turned back to face the Loch. Just in case, she thought.

Thankfully the teenagers remained in their small illuminated spot and, after a time, Sadie's thoughts drifted back to the meeting.

She was impressed with Blane. He presented as quite the leader. Even her grandfather had looked at him with a blatant respect — that said a lot.

Her father had always described Malcolm as rigid and iron fisted. It surprised Sadie that he so easily handed over the reins of the town to this … what did Nan call them?

Sassenach?

Mrs. Learie though, was another matter altogether.

Sadie closed her eyes. The water sang to her disgruntled thoughts as it lapped the shore. Its rhythmic splashing released her from the present and lured her in to the past. She knew she was hoping for the hopeless. Wanting something that would never be, ever again. But it was good to reminisce – on her terms. So, she allowed herself a good memory, one she was in control of.

She was back on her horse. Humid, sticky Natal air whipped at her face as they galloped over the koppies and into the valleys. She was free, free from all the pain, and whole, both inside and out.…

Crunching footsteps on the gravel behind her compressed the air in her lungs and squeezed her heart.

Sadie whipped around, rock at the ready.

"Whoa, it's just me." Blane ducked behind upraised palms.

"Sorry, but you shouldn't creep up on people, you know." She peered toward the group of youths now making their way up the road away from them.

"Always carry rocks around with you?"

Sadie pulled her eyes from the youths to Blane and tucked her hands behind her back.

"I was just coming to see if you were okay. Saw you leave a while ago. What did that ghastly woman say to you?"

Part of her wanted to blurt out just how rude the hefty cow had been. The other part, that hid behind her anger like a lost child, took precedence.

"Perhaps she just asked if I enjoyed my evening?"

Blane laughed, "Seriously? I very much doubt that."

Anger knotted with desire, rode her better judgement.

"I have no need to be the talk of the town, Mr. Buchan. It's not a good idea to be seen alone with you."

"Why?"

"While I don't give myself over to gossips, it's hard to ignore the whispers of a fiancée who's come to visit."

Sadie winced at the sound of her voice.

She sounded no better than a jealous teen, fighting for attention from the Rugby Team captain.

She turned away to hide what she knew shone as bright as a strobe light in her eyes. This man affected her. He stirred stuff; raw, hot, messy stuff, inside of her. Stuff she could never again allow herself to feel. Stuff, which would see her humiliated and hurt, again.

"You're right. You shouldn't listen to the local gossips, because that is all they are, Miss Munro." He shoved his hands into his pockets and turned to walk away.

At that moment, Malcolm strolled out the hall and across the road to where they stood, stopping Blane in his tracks.

"Weel, I'm that please tae be dun wi tonight," her Grandfather said as he draped his cane over an arm, then placed his pipe in his mouth and struck a match.

Sadie dropped the rock and dusted off her hands. "I didn't know you smoked." She waved a blue puff of pungent tobacco away from her.

"Och sorry lass, best ye stand up wind, aye. And no, I only bring this wi me when I know I have a night full o that," he nodded toward the hall behind him.

"Ye did a fine job o convincing the toon, Blane. I congratulate ye man." Malcolm stuck out a hand and shook Blane's.

"Yes well, let's first get that tender in and accepted. In the meantime, I'll be counting on you to watch Mrs. Learie."

Sadie found it hard to ignore the yearning Blane stirred inside of her. It sang to her own desire in a way which made her toes curl in her boots, and not in the bad way either. The scent of his aftershave mesmerized her sense of smell and his deep voice soothed her angst. Not even Darren had been able to elicit such strong reactions from her when they'd been together.

But then Darren had never owned a presence such as this man did. It was more than his physicality which Sadie realized she found attractive, it was also his mind. Hearing him present to the town this evening had shown her a part of him she found she respected, an inner strength which mirrored her own, and a determination as solid as steel.

Malcolm nodded as he sucked on his pipe and blew out another soft blue cloud of smoke. "Aye lad. I'll see to it the ole crone dinnae fuss aboot oor business."

"Well then, I best be off," Blane tucked his hands into his jacket pockets and made to leave.

"I heer ye lady has arrived full of pomp and fancy. Didnae ken ye had a flying contraption on Saorsa?" Malcom queried before taking another drag of his pipe.

The tobacco, although pungent, had a soft hint of cherry and earth to it. It reminded Sadie of Christmases back home. When they'd light a bonfire and….

"It was my brother's helicopter, Sir, and no, she is not my lady. Merely a *friend* come up for a *short* visit."

His emphasis on the words, 'friend' and 'short' caused Sadie to blush.

Nan had been right. Small towns like these did love to spread rumors.

"Oh," Malcolm puffed.

"Good evening Miss Munro, Malcolm."

"Goodnight, Mr. Buchan." Sadie hoped her tone didn't betray her confusion and embarrassment.

She'd never been the type to listen to gossips, but it was different now. She was not used to this strange culture, in a strange land, not to mention, Mrs. Learie's venomous comments. Why would his ex-fiancé suddenly arrive for a visit then?

Ugh, Sadie sighed. It was better to just keep her distance. There were more important things that needed her attention… the Roan.

#

Slipping onto the driver's seat of his black SUV, Blane allowed himself one last glance at Sadie Munro. He should have realized his employees would have mentioned the unexpected and dramatic arrival of his ex, and that as all town gossip goes, the truth of it would be construed. What had caught him off guard was the fact that Sadie had bought in to it. And what had that silly woman Learie said to Sadie to make her wary of him?

Blane squeezed the black leather steering wheel and sighed. While Lairg was another world entirely compared to London, one thing would always remain the same - human nature, and its need to gossip and spread lies!

He watched as Sadie stood beside her Grandfather. Tall and proud in a humble sort of way. The breeze had picked up and played with her long curly locks as though they beckoned to him like a sirens song. Why was it so hard to dampen the feelings this woman stirred?

#

Sadie sat down on the backseat of the old Rolls, leaned back against the head-rest, and closed her eyes. Malcolm started the engine and drove off. She longed to quieten her thoughts and roiled emotions. She allowed the rhythm of the drive to lull her into a peaceful calm.

"So, what da ye think of Blane's plans for Lairg?" Malcolm's question pulled her from her bliss.

"It sounds rather ambitious, but he seems like the type of bloke who could pull it off," Sadie replied.

"Aye, I agree. We'll just have to keep an eye on Mrs. Learie," Agnus pointed out.

"Och, just furget aboot her. She's a boring ole crabbit hag wi nuthing better tae do than annoy people," Malcom said as he turned the rolls onto the drive leading to the manor.

"Och you scoff now husband, but I tell ye, that woman's up to no gud! I ken her sort verra weel." Nan bit back.

Sadie grabbed the lever and rolled the window down a bit. The cool night air spilled over her and washed away the sour, confusing end to her evening.

Movement caught her eye. Sadie sat up straight in her seat. Squinting, she looked to the forest. The faintest

sound of hooves galloping. The brush seemed to part as…
no she was imagining things.

There was no lady atop the horse.

Sighing, she rubbed her eyes and lay back. She was
tired and tonight had seriously tested her inner strength.

Amazing how one's mind played tricks.

#

"Well then lass," Nan leaned down and kissed
Sadie's forehead. "Yew have a good night's rest. I am just
down the hall if you need anything."

"All good Nan, promise. Sleep tight."

She waited for her grandmother to close the door
then threw back the covers. Switching off her bedside
lamp, she hopped over to the bay window.

Donn and Prionnsa followed as she sat down and
peered out over the clearing.

After what felt like half the night had passed,
finally the same warm feeling Sadie always felt around
horses slipped into her heart.

The breeze picked up and brought with it the sound
of hooves stomping the ground. It wasn't easy to hear if
you weren't listening for it.

The roan was here still.

Sadie's insides thrilled when a whinny echoed off
the trees and through the shrub.

The dogs got antsy.

Prionnsa let out a low groan.

"Quiet now, boy. It's nothing to be afraid of. It's
only Blue." Huh, seems her name was to be Blue.

A soft whinnying carried on the breeze to Sadie as
if in acknowledgement. Sadie's heart flipped. Could it be?

Was she being granted a second chance?

Chapter 16

Agnus stood between her beloved roses and whispered a prayer of thanks. It was another blessed day of life in the Scottish Highlands with her granddaughter. The thought made everything around her come to life. The grey sky seemed bolder and the loch brighter. Munro Manner vibrated with the promise of hope and new life.

Sadie had settled in to a comfortable rhythm, although she spent a lot of her time roaming the edge of the wood on the far side of the Manor. Sadie was certainly not the vibrant young woman Agnus had once known. But much had happened since her last visit to South Africa a year and a half ago, and so much loss. It was time to look ahead, into the future and not back. But in order to do that, the ghosts of the past had to be laid to rest.

Agnus decided today was a good day for her and Sadie to spend some time between the roses, pruning, weeding, and chatting.

She made her way indoors and down the long passage which connected the main part of the house to the kitchen. There, she unpacked her pair of spare wellies from the scullery cupboard. *They should fit.*

A pair of wellies in one hand and a basket full of gardening tools in the other, Agnus headed upstairs to wake her granddaughter. There was more to her motivation to spend some time alone with her granddaughter than merely distracting her from her silent musing beside the loch.

Agnus had had a few sleepless nights deliberating over how a day like this would play out.

First, she'd need to ease her granddaughter into the prospect of attending the Munro's annual winter ball. She'd move on to some general questions and then, with some help form above she'd guide Sadie to talk about what had happened.

It was important the lass faced her devils. Not only for her own good, but also because Agnus needed to know, to understand why Sadie carried so much guilt. It was becoming more evident that it was not only survivor's guilt, but something darker eating away at her beloved granddaughter's soul.

She and Malcolm heard it each night when Sadie called out to her dead family. It was enough to drive the hardiest of humans to tears. No, she had to get to the bottom of this, and today was the day.

#

Agnus placed her gardening basket at her feet. "Shall we start off with the damask and beach roses?" No answer.

She looked up and found Sadie standing over at the far side of the garden staring off into the forest again. It wasn't the first time the girl was lost to staring at the trees. Sadie spent most of her days at the edge of the garden staring at the pines, lost to what she and Malcolm feared were traumatic memories.

"Sadie, dear, over here," Agnus called, and frowned when the girl jumped.

Sadie put on a brave face and limped to where Agnus stood.

They slipped on their gloves and Agnus proceeded to teach Sadie everything she knew about her precious roses.

"Why don't you start with the weeding? You can manage on your knees?" She handed Sadie a weeding fork and gardening cushion.

Sadie nodded. "I can manage."

She tucked the padded pillow beneath her bum then began to rid the soil of anything alien.

"So, it's nearing the end of August, and as sweet old Mrs. McPherson reminded us, the winter ball is a big event up in these parts." Agnus inspected her rose tree for aphids and caterpillars, then glanced at her granddaughter so as to gauge her reaction. She caught Sadie's nod. "So, I guess we should head down to Edinburgh one week and find you a dress?"

"It's two months away Nan." Sadie didn't look up from her weeding.

"Aye, but if we're tae find yew a decent dress before the end of year rush, noo is the time."

Agnus kept her pose as Sadie leaned back.

Her granddaughter had paled and her eyes shone bright with fear as she said, "I can't wear a dress. My... my leg, the sc-scars." She pointed to her leg with a shaking hand.

Agnus knelt beside her and gripped her trembling hand. "We wilna let any of that show my darling. I will never put you in such a position. But it's time you realize you are not as broken as you think. You are a blossoming beauty, and one I do not wish to hide from the rest o the world. I know of a seamstress, one who has no ties tae any person up here and who is discreet and wields magic with scissors, needle, and thread."

Agnus gave her granddaughter's hand a squeeze and stood up.

An electric silence floated in on the breeze as she returned to her roses. Was fate this cruel to return her granddaughter in body but rob the precious lass of her soul? No, she could not, would not believe that. Somewhere inside the mangled, traumatized girl who sat on the grass at her feet still roamed the vibrant beauty who was her granddaughter. She would not give up until Sadie was once again whole inside.

#

Sadie knew Agnus Munro like she knew her own mother. Just because she had only seen her Nan twice a year while growing up, didn't mean the woman was a stranger to her. Agnus had oiled the wheel with the mention of the ball and dresses and what not. She would not give up easily. The reminder of the ball was her Nan's first step to her next request.

Her Nan's next move now hung in the air between them. Sadie feared the woman had reached a stage where she needed answers. She knew Nan was worried. She saw it in her eyes every afternoon when she returned from searching for the roan.

"Whatever happened to that pretty boy who used to visit you so often?"

And there it was. Nan wasted no time.

Sadie sat back on her heals and looked around at the delicately tended bushes and trees filled with brightly colored buds and blossoming roses. Sadie looked at her Nan.

It was a chilly day and the sun was playing dodgems with thick wads of grey cloud in the sky. The soft autumn light formed a hazy halo around Nan's head. It gave her the look of one of those saints depicted in the glass of church windows.

"He left, Nan." She looked away.

One could see the west edge of the woods from here. She rubbed at her chest bone. The mare was back. She could feel her.

"Left for where? To travel? Will he be dropping in?"

The question annoyed Sadie and she laughed nervously. "I doubt that, and I don't know."

Perhaps if she were blunt enough she'd put Nan off? She didn't want to talk about this. It was enough she should come to terms with being shown off in a few months at the ball.

"He took one look at messed-up me, knew what was good for him, and ran. Just like your friends will run when they see me in a dress at your ball." Hot bile dripped off every syllable.

She was acting like a spoiled brat. But before she could swallow her pride and apologize Nan added.

"Och, what a fool. I never thought he'd amount to much."

Agnus didn't so much as glance at her as she spoke. Instead she continued faffing over her roses.

Sadie sighed. No use in saying anything more.

Sadie returned to the weeds. There weren't many, but she enjoyed the monotony of tilling the soil. The scent of wet ground drifted up her nose and Sadie had the sudden urge to dig her hands into the damp flesh of Mother Nature and connect with something solid.

All Nan's questions had her head spinning and Sadie knew if she didn't hold on tight, she'd be flung off the fragile axis on which her life was so precariously balanced. She pulled off her gloves and plunged her fingers into the ground.

"And you, my dear? How do you feel about it all?" Nan pressed on.

Stop Nan, no more! She wanted to plead.

She froze when Nan knelt down beside her and placed an un-gloved, warm hand on her shoulder. "Och lass. I know it hurts, but you need tae let it out."

Sadie pulled back. "Let what out, Nan?" Ice edged her tone.

Sadie cringed at the way she'd just spoken to her grandmother. But, all the hurt, the fear, the loss seemed to reach boiling point and she could no longer keep a lid on it.

"The hurt lass. It's eating ye up inside. I hear it in the night…"

Sadie stumbled to her feet and rounded on her nan. "And why weren't you there?!"

Agnus gave Sadie a puzzled look.

"The funeral. The hospital. Me. You didn't bother to come, to say goodbye…"

Agnus touched a shaky hand to her neck. "We…we… I thought ye were dead! We didnae ken ye'd survived… and the funeral, wot wi yer grandsire's stroke and…."

She barely gave Agnus a chance to explain. She had to get away. The look of anguish in her Nan's eyes hurt too much. How would she ever be able to tell her grandparents it was her fault. It was all her fault. If only she'd listened to her father. Not been so damn pig headed. Not tried to save those silly horses. If only…

Sadie turned and ran as fast as her faux leg would allow.

#

Agnus swallowed her guilt. The question had only arisen once since Sadie's arrival, and that was the morning Blane had delivered her granddaughter to her front door. It was an unanswered question Agnus had chosen to forget. More likely sticking her head in the sand, out of shame, she realized now.

Yes, she hadn't gone, hadn't even known when it would be or that Sadie had survived, but that was not an excuse. It was hard for them to face what had happened that day and the ones that followed. Malcolm had suffered a minor stroke on hearing of the heinous murders. She wasn't about to leave his bed side, and she knew she wouldn't have had the strength to bury her son, daughter-in-law, and grandchildren on her own.

Had they known Sadie had survived, well that would have been a different story entirely. But why had Sadie not contacted her?

Her heart broke a little more for her granddaughter. She watched as Sadie stumbled away from her, white as a sheet, not shedding a single tear. To run after her now would be a mistake. She needed space. But the girl was keeping something from them, a burden so great it was suffocating her, and it was probably the same reason she'd not called, but merely arrived on their door step.

Enough was enough. She would fix this. She had to save that girl from herself. The Devil be dammed! She would pay for her own sins later.

#

Sadie clung to the cold red rock of the house, afraid if she let go of the solid mass, she'd crumble to dust. The air had fled her lungs and left her gasping. What did Nan want from her? A bloody confession? And then what? Probably exile.

Sadie turned and pressed her back into the wall, then slid to the ground. She was alone here on the far side of the manor, just beyond the court yard. Alone to face her demons. She tried again to suck in a mouthful of air, but instead of fresh highland oxygen, smoke and burnt flesh invaded her senses.

It burned her throat. The screams of the horses, the pleading of her mother, the horrors of hell, all assaulted her mind. Sadie slapped the sides of her head with her hands.

"No, no, no." The words struggled up through clenched vocal chords over and over and, just when she thought she was lost to the nightmare, stomping hooves and the high-pitched whinny of the mare broke through her delusion and pulled her back into the present. She fell forward onto her hands and knees and looked up in time to see the blue roan gallop off into the depths of the forest.

"Lass, are ye right there?" Mrs. Perkins voice rose softly. Sadie twisted and fell onto her bottom.

"Um, yes…thank you." Her cheeks burned.

Mrs. Perkins stepped forward, a basket of long green stems under one arm as she held out the other hand. Concern creased the skin between her eyes.

"Come on then. Its tea time and yer Nan is by herself."

Sadie took the proffered hand and gave the housekeeper a wobbly smile, grateful that Mrs. Perkins hadn't made a scene about the state in which she'd found her.

"Come wash yer hands first." Mrs. Perkins pointed to an outside tap.

The water was icy, but the cold tempered her residual panic. Sadie looked up to where her grandmother stood, trimming the dead roses. Though she owed her an apology, she wasn't sure what she would say. Reluctantly, Sadie followed the housekeeper back to the roses where Mr. Foggart was serving morning tea with slices of the most beautiful cream and strawberry cake Sadie had ever seen.

"Ah there you are. Just in time for some Oolong and Mrs. Perkins' bake," Agnus smiled at Sadie as though nothing had transpired a few minutes earlier.

How did she do that? Pretend all was right in this broken world?

Mrs. Perkins greeted Nan and headed back into the house behind the butler.

The pair sat on the granite garden bench in silence and enjoyed the tea and cake.

After tea, when Mr. Foggart had retrieved the tray, and they were once again alone, Sadie leaned forward and took her Nan's hand in her own.

"Nan, I'm sorry."

Agnus smiled. "I know, dear, and I should probably not have pushed so hard, but…"

"You need to know," Sadie finished.

"Aye."

"Just… I can't."

The hurt in her grandmother's eyes twisted her guts.

"But." This was so hard. "Perhaps Selwyn, Dad's solicitor, could?"

"Perhaps." Agnus folded her hands on her lap, "I'd prefer tae heer it from yew. You need to…"

Sadie shook her head.

Nan looked out over her rose garden. "I owe you an explanation." She glanced at Sadie.

"You owe me nothing."

"Oh aye, I do. We do." She turned her body toward Sadie. Their knees touched as she leaned forward and placed her hand on Sadie's knee. "Ye see. That phone call, ye grandsire answered? It aboot brought him tae his knees. I dinna think he heard the whole message, but, only that Stewart and his family had perished. Then he had his stroke. I wanted to go to the funeral, but I couldn't lose the last person in the world love. As far as we knew, no one had survived. And frankly, I couldnae face that terrible place with oot any of ye in it. So, I said my goodbyes on the shores of the loch and prayed tae God tae forgive me fur not comin tae bury my sweet son and his family."

Agnus bowed her head, as tears streaked her rouged cheeks.

Sadie took her hand in both of hers holding them to her face. "There's nothing to forgive Nan. You did what any person in your shoes would have done."

Agnus nodded and pulled her into a hug.

Sadie knew she was putting herself at risk. Selwyn didn't know Sadie had acted against her father's instructions. It was her fault Obaje had come to their farm. Her fault her family, all their stock, and their workers were slaughtered. But things had a way of coming out. And sooner or later, Sadie knew she'd have to face the music.

Chapter 17

"Enjoying the rare sunshine?" Blane asked as he strolled toward Sadie who was perched on the bench beside the loch.

She turned her head and gave him a luminous smile.

"Where I come from there is too much of it."

"Do you miss it?" he asked sitting beside her.

Her face paled a little, and her eyes darkened causing Blane to regret his question.

"No." she said then looked back out over the loch.

"I owe you an apology," she added.

"For?"

"I acted like an absolute cow the other night. You were being nice and I…" She glanced in his direction then back to the loch.

"It's no worry. I'm certain you're still feeling the after effects from jetlag… that and the fact your grandmother introduced you to the entire Lairg in one night. Any person would be crabby after that. But I do think I owe you an explanation."

Blane found himself lost in the large smile Sadie rewarded him with. It warmed her face and the yearning chasm in his heart. The tip of his index finger itched to stroke her lips then trail its way up to connect the dots sprinkled across her nose and cheeks.

"Whatever for?"

"Cybil's arrival… it was…" he began to explain when Sadie shook her head.

"What goes on in your private life is entirely that… private. No need to explain." Her smile had faded, and her eyes grew guarded.

Blane felt a chill enter his chest at the loss of her smile.

"Malcolm reckons you guys have a lot of work to do for the tender." She said again.

"Yeah, but it'll work. And when we win the tender
and turn Lairg in to the bustling farm town it is meant to
be…" he stopped when he realized he was blabbering.
"Don't stop. I enjoy hearing you talk about what
you love."

Her eyes like crystals and gems drew him in.

The way the sun bounced off her fiery tresses, and
her sweet soft smile. She was utterly sincere and genuine in
her request to hear more. These were qualities which
lacked in many humans these days, but ones she wore as a
goddess would her crown.

#

Blane jumped into his Rover and pressed his thumb
against the start button. It was the perfect end to what had
been a long day. One filled with de-worming sheep, and
then sitting down with Malcolm Munro and sorting out
paper work for the town's tender. He'd finally given in to
the burning urge to follow her out to where she now sat
beside the loch. It had been pure torture seeing snippets of
her as she strolled along its shores and played with the dogs
while he was stuck inside discussing technicalities with
Malcolm. Never in his life had a woman elicited such
strong feelings in him. They were both strange and
unnerving at the same time.

As he drove out the gates of Munro Estate an SMS
alert pinged. Blane grabbed his phone from his pocket –
Cybil!

His elated mood morphed into a dark and sullen
energy. The thought of Cybil simply arriving two morning
ago, without any warning or invitation, burned hot and
angry in his mind. What did she hope to accomplish? They
were done, over, history! There wasn't the slightest chance
he'd ever take her back. Their ideologies and personalities
were like oil and water. Simply incompatible. Why
wouldn't she accept it?

Blane had tried to make a point to sit and talk sense
into Cybil's stubborn mind, but each time he'd managed to
corner her, she'd cleverly evaded the subject. God, he
should just call Michael, and have his little brother come

collect her. What was this woman up to? Why couldn't she understand his life no longer centered around prissy princesses, the latest German sedan, and closing deals.

Blane turned on to the main road and floored the accelerator. It was his way of ridding himself of his daemons. The torque of the five liter, V8 motor vibrated through his body. He'd never tire of this sort of power. Blane felt the grin spread across his face as he left a dust trail behind him speeding toward Saorsa.

Blane slowed the SUV down and drove around the back of the large manor house then pulled into his run-down garage and forced his mind back to the here and now. He would need to have it refurbished soon, before the roof caved in.

Saorsa had been in a sorry state when he'd purchased it from the Ross family two years ago. Since then, he'd had extensive renovations done to the ten-bedroom manor house and all its contents to bring it back to its former glory. The farm now employed a handful of locals, and the sheep, which at first proved to be a challenge, now earned their keep and then some.

Finally, Saorsa was carrying itself and he no longer needed to plow any more of his personal funds into the estate. Blane had many plans for his estate and the nearby village. He didn't want to see large companies buying up and building over the beautiful moors as they had so many other places.

To keep that from happening, the village needed to thrive, and the younger generation given a reason to stay, instead of heading off to the big city. He hoped his proposal to the Department of Agriculture and Environmental Research at Edinburgh University was a success. The influx of students and lecturers to the area would do wonders for the fading town of Lairg, and the preservation of natural as well as farm lands.

His phone beeped again. Blane let out a heavy sigh then opened the message.

Wondering how Cybie's settled in?
Are you coping?

His mother. He knew she didn't like Cybil and did not approve of the woman's stunt to try and win him back. Another beep.

Don't you bed her! She'll trap you that way.

Blane rolled his eyes as his thumb tapped the screen fervently.

Mother, enough! I'll handle it.

She'd warned him Cybil wasn't his type. At the time, he'd been angered by her words. But like the good mother she was, she had supported him when he'd announced his impulsive proposal to the Lady Cybil Acton. He began to understand, too late, what his mother had meant.

His father had never said a word, not until he'd told them both of his plans to end his engagement, leave the company in his younger brother's hands, and head off into the highlands.

His father's prophetic words echoed down the dark hallways of his memory.

"You be careful now son. She'll find a way back in to your life. Women like her always do."

Blane entered his house through the back door. He left his loafers in the scullery then made his way toward the fire place to check on the tiny ewe he was nursing back to health. She bleated then returned to her peaceful position curled up near the fire. Unlike the other sheep, Matilda was quiet and docile. He could leave her alone in the kitchen knowing she'd not cause any problems. Blane knelt beside her and rubbed her head.

"That's a good lamb now," he whispered as he looked toward the flames in the old stone fireplace.

Blane wondered what they'd make of Sadie? A vision of his mother sitting beside Sadie on the bench by the loch, chatting and laughing flashed before his eyes.

He promptly pushed the thought from his mind. He had to sort out his personal life, tonight. That involved confronting Cybil and sending her packing to London, as in yesterday.

He washed his hands and face in the scullery before he went in search of Cybil.

He found her in the study, sitting in the red settee with a book. Her pretense at blasé relaxation was skin deep; Cybil only ever read fashion magazines and rarely lounged in settees. She looked up as he entered, the cold blue of her eyes bright, even in the soft glow of the corner lamp, and her cheeks flushed.

She was a pretty little thing, fine boned and fair, a proper, social climbing English lady to the marrow, but no longer one he loved or wanted in his life.

"Good evening, stranger." She placed the book on the seat beside her and rose to walk over to him.

Stretching up, she wrapped her thin cashmere covered arms around his neck and kissed him. Blane peeled her arms off and stepped back. Cybil acted as though nothing was amiss.

"Have a good day?"

"Busy, and you?"

"Oh, just getting used to the…um… the fresh air." Cybil smiled, but its warmth did not reach her arctic blue eyes.

She paused a moment when Blane didn't respond. "You must be tired. Shall I run us a bath?" she stepped closer running her index finger down the front of his shirt.

With care and as much grace as he could muster, Blane, gripped her shoulders and pushed her away.

"Cybil, we need to talk."

Her seductive gaze quickly melted into a panicked glare, and her lips pulled tight as she raised her hands to cup his face.

"Shhh," she tried to stop the words from tumbling out of his mouth.

"Cybil. I'm sorry I left you when I did," Blane began.

"I know… and it's alright. There is no need to apologize baby. We can simply move forward from here…"

Blane let go of her and stepped away pulling his hand through his hair, loosening the tie keeping it in a neat pony tail and causing his dark curls to cascade around his face.

"God dammit Cybil. There is no moving forward, or back. There is simply no moving anywhere with us as a couple. I thought I'd made myself clear before I left London!" He didn't mean for his voice to peel across the room like thunder, but his patience was wearing thin. How else was he to make her understand?

"But we share such passion. We're good together and I'm not only talking about the bedroom my love." She reached for him, but Blane stepped away.

"Cybil, face it. The only passion there ever was between us, is in the past. It was lust Cybil, and lust is no foundation for a marriage." Regret scorched his heart as he watched his words cut her.

He didn't want to hurt her any more than he already had, but she had to come to terms with the truth.

She walked over to the drinks trolley and poured a stiff shot of Whiskey for herself, downed it, then poured another and turned to face him.

"Fine, but I'll return to London on my terms. It's been hell with all those ditzy back stabbing bitches. You buggered off, left me to face… face them on my own. I need time and this… place… is as good as any."

\#

Blane made sure Cybil was comfortably settled in her bedroom before making his way back to his study where he poured himself a whiskey. The amber colored liquid bit into the back of his throat as it ran down into his belly. Its warmth reminding him of a lingering, sharp, green gaze, and flaming hair.

Sadie…

She refused to leave Blane's thoughts in peace.

He'd never experienced a conversation with a woman who wasn't constantly worried about her looks, her social gatherings, gossiping, but actually listened to him, even if it was about the tender. There were many sides to

Sadie Munro and Blane couldn't help but want to get to
know them all.

Chapter 18

Sadie stretched her arms out above her head. Prionnsa, as always, lay at the foot of her bed and groaned when Sadie prodded him with her toes. She'd fallen asleep in the early hours of the morning after spending most of her night sitting at the window, reading and waiting for the mare.

She reluctantly opened one eye. The sun was lazy, hiding below the horizon with only a few errant sunbeams showing its promise it would soon warm the earth.

Sadie's mind and heart felt a little numb after the confrontation in the rose garden with Nan the day before. Strangely though, seeing Blane yesterday afternoon had eased some of her anxiety.

Last night, she'd phoned Selwyn. First, she'd tackled the question nagging her since her arrival.

"Why did you lie to me?"

"Lie?"

"Yes, Selwyn. You told me more than once you'd left a message and received no reply. Nan and Malcolm only got that one call from you. And you didn't even tell them I lived!"

A heavy silence suffused the conversation.

"Sorry Sadie. But …" His sigh travelled across the wireless airwaves into Sadie's ear. "I was trying to protect you. As far as I knew or understood, and from what your father had told me, your grandfather was a block head and the chances were, he'd turn you away. I wasn't sure how you'd handle that. I didn't say anything because, frankly, I expected you back on my door step within the week. And besides, when you didn't make an effort to contact Agnus of your own accord, well… I took it as a sign."

"Agh, Selwyn. It's all worked out in the end. It was never your choice. You had no right to make that decision for me… I know you care… I know you are hurting too, but, this wasn't right!"

Where once their friendship was based on trust and loyalty, it now stood on shaky ground.

"Is that why you're calling?" his voice had grown softer and bordered on distant.

"Yes and… Will you speak with Agnus and Malcolm?"

"Of course, my girl. But first, tell me, is the Scottish air doing you good?"

His voice, husky from years of smoking, usually comforted her. But her anger at his blatant betrayal burned its way up her throat as she cut the conversation short.

"Selwyn, please if you could just speak to Agnus and Malcolm?"

"Certainly,' he answered.

Sadie dropped the phone on her bed, then made her way over to the window. Her mother would have given her what for, for the way she'd just treated Selwyn, but her anger was too close to the surface to ignore.

Yes, why hadn't she made an effort to call her Nan when she'd heard nothing more?

Chapter 19

Stepping out in to the passage, Sadie's eyes fell on the only other closed door in the passage — her dad's bedroom.

A shudder ran up her legs and curled tightly around the pit of her stomach. A piece of her father was still here. Yet she was too much of a coward to ask about him. Why had they kept his room just as he had left it all those years ago?

No, no more remaining stuck in the past. Besides, today was an exciting day. A day filled with possibilities. Too excited to eat, she skipped breakfast and made her way out to the log, which lay conveniently close to the forest on the far side of the house.

Over the last week she'd spent every morning and afternoon patiently waiting for the mare. Blue had made her presence known, but always kept her distance. Today would be different though, she just knew it.

She sat down and straightened out her left leg. It was a good day, pain wise. Also, she hadn't dreamed of the farm last night. She'd only had one dream, a good dream — riding the mare.

Sadie closed her eyes and allowed her mind to step back into the dream….

The collective thudding of hooves pounded the rich soil. One hand gripped the blue-grey mane. The other rubbed the sweat stained muscles of the mare's neck. Sadie's body was whole and healthy. The smell of horse and freedom filling her nostrils and her soul, the connection of two hearts beating as one.

The sun stretched out its long glowing arms and finally rose above the peak of the distant mountain, spreading warm fingers across Sadie's back. She opened her eyes and waited. This is what it would be, a waiting game. One of patience and of earning trust. Sadie rubbed her chest bone, she knew the mare was close by, she could feel her.

It was deep into the morning when she returned to the here and now.

Footsteps crunched up the gravel and mulch behind her and drew her out of her meditative state. Sadie turned to find Malcolm, two mugs of tea in hand, walking to where she sat, black spaniels in tow.

"Is the bench not more comfortable?" he smiled. "You spend an awful lot of time just staring off into nothingness lass."

They shared most tea times together at their bench on the loch's shores these days. They never spoke much, didn't need to. Sitting, contemplating life together in silence over a steaming cup of freshly brewed tea leaves was all they needed.

Sadie shifted to make space for her grandfather on the log. The dogs settled down at their feet. Malcolm handed her a mug and they sipped their tea in silence. Her grandfather rubbed his chest bone every so often.

"Everything okay?" Sadie asked.

It wasn't good to have an oldie rub the spot close to their heart the way he was.

"Aye lass, just a twitch, dry skin probably," Malcolm tipped the remains of his tea on the ground beside him.

Sadie considered him as a conversation she'd had with Nan slipped back in to her thoughts.

"You sure it's not something else. I feel it too, you know."

Malcolm's cheeks flushed, and his grey eyes lit up. He looked out into the forest, then shook his head.

"Weel see ye at lunch then, aye?" He held out his hand for her cup.

Sadie sighed, and proffered a small smile. "Thank you."

Perhaps not.

"Tighinn." He slapped a free hand to his thigh.

Sadie had learned it was Gaelic for *come*. Prionnsa and Donn looked up, then to Sadie.

"It's alright. Off you go and give the old man some attention now." She looked up at Malcolm and gave him a cheeky smile which he rewarded with one of his own.

#

Sadie stood up and stretched. The mare was stubborn, far more so than any other horse she'd ever had to work with. She thought of telling Blane that the horse was still alive.

Her stomach flipped. It annoyed her the way her body reacted each time she came near him, thought of him, or heard his name in a conversation. No, he did not need to know about Blue, not yet. Best to leave him and his 'unexpected' guest to it.

Her mind drifted back to the present. Why was the mare being so stubborn? The horse was close enough for Sadie to feel her in that soft spot in the center of her solar plexus, but too far away to pin point her exact location. Fear trickled into her heart. What if the horse had injured herself? No, she'd heard her last night.

A whinny and hoof stomping echoed through the trees. Relief flooded Sadie's veins. She turned to look but could see no more than the grey outlines of tree trunks and foliage.

Sadie skulked toward the edge of the woodland. There, to the left, where the canopy broke away and allowed thin fingers of autumn sun to poke through, stood the roan. Sadie swallowed a gasp. God, what a beauty. With her neck arched she was every bit the magnificent Queen of the Equines. Even in the dim light of the forest Sadie was able to admire the mare's toned build and exotic stature.

The delicate rays of light hugged the dark grey and blue of the roan's coat. Her mane shimmered like the night, but her legs were covered in mud.

The roan turned her head. Her large eyes looked right into Sadie's. Sadie hoped the horse hadn't picked up mites or injured her heels and fetlocks. By the looks of it she was rather healthy. This was strange for a horse lost to the wilds.

Fear and elation tumbled through Sadie's innards. Every cell in her body called for her to let go of her doubt and dread, and for her to reach out to this poor, lost animal.

Her legs wobbled, and her breath hitched. Could she dare to use her gift once more?

Her gift, as Mom called it, allowed her to connect with animals on a special level, especially with those who were hurt or traumatized. Sadie was the person her father would ask to train the skittish equines. Through concentration and a song she was taught by Nomvula, her Zulu nanny, she always managed to pull the most paranoid of thoroughbreds out of their anxiety-ridden worlds.

But she was no longer the whole one. Would it still work? Excitement rippled down from the crown of her head into the toes of her foot. Yes! If only to save the horse and return her to her owner.

An unbidden image of the tall, bearded Englishman flashed in her mind's eye. She pushed it away.

This could take all day. It could take a few days. But then, there was no rush and Sadie liked to believe she'd mastered patience a long time ago.

She welcomed the familiar sensation stirring inside her chest. Careful not to make any sudden movements, she stepped backward. The back of her knees touched the log and she sat down.

Her heart flipped. It'd been months since she'd been near a horse, not since… She pushed the dark memories from her mind. She couldn't slip back into the nightmare she fought so hard to forget. Not now, not when this mare's life depended on her.

Sadie kept still, closed her eyes, and let go. Entering a state of complete ease, she envisioned a golden string drifting from her solar plexus toward the horse. It was hard, harder than she remembered, and not as bright, but Sadie persevered. It wasn't easy working with broken tools.

The mare's fear was palpable. It stirred her own deeply buried trepidation. Sadie pushed the unnerving emotion away so as not to allow it to become her own, but a dank cloud began to form around her. If she concentrated long enough, she could stay the fear and the mare would come to see Sadie as friend, not foe.

Wading through the thickening fog, Sadie focused on the connection they already shared through their dreams.

She took a deep breath and opened her mouth. Flames sprung up around her and the sound of men, woman and horses invaded her inner ears. Her voice cracked, the words of the song evaporated from her mind and the fog settled over her. *It's not real.* She reminded herself as she reached deep within. Nothing. Sadie fought the nightmare. She clawed her way to the surface and the light. When she opened her eyes, she felt the snap and separation of the connection with the mare.

She couldn't do it; she simply could not go back to what was.

"I'm sorry," she whispered and walked away, frustrated, and broken.

#

Sadie stomped in through the back door, dropped her boots in the scullery, and made her way into the kitchen. Failure burned the back of her eyes.

Mrs. Perkins stood at the kitchen table putting together the finishing touches for dinner. Sadie couldn't face anyone after her disastrous attempt, not that anyone knew what she was up to, and made no eye contact as she strode past. She wanted to get to her room.

"Yer goin tae give up that easy, lass?" The skinny middle-aged woman did not look up as she plonked a dollop of salted butter onto the potatoes.

Sadie froze, turned, and faced Mrs. Perkins.

"I saw her that day," she said, fidgeting with the baby carrots.

"Who, the mare?"

"Nae lass. Rhiannon, the Goddess. I saw her when I did gaze upon yer eyes that first day ye did arrive." She turned to Mr. Foggart. "Let Himself know dinner is served. The Mistress should be with him in the library." Then she bent her knowing gaze on Sadie. "Weel off with ye then. Go wash those grubby hands afor ye eat my food."

Sadie didn't move. "The Goddess?" A diluted memory rose to the surface, a dream. As a child, a tall woman in an emerald green dress, and hair as black as a starless night sky, often visited her in those early hours between sleep and wake. It was the same woman her mother's nickname for her came from, Epona.

Mrs. Perkins stopped what she was doing and looked back at Sadie. "Aye lass. She is inside of ye, riding yer blood and tempering yer spirit. Dinnae push her awa like ye grandsire has, aye? Find her and ye will find the mare. Noo off with ye."

Sadie found her body refused to move. She had to know. "Like Malcolm? The Goddess? And where did you see the mare?" The words tumbled from her mouth as Mr. Foggart walked back into the kitchen.

"Himself says tae wait wi the dinner. There's an unexpected guest."

"Och, fur the love of all things holy! Off with ye lass, we can speak of these things another day."

Sadie stood a moment longer. She needed to digest all Mrs. Perkins had thrown at her.

As her mind calmed, it registered Mr. Foggart's words. Guest? Sadie wondered who that could be.

Mrs. Perkins muttered on about spoiled trout and squishy tatties as Sadie turned and strode from the kitchen, still in her socks, down the long passageway that led to the kitchen.

#

"Yes, Sir, I thought if we…"

A surge of fire ran through her body at the sound of the voice. *Bloody hell!*

She cursed inwardly. *Could she not react like a silly school girl every time she was near the man!*

"Good evening, Sadie."

Blane's gaze enveloped her before they travelled the length of her tall frame and squinted when they reached her feet. Sadie looked down and quickly tucked her misshaped foot behind her leg before looking him squarely in the eyes. "Good evening, Mr. Buchan."

"Why don't you join us for dinner, Mr. Buchan?" her grandmother invited, drawing his attention back to Agnus.

"No thank you, ma'am. I just came to discuss town matters and a sickly ewe with Mr. Munro. I need to get back." His eyes fell to the floor as he tucked both hands into his pockets. "I … have a guest waiting."

Cybil? Sadie wanted to snap, tasting the bitter bile of jealousy on the back of her tongue.

"Och, is the poor dear fitting in?" Agnus asked.

Blane's head snapped up and a light filtered into his dark gaze. It poked at something familiar in Sadie. "Yes Ma'am. She was an unexpected birth. An anomaly. She struggles more, seems to catch the slightest bug." A tenderness warmed his tone, one which spoke of a deep love for animals.

Sadie found a new respect blossoming for the man. He genuinely loved his animals.

Agnus placed a hand on the tall Englishman's shoulder. "I meant yer guest, dear."

Sadie bit her lip as Blane's neck turned a soft pink. She rubbed her cheeks, sure hers had turned in color also. She, like Blane, had thought Agnus had asked after the poor lamb.

"Well then, why don't you and your fair guest join us tomorrow evening then? You will be free?" Agnus suggested.

Sadie's back stiffened. She noticed Malcolm's lips tighten and pale.

A nervous smile swept across Blane's face. "Um, I don't…"

"Nonsense, we'd love to meet her." Agnus declared.

Even Blane Buchan knew better than to fight it.

"Then it would be my pleasure." Blane smiled, but the skin under his cheeks paled. He seemed uncomfortable at the thought of bringing his 'guest' to dinner. Why would that be?

"Wonderful. Well you two had better finish then. I don't think Mrs. Perkins is very happy waiting on us while her food gets cold."

And with that, her grandmother slid her arm through Sadie's, leaving Malcolm to see Blane out.

"Why did you invite them, Nan?"

"Och, why not, my dear? Blane is our neighbor and, if Annie's Chinese whispers are correct, the poor man needs some relief from the demands of his 'guest'."

A mischievous twinkle flickered in the corner of Agnus' eyes.

"Want to slip on a pair of shoes before we sit at table? I doubt he noticed. Those socks are dark and thick."

Said's heart dropped. What if he had noticed the oddness of her fake foot? If he had, he hadn't shown it. And what in the seven heavens was the horrid feeling that washed over her each time Blane's 'guest' was mentioned? She'd never experienced jealousy over anyone before. This was both strange and annoying.

Sadie made a mental note she would go out of her way to be kind to the woman and push the strange feelings broiling inside her deep into a dark forgotten corner. They were not welcome and only served to hurt and cause problems.

Slipping her arm out from Agnus's. She said, "Malcolm didn't look too keen about the dinner either."

"Och, that's just because your grandsire is no fan of Sassenachs." She winked and made her way to the dining room.

Sadie had learned that the term not only meant a person not from Scotland but probably someone they didn't like. Is that what he had thought of her mother?

"Well if Blane's tender is accepted he'll have to deal with a fair few more of them." Sadie said as Agnus chuckled.

"Aye lass. His worst nightmare has become his beloved toon's savior."

Sadie made her way up to her bedroom and grabbed her shoes. Her conversation with Mrs. Perkins earlier in the kitchen came back to her. What had she meant by 'she had seen the Goddess in her eyes'?

Why would Mrs. Perkins mention it to Sadie? She'd never mentioned her special gift, unless Nan had? Also, what was the Goddess's connection to Malcolm? He didn't strike Sadie as the type to indulge in fairy tales.

Feet shod and hands washed, Sadie made her way back down to the dining room. She sat opposite her Nan with Malcolm to her left as he ranted.

"Did ye really have tae invite him and his woman tae dinner, wife? I dinnae mind him, but who knows what this woman is like."

"Yes, my darling. It's been forever since we've had anyone over and it would do you good to enjoy the company of more than one outlander."

"Dinnae be daft woman."

Agnus held up her hand as Mr. Foggart entered with their plates of delicious trout. Malcolm didn't say another word.

Sadie broke the hungry silence. "So how are the plans for the research students and grants coming along?"

"Ye mean the tender? Weel its tae be a big story. The University in Edinburgh must be convinced tae move their Department of Agriculture and Environment up here for research and the students' practical experience is worth their while. Blane reckons it might take less than a month tae get the paper work in order." Malcolm's face lit up like a little boy before lifting a trout-filled fork to his mouth.

"Malcolm no need to shove yer gullet like a swine," Agnus scolded.

He winked to Sadie causing his wife to sigh and roll her eyes.

Chapter 20

Sadie sat at the large table and watched as Mrs. Perkins shelled peas. She reached forward, pinched a few of the tiny emerald pearls, and popped them into her mouth. Their crispy freshness burst over her tongue, reminding her of days spent cooking with Grace and Mom. It was becoming easier to think of them now, not a lot, but this memory brought some joy instead of the usual searing guilt and grief.

"Ooh, these are good." She leaned forward to grab a few more.

"That'll be enough lass," Mrs. Perkins warned, "or ye'll ruin yer appetite. Shouldn't ye be upstairs making ready fur this evening?"

Sadie slumped at the mention of the dinner and their expected guests. She wasn't in the mood. She'd spent the day in Lairg with Nan.

Their first stop was Nan's bridge club. Sadie hated card games. Thankfully they'd had four players, which left Sadie comfortably seated at Mrs. Higgins' fire place with a book. From there, they called on some of the older residents. Agnus took it upon herself to make sure those who either had no family, or whose families simply didn't care, were looked after.

"It's our duty as head of the clan, lass," Agnus explained.

Also, they made a few other calls on homes who might be interested in taking in student borders, should the town's tender be successful. Sadie had drunk so many cups of tea and eaten so many homemade biscuits and shortbread, she thought she'd turn into a biscuit wielding tea pot by sunset.

To round it all off, she'd bumped into dear Mrs. Learie outside the post office. Nan had popped inside to collect correspondence and buy more stamps and envelopes while Sadie had stood outside waiting. Nothing was said, but the look the old crone had given her was straight out of a horror novel. Sadie couldn't let go of the thought the woman was far more devious than anyone realized.

"What's on yer mind, lass?" Mrs. Perkins asked without looking up from her meal preparations.

"Malcolm. You mentioned the other day…"

Mrs. Perkins held up her hand. "Annie," The girl looked up from her potato peeling. "Go start Ms. Munro's bath and sprinkle some o my mix on the fire, will ye?" She then turned her attention back to Sadie, who was about to protest against Annie drawing her a bath, held up her hand, and only spoke again once Annie was out of the kitchen.

"Careful whose ears are aboot when chatting lass. Ah, yer grandsire, eh? Ye mean, the mention I made o him rejecting his gift and all?"

Sadie nodded and managed to swipe a few more peas from the bowl.

"Aye, weel Himself was born in a time when such things were a great taboo. It was believed if ye were touched by the faeries, ye was touched in the heid, ye ken? So just afor he was sent off tae school doon in Edinburgh, his mammy, yer great grandmother, sat him doon. She made sure he wouldna ever again mutter a word aboot the Goddess or how she spoke to him through wee creatures."

A pea lodged itself in the back of Sadie's throat at the mention of the Goddess and her grandfather talking to animals. She coughed, and Mrs. Perkins slapped her a few times on the back. "There, there noo, no moor fur ye then."

Sadie struggled to take all this in. Perhaps it was not a good idea to have asked. Faeries and voices? She knew she had a gift, but she'd never had some ethereal being speak to her through animals.

"Yer family, the Munro bloodline, has a strong history wi the Goddess. It's buried beneath myth and legend noo, but it's there. There's a book, ye nan will ken where, that teels aboot the verra first Munro, a daughter of the forest, Fenella, hoo was given the task of keeping the forest an all its creatures safe. Hoo she were able tae understand the smallest chirrup of the swallow, and the softest grunt of the badger. An by her side a white stallion who never grew old. An as reward, when her hair had turned grey and her skin tae leather." Mrs. Perkins voice dipped and lulled as she told the tale and Sadie found she was captivated by tales of her ancestors and the fairies.

"Rhiannon did come tae collect her and take where she would forever be whole and young."

Sadie sat stunned, both by the tale and by the way Mrs. Perkins tone had slipped in to a near hush as she spoke her last words. As though, like Sadie, she wondered if her family had been granted the same as they'd crossed over.

This was a lot to take in, if she were to believe the tale as truth. She needed some space, some fresh air.

Sadie placed both her hands on the kitchen table and made to stand when Mrs. Perkins said, "Why'd ye think ye sire and Malcolm fought so much? Stewart, may he rest in peace, he believed in her and Malcolm forbade it. It's taken yer grandsire that long tae forgive himself fur pushing his only bairn awa."

"I knew Dad had something special, but…"

"Oh, aye, not near as strong as Himself or yers, but he had some of it."

Sadie rose slowly from the chair. Wow! This was insane! Intense! And mind blowing. She'd known her dad was as good with animals, but never had she thought of her ability or her dad's, to connect with animals as something more than just a knack, or personality trait.

And her dad had sure as heck never mentioned anything about faeries, goddesses or ancient relatives who had been gifted by the goddess. Although he'd always encouraged her gift. She'd thought the fact her mom had likened her to the Celtic Goddess was an endearment.

A conversation she'd had that first day she'd arrived came to mind. Nan had told her she shared the gift with Malcolm and that Malcolm had long ago forsaken his -- how could she forget?

Sadie turned to make her way to her room when Mrs. Perkins said, "Ye both have naught to ask for forgiveness, ye ken. Sometimes life is what it is, cruel and harsh. But Rhiannon would help ye understand and heal. Call on her. Dinnae be afraid lass. Noo go up, yer bath water is getting cold."

#

Ideas of magic, gifts, and beings with power tumbled around inside Sadie's mind as she sat on the edge of the bath and slipped her prosthesis off.

The trade men had done a great job on the bathroom. The fancy clawed foot bath had been replaced by a more practical, and less slippery one. Beside the bath stood a stool where she could sit and undress, and on its sides, both inside and out, well-placed handles, so Sadie managed to get in and out with ease.

A shower, with handles and a seat, stood on the opposite side of the bath. When Sadie had mentioned a shower worked best, Nan said, "There are times where one simply needs to soak away the troubles of the day."

Today, was just such a day.

She sighed as she slipped into the hot water. Annie had thrown some dried rose and sandalwood on the fire in the bathrooms fireplace, which created an aura of complete relaxation. Sadie's thoughts drifted.

She smiled. Clever Mrs. Perkins.

Sadie inhaled deeply and allowed the hot water to soothe her body as the incense drifted up her nose and infused with her blood. Her thoughts quieted, and her heart beat slowed. Mrs. Perkins had told her to find the Goddess within and she would find peace. But how would one do that…

Tall pines surrounded her and formed a canopy above her head, which hid the bright night sky, but the moon still managed to light the way with its silvery slivers of light.

Sadie… a voice like a hundred chiming bells beckoned to her. Strange fingers of mist twisted and curled around the trunks of tall trees and green shrubs, then snaked toward her and wrapped themselves around her legs… her body was whole!

Sadie was not frightened. In fact, she had never felt so… safe.

The voice called again, and Sadie found herself moving toward a small clearing. She had never seen anything so beautiful in all her life.

Standing in the center of the opening -- the whitest stallion she had ever laid eyes on.

His mane, like a river of diamonds, flowed down his neck. His tail, thick and glossy, touched the ground. Sitting astride his back, a woman with hair like the flames of a bonfire. She was naked from the waist up, with her tresses draped gracefully over her breasts. Sadie knew her. She'd seen her so often in her dreams as a child. Although she took many forms, something inside Sadie always recognized her.

Sadie stepped forward and the woman turned to look at her. Her gasp echoed through the forest. The woman, her horse, the forest, and the pale moonlight vanished. Sadie, flailed in the water and came to sit up coughing and sputtering.

Wiping her face with the washcloth she took a deep breath. How silly of her to fall asleep in the bath. She could have drowned! Sadie leaned forward and grabbed the cake of handmade lavender soap to wash.

What a powerful dream. She could still smell the forest and see the woman's face, her – face! She stopped what she was doing and allowed her memory to drift back to the moment the woman had looked at her. Green eyes — her own — staring back at her, into her, through her.

Sadie shuddered.

A knock at the door made Sadie jump. "Who is it?"

"Just me lass. Yew had better hurry. Our guests will be here in half an hour," Nan reminded.

Oh, bother.

Chapter 21

It was well after sunset when Blane and his 'guest' arrived.

"Aboot bloody time," Malcolm grumbled as he, Sadie, and Nan congregated in the foyer to meet their guests.

"Noo Malcolm, behave," Nan whispered a warning.

Mr. Foggart opened the door to reveal Blane, and a shorter, blonde woman.

"Good evening Mr. and Mrs. Munro." Blane, shook first Malcolm, then Agnus's hand, before he turned to Sadie. "Good evening, Sadie."

His molten gaze and brilliant grin held her attention a moment longer than necessary. There were those damn stampeding buffalo stomping around her stomach, again!

"Hi." Sadie forced herself to break away from the spell his eyes cast and turned her attention to the shorter woman beside him.

A sour taste spread itself across her tongue and pinched the insides of her cheeks. It wasn't because the woman was his ex-fiancée. No, there was something about her that flipped the switch on all Sadie's warning bells.

The slim blond wore her hair in a perfect bob, with immaculate make-up, which emphasized sharp cheek bones, and tight, thin lips. Dressed in the latest haute couture and heels from hell, she had to look up at Sadie. A groomed and penciled eyebrow arched as sharp blue-grey eyes measured Sadie and sliced through any pretense of potential niceties.

Not taking her eyes off Sadie, "Aren't you going to introduce us, darling?" the woman asked.

Her nasal British accent reminded Sadie of nails scratching a blackboard.

"Ah, yes. Sadie Munro, this is Lady Cybil Acton."

A lady, nogal?

Sadie suppressed a smile when she thought of how their neighbor, Oom Dirk would have reacted to that introduction. Where she came from there was no such thing as airs and flair's, as Mom always put it.

"Sadie, it is a pleasure to meet you."

Cybil held out her hand and proffered a squishy hand shake, her tone measured and her words calculating. Sadie would have none of it.

She gripped the pretty hand and shook. She didn't do squishy handshakes and smiled inwardly when Cybil rubbed her hand with the other. Sadie knew she was knee jerking, but something about the woman irked the nonsense out of her.

"Good evening, *Cybil*. Nice to meet you and welcome." She plastered on her best fake smile. It was hard to pretend to like a person when you didn't. How did Nan do it?

"Well, shall we enjoy a wee sherry before dinner?" Agnus motioned with her hand toward the open doors leading to the library.

Sadie slipped her arm through Malcolm's. Agnus, ever the hostess, slipped hers through Cybil's at the same time as she threw both Malcolm and Sadie a warning glance. Blane followed on his own as niceties about Cybil's flight up and how she was settling in, were exchanged.

#

Blane kept an eye on Cybil as her gaze trailed over the interior of the manor and their hosts. Her hands, tucked neatly behind her back, blanched as she gripped them together. She was sizing up her prey.

To everyone else she presented as calm and appreciative — everyone that was, except for Blane. It wasn't hard to sell a pretty smile and the odd compliment, a skill most women in her class and background had down pat. The telltale tremor at the corner of her mouth told him not only was she enjoying the company but she'd sensed his attraction for Sadie.

He'd hoped he'd been able to temper his growing feelings but being in the remotest vicinity of Sadie Munro was enough to heat his blood and send his nerve endings on a synaptic rampage.

Cybil had a sixth sense for this, especially when it came to him. Their time together in London was marred by many a cat fight, or Cybil going out of her way to destroy the reputation of any woman she deemed a threat. He'd have to watch her closely.

God!

He cursed himself inwardly. He'd been too polite, and kind not to pass on Agnus' invitation to dinner. By allowing Cybil to accompany him to his neighbors this night, he'd given the woman a foothold, and he knew beyond any doubt she would use it to further insinuate herself in to his life. But his good nature had not allowed him to keep the invitation, which was meant for her also, from her.

The butler served them each a sherry, which did nothing in the way of dampening his edginess. Blane split his attention between Malcolm's conversation and the way Cybil looked at Sadie. Her face wore a hooded expression. The one he knew all too well.

Sadie stood at least a head taller than her. Her hair hung lose down her back. They reminded him of late summer evening sunsets over the Loch. Her navy trousers and cotton top complimented her figure and... Blane swallowed hard when Cybil turned her knowing gaze onto him.

Cybil made her way over to him not breaking her gaze for a moment when Malcolm steered the conversation toward the tender. Blane bit his bottom lip. He did not want her to know about any of his business, or ambitions for Lairg.

"So, Lady Cybil, how are you finding Saorsa and the highlands? Quite a change from the hustle and bustle of London, I expect?" Agnus had come to stand with them.

"Oh yes... quite."

Blane didn't miss the ice in her voice or the cold glance she threw Sadie, who was making her way over to them from the window where she'd stood staring out in to the darkness.

"Your plans for the town sound very…um…ambitious, darling. Care to tell me more?" Cybil gave him a hard glance as she placed her empty sherry glass on the butler's tray.

"Well there's not much to tell yet. We're only in the beginning stages." Blane shifted from one foot to the other.

"Plans you'd be able to orchestrate from your London office?"

An uncomfortable silence draped itself over them all. He didn't miss the questioning looks in both Malcolm's and Agnus's eyes. What in the seven hells was Cybil up to?

\#

Cybil jumped, and Agnus spun around on her heels as what sounded like the chanting of an angry gaggle of geese barged through the open doors of the library.

Mr. Foggart stood just beyond the entrance, dressed in his Kilt regalia, chest expanded and eyes sparkling as he placed his lips on the blowstick of his bagpipes and began to play a familiar melody.

"Liewe donner!" Sadie cursed before bursting out in laughter.

Agnus'd never thought to hear such joy from her beloved granddaughters heart again.

"Since when do we start dinner off wi the pipes husband?" Agnus battled to keep her voice steady as the urge to laugh at her husband's cheeky gesture threatened Mutiny. Blane turned to hide his grin, which only caused to egg on her own inner mirth.

She knew Malcolm would do something to tip the apple cart, he always did with outlanders, but she'd not been able to put her finger on it.

"Och wife, thought it were time Mr. Foggart got sum practice afor the ball eh." He winked and made his way toward the dining room.

Agnus patted the tightly wound blond on the shoulder. "Och dearie, I forgot the large city folk are no longer accustomed to oor highland etiquette. We're still a little old fashioned, ye ken." Agnus explained.

Cybil nodded, and her lips pulled tighter as she attempted a small smile, while her eyes darted from Blane, to Sadie, to Malcolm, and back to Blane.

It was odd to think a man such as Blane Buchan was attracted to such a cold creature? It also didn't escape Agnus's notice that Cybil saw Sadie as a threat. Somehow, Agnus suspected, Cybil would see any woman stronger than herself as a problem to be dealt with. Had she been foolish to invite the lass to dinner? She'd noticed the chemistry between their neighbor and Sadie unfold this last week, and her first reaction had been to ask him to stay away. Sadie was not yet whole enough for complications of the heart. Agnus had decided a subtler approach would suffice. She'd hoped if Sadie saw Blane with Cybil, all be their engagement broken off, it would create a degree of separation. Instead, Agnus feared she'd selfishly opened a whole new kettle of fish.

Agnus tucked her hand beneath Cybil's elbow and led the party through the open sliding doors to the side of the library and in to the dining room.

Cybil was seated opposite Blane, at Malcolm's left hand, and Sadie to Cybil's right. Blane sat to Malcolm's right with Agnus beside him.

Mr. Foggart, still dressed in his kilt, walked in with Annie behind him, both carrying trays with their starters.

"Red deer carpaccio with spring onions, olive oil, grated Parmesan cheese, and black pepper," the butler announced in a deep brogue.

He and Annie placed the plates before them. The room fell silent as everyone took in the beautiful aroma.

"Thank you. This looks simply marvelous." Cybil raised her glass of red wine. "And thank you for your gracious hospitality, and the kindness you have shown Blane."

Everyone raised a glass as Cybil smiled at Blane. It was cold, measured, and didn't reach her eyes.

The butler and Annie returned to remove their plates.

"What is it you do to keep yourself busy up here?" Cybil turned to face Sadie.

"Nothing yet," Sadie answered calmly, her face giving nothing away. Agnus smiled inwardly.

"Still finding your feet? I take it you're not from around here?"

A ripple of something fluttered across Sadie's face. "Yes, you could say that."

"And when you have found your feet?" Cybil prodded.

"Cybil, I'm sure Sadie's plans are no concern of yours," Blane intercepted.

Sadie smiled and nodded. "I suppose I will learn the ropes from my grandfather."

"Slainte!" Malcolm, cheeks flushed with pride, raised his glass and winked at his granddaughter. "Of course, ye will lass."

Agnus noticed the tremble on Cybil's lips as she tried to smile before she took a sip of the deep red wine.

Agnus sipped from her own glass. It was a good wine, dry and sharp. It emphasized the venison they'd eaten, and Agnus suspected was the only warmth that would reach the hollow cockles of the English woman's heart.

The main meal was served, and with it, a delicate silence.

Steaming ox tail cooked in red wine and seasoned vegetables was placed before each of them. The savory aroma delicate enough to make the most uncomfortable of persons feel as though they'd just returned home from a long, cold journey.

Agnus was grateful the excellent cuisine made up for the awkward atmosphere. Mrs. Perkins surely knew how to put together a decent plate.

Each person made inroads into his or her dish. Agnus tried to ignore Malcolm's grunts and slurps, not wanting to reprimand him in front of guests. She raised her eyebrows when she noticed Blane eating with the same highland gusto.

Cybil barely touched her plate.

"The food not to your liking, Lady Cybil?"

"Oh no," Cybil dabbed at her mouth with her napkin. "It's delicious, but I am afraid your delicious carpaccio filled me, and I have no room left."

She turned toward Sadie with a faux smile. "Where did you say you came from?"

"I didn't." Sadie dabbed her napkin across her mouth.

Agnus hid a smile as Cybil suppressed her indignation.

"South Africa."

"South Africa? It's not a country I am familiar with. Though I have come across some migrants from the country. Is it as uncivilized as some expats make it out to be?"

Sadie frowned over the top of her wine glass.

Agnus glanced at her husband, who was as oblivious to what was going down as a sheep was to a bumble bee sitting on a dandelion. Blane on the other hand had taken notice, his expression blank but his eyes were all fire and brimstone.

Blane made to say something, but Sadie beat him to it.

"It is a dangerous land. But so is any country where it's people are robbed of their basic needs by an uncaring and corrupt government. One which manipulates the mass of uneducated souls, of their own making, into acting out their hatred, so they may gain nothing but more empty promises. Unfortunately, they are robbed of foresight and cannot predict this will bring about their own demise, just as it had Zimbabwe. If, to the rest of the world this creates an image of white South Africans living it up and those of color living like uncouth villagers, it is due to their own ignorance at believing the drivel spread through twisted news reports, and public officials wishing to spread their propaganda."

"Then pray tell, what is the truth?"

Agnus bit her tongue when an old Scottish curse landed on it. Instead she would change the subject, but before she could Sadie placed her knife and fork down on the table. Her granddaughter's eyes shone as bright and as dangerous as one of those big African cats.

"That violence and corruption never take in to consideration the color of its victims' skin. That evil knows no bounds and only looks to serve itself and its own coffers *Lady Cybil.*"

The air around the table thickened to the point, Agnus feared, that the slightest spark might set everyone present alight. Split seconds of silence hung from the ceiling like a ticking time bomb.

"Well now, why don't you tell us more about yourself, dear?" Agnus' gentle voice sliced through the uncomfortable moment.

#

Sadie gulped down the last of her wine. With her appetite ruined she sat back and merely observed the small talk taking place around the table. She only nodded and smiled when Cybil made to include her or dropped a perfectly timed innuendo.

"Well Blane did promise to take me out on his four-wheeler motor bike and show me his property. Motorbikes can be so thrilling and personal… do you remember our trip to Italy and that silly pink moped, Darling?"

Blane did not answer but smiled and sipped more wine.

"Have you been? Out on the four-wheeler?" she turned to Sadie.

"Ghilley has a small utility vehicle." Sadie answered.

"Oh, so you have not been over to Saorsa?" Cybil asked again.

"I've not had the time to." Sadie smiled then turned to chat with Malcolm who was in the process of shoveling a heaped dessert spoon of sago and baked pudding into his mouth.

Normal conversations should not be a means to get under a person's skin. The woman was out to prove a point while she was fishing for information.

She'd given Sadie the impression of a spoilt princess who always got what she wanted and beware if her terms weren't met. Sadie smiled inwardly at the image of the blonde stomping her feet and throwing a tantrum like a spoilt toddler. Yup, that was just what Cybil Acton struck her as. A temperamental toddler. Was this really Blane's type? Weak, sooky, spoiled women?

The rest of the dinner passed with little consequence. Malcolm and Sadie, only spoke when spoken to, leaving Agnus to initiate most of the chatter. Blane did not utter another word.

"Well it was nice to meet you, Lady Cybil. How long will you be visiting?" Nan took one of the prissy English woman's hands in hers.

"Oh, …" She threw a puppy eyed glance toward Blane. "I suppose until my welcome runs out?"

Sadie watched Blane's face. Like Nan and Cybil, he hid his emotions well behind his calm façade, but his eyes… if fire could chill the soul, then that was exactly the look Blane was giving Cybil at that moment.

"Well then, please feel free to come over at any time if you get too lonely at Saorsa. Goodness knows the highlands are nothing like London." Her nan smiled then gave Cybil one of her warm hugs.

"Yes, of course."

Cybil shook Malcolm's hand before turning to Sadie. "It was a pleasure to meet you too, Sadie."

Sadie nodded. "I hope you enjoy your time up here. Take care."

Why was it so hard to be nice to a person who was clearly the ice queen's twin sister? How did Nan do it?

Mr. Foggart closed the door once the guests had left, and Sadie began to make her way upstairs to her room.

"That woman is trouble. More trouble I fear than even our dear Mr. Buchan can handle."

Sadie turned back to face her nan. "No, she's just spoiled."

"Och lass, I've met a few lassies like her in my life. And you, my dear, should tread carefully."

Sadie frowned. "She's just like any other prissy Prom Queen, Nan. I doubt she can do any harm."

"Oohooo don't be too sure lass. That girl sees you as a threat." Agnus smiled.

"But I'm not interested in Blane, Nan, and I am certainly no threat."

Nan's eyebrow arched. "If you say so, my dear."

Sadie opened her mouth, but the words tumbled around in her head and would not fall in an orderly row.

"Hahaha, lass, relax. I doubt you'd have much more to do with them anyway." Nan's words came out more like a request than an observation. Did Nan think there was something between her and Blane… surely her attraction wasn't that obvious? Ugh.

"You stood up to her well enough dear, but I am afraid to say that would only fuel her insecurity."

"She has absolutely nothing to worry about Nan. Besides, Blane made it clear a couple of times during dinner that she was merely up for a visit, as a friend. Seriously, I'm a nobody, a broken nobody, and she…"

"Yer nothin of the sort young lady. Ye are a Munro and dinnae ye forget it, aye! That wee Sassenach will head home soon enough." Malcolm patted her on the shoulder as he walked past and made his way up the stairs. "Commin tae bed then?" he called over his shoulder.

Agnus shook her head. "Och lass," she sighed, "I ken it's hard, but it's good practice for the winter ball. Pretending to like a person you really want to spit fire on is one of the hardest skills to accomplish, but necessary in all forms of life."

"About the ball, Nan…"

"Oh no, yew are attending my ball, come hell or high water. We've already discussed this, and I have set a date for a fitting down in Edinburgh." She gave Sadie a hug and a kiss. "Now off with you. I can see you're tired."

Sadie smiled then hugged her Nan and left for bed.

Chapter 22

The drive home was a quiet one. Blane's anger at Cybil's calculated innuendos burned hot and white in his chest. She'd asked for time. He'd given her that, but why was she playing so hard to maintain the illusion they were still a couple of sorts? It had been both embarrassing and tiresome having her dine with them this evening. When at last he'd had enough of her insinuations, he'd, in as kind a way as he could manage, reinforced the truth, that he and Cybil were merely friends, and that she was here for a short sabbatical from the rush of London society. Cybil had about sliced him in two with her eyes.

Even now, her mouth was pulled tight and her cheeks were flushed enough to show through the paint on her face.

Blane parked in the shed, then turned in his seat to have his face-off with Cybil, but, before he could utter a word, she slipped from the car, and slammed the door. He watched as she walked past the back door, which was closer, and unlocked, and made her way, in the dark, to the front of the house.

He got out and closed the door. He would not run after her. Slowly, determinedly, he made his way to the back door and let himself in. Cybil's distant pounding on the front door echoed through the large home.

"There, there, how are you tonight, my wee lamb?" Blane knelt and stroked the sickly lamb's head. Well she was far stronger than when Mac had first brought her up from the paddocks.

More pounding followed by, "Will one of you blasted servants open this door!"

"Well, I'd better let her in before she blows the house down." Blane patted the tiny ewe before making his way to the front entrance via a long passage, just in time to see his butler rush from the employee's quarters as he tied the belt of his night coat.

"Why not the back door? It's always open and right across from the shed." Blane scolded as Giles unlocked and opened the front door, before stepping back with perfect servility.

"Because I am not one of your servants!" Cybil pushed past the sleepy butler with no thanks or pardon. "You could have dropped me off here before parking your car in that run-down piece of rubble, Blane."

"Thank you, Giles," Blane said apologetically.

The middle aged, plumpish man nodded. "Will ye be needin' anything, sir?"

"Thank you, no. That will be all for tonight." He waited until the man disappeared then followed Cybil into his study where he found her wiping away her tears.

"Oh darling, you have no idea how hard it's been for me. Why are you being so cruel?"

She walked up to him. Her ice blue eyes stared up at him, pleading.

It did not affect him as it would have. Instead, he felt irritated; his patience with her was running thin.

"Then leave Cybil. There is nothing keeping you here."

"Go home with my tail between my legs? I'm already the gossip of all our friends. You left me for this!" She waved her arms around her as she flopped down into a chair covered her face with her hands and sobbed.

Blane considered her a moment. She was right, the vile gossip, which ran rampant in his old social circles would've cut her to shreds, though he knew she gave better than she got. But he couldn't have her stir up nonsense and treat his staff like mud beneath her boots either.

"Fine. But I'll not have you treat my staff the way you treat yours. You'll find your own way around, and Cybil… If I hear one more rumor about us which includes the word engagement…," Blane inhaled deeply as he rubbed his bearded cheeks with his hands. "And I won't have you targeting Miss Munro…" He held up his hands to silence her when she made to interrupt. "You can stay a while longer Cybil, to heal. This world with all its glory is as good a balm for a bruised ego as any. One week. But that is all, understood?"

Blane walked over to the tray which held the whiskey filled crystal decanter. "A drink?"

"You're right. I can learn something from these… these, folk and get over my embarrassment. By then I'd have arranged the greatest Christmas party to beat any I've thrown previously, and I can start my life anew."

"I said a week Cybil. Besides the Munro's throw a ball every year. Best you plan to outdo yourself back in London." Blane said then downed his dram.

He did not miss the arch of her eyebrow at the mention of the Munro ball.

Chapter 23

Sadie woke with the dawn. She'd sat up most of the night researching Gaelic lore and language. She found she had quite a hunger for the Munro family history. Most of what she'd found read like a faery tale and the rest was made up of long lists of the names of all her forefathers and mothers.

When she'd finally laid her head on the pillows, dreams which varied between mystical and monstrous had plagued her rest.

A soft knock at her door. "I'm awake Nan."

The door opened, but instead of her Nan, Mrs. Perkins stood there with a tray.

"Thought ye might like an early start?"

The housekeeper walked over and placed the tray on Sadie's bed. "Some peppermint tea and fruit," she said before she turned to leave.

"Mrs. Perkins."

"Yes, me dear."

"How did you know?"

A smile as bright as the moon spread across the housekeeper's face. "Och lass, ye'll not be the only one blessed wi a gift, aye?"

Sadie wiped her hand across her eyes as Mrs. Perkins winked. For the merest moment of a moment she swore it was the goddess who stood smiling back at her before the housekeeper turned and left, closing the door behind her.

#

Having dressed and greeted her grandparents, Sadie made her way to her log. She'd ordered the dogs to remain with Malcolm. It was a bright morning, not a cloud in sight, but to her Natal bred bones, it was chilly. Sadie pulled her jumper tight around her shoulders and sat on the old stump facing the woods.

"Okay Blue, it's now or never, my girl."

Today she would approach the situation differently. Inhaling, holding her breath tight against her diaphragm, then slowly releasing it, she settled her mind.

She allowed memories of Mom, Grace, the farm...Dad and Stephen to dance across her memories like brightly colored ribbons in the wind. She held onto the laughter they'd shared, and their love which she clung to like a life jacket. A soft, low hum drifted from her lips.

And when she was confident her voice wouldn't fail, she began to sing as she reached out with her heart.

She chose the song her Zulu nanny, Nomvula, had sung to her. Sadie had been afraid of the dark as a small child. Nomvula would unwrap the blanket from her waist and place it on the floor. She'd sit on it, and Sadie would climb onto her lap as she sang the lullaby. The tune, and the words, would wash away all the shadowy monsters.

Perhaps they would do the same now.

Sadie drew in another deep lungful of crisp morning air as her fingers gripped the damp wood beneath her, opened her mouth and allowed the words and the melody to carry off in to the forest. Her voice wobbled, and caught, but soon the tune flowed, and the song came to life. As she sang, memories of her childhood came to life before her eyes.

Grace chasing her and Stephen out the kitchen when they stole her freshly baked buttermilk rusks. Her father handing her the reigns of her first horse to train by herself. Her mother, smiling at her as she trotted past the back of the house on her pony.

So many faces. So much loss. The pain glowed inside her like hot coals, but before its heat could consume her, the face of the Goddess took form before her. The pain settled and only the love of what was good remained.

A whinny, and hoof stomping, drew Sadie into the present.

Sadie hadn't realized her eyes were shut. Slowly, for fear she might be dreaming, she opened her eyes one at a time, all the while continuing to sing.

Thula thul, thula baba ...

Blue stood just beyond the last tree, sunning herself in the early Autumn rays. Still singing, Sadie gave her a good once over. Beside a coat of mud, she'd obviously been rolling in it, Blue looked fine. She was not nearly as underfed as Sadie had feared. The heather and ferns must be nutritious.

Sadie stopped singing and began to hum as she reached out with her spirit. She imagined herself making her way toward the mare. The horse's ears drew back flat on her head. She snorted and stomped her front hoof, nodding her head up and down.

"Okay girl. Tha Epona còmhla riut. Tha thu sàbhailte." She spoke the Gaelic words she'd memorized from a book she'd read last night. It was a short confirmation of the Goddess keeping them safe.

In her mind, Sadie pulled back a little and the horse calmed. When she was happy Blue was more relaxed, she began to reach out again. Eyes shut, she hummed, withdrawing when Blue got agitated. Sadie's limbs grew cold and numb, but she would not give in even if it took her all day.

A tingling sensation grew inside of Sadie's solar plexus telling her the mare was conceding. A soft musky breath wafted over Sadie's face. Slowly she opened her eyes to find the mare standing in front of where she was sitting on the log. Excitement galloped through Sadie's veins. She'd done it! All was not lost!

"There you go now. See, I don't want to harm you," Sadie whispered.

Blue nodded, snorted, then whinnied. Careful not to startle the horse, Sadie stood up and stepped toward her. The mare whinnied then sniffed her left leg before gently nudging it.

"Yes. I'm as broken as you are girl." Sadie murmured.

The two stood in the sun, Sadie leaned her forehead against the mare's, her hands rubbed the dusty mane and neck. They remained as they were for quite some time.

Except for Blue's ears twitching and turning, neither one moved closer or further apart.

The sun shone dead over head when Blue decided she'd had enough connecting for one day. She promptly turned around and galloped off into the forest.

#

"Gud God, such a bonnie sight I never would believe..."

Malcolm stood, his walking stick in one hand, and two spilling cups of tea in the other. He placed the mugs on the seat beside him and clenched his hands under his arms to stop them from trembling. His eyes must be lying, or his mind deserting him. His shoulders rose and fell as he drew in deep breaths. The spot above his heart ached. Did he just see that? If he didn't know better he'd say it was Rhiannon and her stallion standing there beside the forest! The legend was true. His mother had lied. He had lied to himself all these years!

Jealousy, fear, anger, and dare he say hope, filled an old gaping wound in his soul. He watched as the horse turned and trotted back into the forest. His granddaughter made her way to him at their bench beside the loch.

"You're late out with tea."

"Ah - yes. It's turned oot to be a lovely day has it not?" Malcolm fumbled over his words, still in shock as he handed Sadie her now half-filled mug of Oolong.

"Are you okay?" Sadie gripped his shoulder.

He looked up into the flushed face of his granddaughter. "How did ye do that?"

He watched as first surprise and then pride fluttered across her beautiful freckled face, and for a wee moment it was Stewart looking back at him.

They sat down. "The same way you used to, Oupa."

Malcolm spluttered, spitting tea over his lap. He wasn't sure what surprised him more, her canny answer or that she hadn't called him Malcolm but had instead used an endearment native to her mother tongue.

"Perhaps once, long ago lass." He fidgeted in his jacket pocket for his handkerchief and dabbed at the stains on his trousers. "But no anymoor."

"Perhaps you could again?" She did not look at him, but stared intently out over the water, her mug cupped between her hands.

"Are we tae tell Mr. Buchan ye found his beastie?"

"Not yet."

Malcolm nodded.

Granddaughter and grandsire sat back and enjoyed their tea in silence. Malcolm thanked his lucky stars for the blessings and his second chance. In her bountiful grace the Goddess had forgiven him for turning his back on her and he would make sure to show her, his humble gratitude from today until she beckoned him from beyond the veil. They finished their tea, and Malcolm left Sadie by the side of the loch as he always did.

He made his way back to the house, leaving the two empty mugs in the scullery. Agnus met him at the door of the study. The frown on her face told him it was urgent.

"What is it?"

"The lawyer, the man who took care of all Stewart's business in South Africa, called while you were having tea with Sadie."

Malcolm pulled the door of the study closed. No one in the household needed to know any of this.

"Aye?"

"We need to set up a skype account."

"A what? Bleeding man o the law. Wants money first eh? Chancer!" Malcolm huffed placing his balled hands on his hips.

Agnus laid her hands on his shoulders, the effect immediately calming him.

"No ye daft laly. It's a program on the computer, so one can converse with another from far away. I've asked Annie to open us one and connect to Mr. Goldstein's. And no, she and no one else has any idea who the man is."

Malcolm squinted. *Och, this technology.* He doubted he would ever grasp any of it.

"Fine if ye think so. But when will we sky him?"

"Skype, darling. Saturday evening at seven."

Malcolm turned from his wife and plodded toward his desk.

It would be good to find out what happened to his son and family. And while it could give them some much-needed closure, a slithering feeling deep in his belly told him he'd not like a single word the man had tae share wi them.

But for now, he had another, joy filled matter to take care of. He pulled a little too hard on the top drawer of his desk causing a few pens and a writing pad to spill from its shallow belly. He reached inside for a faded, red leather-bound book.

"What are you up to old man?"

Malcolm looked up to where his wife had gone to sit. It was her favorite spot, perched like a girl of twenty on the bay window bench. "I need tae order some tack and lumber."

"Tack and lumber? What in Heaven's name for?"

"If oor lass is doing what I think she is, we'll need a stable for that mare and soon."

"Stable? Mare? What mare?" Agnus asked in astonishment.

"Oh aye, it still feels it was a dream. This morning when I went tae meet the lass for tea... I found her, Aggie. She was standing oot there on the far edge, just standing and what would be standing afor oor wee lass?"

Agnus shrugged.

"That runawa beastie of Buchan's."

Agnus gasped. "Oh thank God. Here I thought oor girl was losing her mind just starin oot at naught all day! And ye saw the mare did ye?"

"Oh aye. Oor granddaughter has the gift and tis strong as ever I've seen it."

"Have ye told our neighbor yet?"

"Nae, she said tae wait." Seeing the look on his wife's face, Malcolm, was quick to add, "Neither will come tae any harm. If anything, it's a good thing wife. Dinnae say a word tae anyone ye hear."

For once, Agnus agreed.

Chapter 24

Sadie wasn't in the mood to make the trip. Going in to town meant she'd have less time to spend with Blue.

"Why do you need me to come with you?" Sadie asked over her breakfast tea as they all sat around the table while Malcom shoveled heaped spoonful's of porridge into his mouth.

He swallowed, slurped his tea then answered her.

"There's a package I need ye tae help ye Nan wi, while Blane and I wrestle that confounded Learie at the toon meet, lass."

It was the beginning of October and the weather was definitely cooler than she was used to. Sadie found the early mornings crisp, but by mid-morning it was warm enough to walk around in a long sleeve shirt and jeans. However, Sadie had learnt to never leave the house without a jacket and a 'brollie'. She grabbed them off the hook of the coat rack in the scullery and followed her grandparents to the Land Rover.

"It needs a wash, Oupa." She avoided the thick crust of mud along the four by four when she pulled open the back door.

"Weel feel free tae grab a bucket an' water from Ghillie when we're back, lass." He winked as a cheeky smile stretched across his well-worn face.

Sadie smiled. She enjoyed their friendly banter. Had he and Dad ever shared something similar?

Malcolm drove like a bat out of hell, knocking them about as he hit a few potholes. Sadie had hoped Nan would drive. While Malcolm had recovered sufficiently after his stroke, sitting in a car with him driving like a crazed Scot made her nervous.

"Hell's sakes, husband. There'll be noothing left of us by the time we reach toon. Slow doon!" Agnus warned, but Malcolm kept his foot on the accelerator, only slowing once they reached Lairg.

They drove past the town's inn.

"I thought you had a meeting this morning?" Sadie asked.

"Aye, package first." He winked over his shoulder as he turned left into a narrow-tared lane and drove east to the edge of the town.

Sadie leaned forward from the back seat, and frowned as she studied her grandparents' faces, which as usual, revealed absolutely nothing. What were these two up to? Agnus had come home with large 'packages' on her own before.

Sadie glanced back and spotted a black Rover pull up to the Inn.

Blane…and was that?

Her heart dropped like a block of lead to the floor of the car.

She'd seen him twice since the uncomfortable dinner more than a week ago. He'd come to sit beside her at the loch after the meeting with Malcolm. The first few minutes were uncomfortable the first time. But Blane broke the silence with a short funny story he'd heard from one of the locals. He'd had her in stitches. She'd also begun to realize Blane Buchan, the suave, confident, Scottish born, Englishman, was more than an ambitious Midas. He'd given Sadie small glimpses of the real man behind the beard, and burning gaze.

Like her, he desired an inner peace. He had a passion for people, and his country of birth, and he loved animals. But, there was still the fact his ex was 'visiting', Nan was right, she needed to keep her distance.

Malcolm's four-by-four hit another bump in the road which jolted Sadie back to the present.

"Come, let's get this over with so I can get to my meet," Malcolm said as he parked outside the town's co-op.

"I thought we had to collect a package?" Sadie blurted as she hopped from the back seat out of the car and onto the side walk.

"Aye," was all Malcolm replied. There was an uncommon twinkle in his eye. A joy she had never seen before, danced across his face. He even had a bit of a bounce in his stride. What was up? Was it good news about the university?

She followed her grandparents into the large warehouse-type outlet.

"Aye, Mr. Munro. It's arrived and let me tell ye it's been that hard tae keep it hushed. I see ye parked close by. Once ye and the lass have peeked and are satisfied, I'll have Derek load it in the back of the vehicle, aye?"

"Oh Aye." Malcolm turned to Sadie. "Come on, we don't have time tae waste."

Sadie followed the men to the store's back room while Agnus remained behind and chatted with the owner's wife. What was Oupa up to, and what was the owner on about? Keep what secret?

Sadie's heart jumped into her throat and for a split second she hesitated.

She felt Agnus' warm hand on her shoulder.

"It's safe lass. Go on now."

At the back of the co-op, to the left, was another storage room. It was dark and musty. The tin roof had a few holes which allowed sun motes to drift down and tickle the dusty concrete floor.

The store owner, Mr. Smythe, flicked a light switch and led them to the far corner.

Sadie gasped, turned to Malcolm, then back to the wooden stand containing two saddles. One was a brown collegiate, an all-purpose English riding saddle. The other, also brown, a close contact Bates saddle. A variety of Numnah, three different bridles, halters…. Everything one would need, when one owned a horse.

Sadie turned around. "Oupa?"

"Weel we cannae have ye fix the mare with no proper tack tae help ye?"

Sadie wrapped her arms around his barreled chest. "Thank you."

Malcolm cleared his throat and dug a hanky out his jacket pocket. Sadie stepped away as the old man wiped a tear.

"Och, Smythe, the dust in heer is awful."
Sadie wiped her tearless eyes.
"Does Bla- uhem, Mr. Buchan know?" Sadie asked
as she ran a hand over the seat of the new saddle.
"Nae. But I thought it a good idea tae tell him afor
Ghillie begins tae repair the old stables?"
"You're going to build her a stable?"
Malcolm smiled. "Aye lass. We cannae have the
mare livin in the wild, not wi winter roond the corner."
Sadie smiled and nodded. "Thank you. I'll chat
with him tomorrow perhaps?"
"Aye. Well then, Smythe, I think we'll take the lot.
Ye man can load it up."
He handed the Land Rover's keys to the store
owner whose smile was akin to that of a Cheshire cat.
\#
Blane held his breath and slowly released it before
he hopped out the car, walked around, and opened Cybil's
door. She'd been determined to accompany him to town.
"I need a change of scenery Blane. I promise not to
interfere or get in your way."
He proffered a hand as she slipped off the seat onto
her expensively booted feet. The town council was to
discuss the tender for the university up in Edinburgh today,
and Mrs. Learie was proving to be quite the force to be
reckoned with. He honestly didn't have time to cope with
Cybil as well.
"Well the Inn serves hot meals and tea, then there's
Joy Blossoms café down the road, I'll SMS you when the
meetings done," he explained as she shut her door.
Cybil plastered on a smile and slipped her taupe,
Valentino coated arm through his as they made their way
across the road and toward the Inn.
"Perhaps I'll try out the local pub?" she tried to
wink and Blane bit back a sigh as her left eye scrunched
and popped open wider than the right.
The members were seated around an oval
mahogany table in the "conference room" of the Sheep
Heide Inn.

He'd left Cybil seated at a small table with a high back chair and a pot of tea. He'd smiled inwardly when she'd tried to order something besides tea. "I'd rather have a three-quarter skinny latte, no sugar, thank you."

He knew how much she hated tea.

The inn keeper's wife, a plump, gentian-violet haired woman, squinted at her.

"Och, lass. We dinnae do skinny anything's aroond here. But tell ye wot, I'll just bring yew a pot o Earl Grey, eh?"

Blane left Cybil to sulk as he made his way through to the 'private meeting room' of the Inn. "Ah Blane," Mr. Ferguson waved to him. "Malcolm is running a wee bit behind. Said he'd be heer in a few minutes."

Female voices and heavy footsteps Blane would know anywhere caused those members of council already present to hush their tones. Blane turned, and so did all his hopes of keeping his plans for Lairg from Cybil.

Mrs. Learie had Cybil by the elbow as the pair walked through the door and made their way straight over toward two seats set apart from the meeting table.

"Och ye dinnae say, Lady Cybil?"

Blane eyed the staunch matron. The woman had done her homework.

Blane sighed inwardly as he watched their exchange.

The last thing he needed was Mrs. Learie nosing around his personal business.

Cybil glanced toward Blane, a sharp twinkle flashing across her bright blue eyes.

Blane walked over to where the women stood as Malcolm Munro strode in, took one look at the women, shook his head and went to stand at the head of the table.

"Best we get seated, Mrs. Learie, it looks as though we're about to begin," Blane motioned toward the table.

The robust woman with her stiffly coiffed hair was not to be told what to do. She merely nodded to him then turned her dark eyes back on Cybil. "Weel, I am pleased tae see ye here. Are ye visiting long?"

Blane's heart tumbled into his boots.

"Well, that's up to Blane," Cybil batted her eyes and gave him a soft smile.

"Och lass, heer in the highlands everyone is as welcoom as long as they like. I tell ye wot, we should arrange to meet over tea one morning, aye."

"That would be lovely Mrs. Learie." Cybil's smile reminded Blane of all kinds of fake.

"Weel folks, shall we begin? We dinnae have all day tae stand aroond and chin wag, eh?" exclaimed Malcolm.

"I, Malcolm James Stewart Munro, Laird of the clan Munro, and the lands as beholden to us, hereby call this meet tae order."

Blane caught the devious grin which crossed Cybil's face.

Chapter 25

A sharp chill wrapped itself around Agnus's heart.
It had been a happy few days, what with Malcolm's
surprise for Sadie, and the workmen renovating the old
stables. The mare still ran off into the forest when Sadie
tried to lure her closer to home, but according to her
granddaughter, it would take time.

But Agnus feared that tonight, much of their hard-
won peace and healing would be shaken to its very core.
With a sigh, she turned and made her way to the study to
meet Malcom.

She'd told Sadie they were scheduled to chat with
Selwyn Goldstein. Her granddaughter had paled, refused
dinner, and closed herself up in her bedroom. It was left to
Annie to assist them to set up the fancy computer they'd
bought to call her son's solicitor and good family friend.

Agnus walked up to Malcolm and wrapped her
arms around him. The familiar scent of his aftershave and
the warmth of his body soothed some of her anxiety before
she went to sit down at his desk. Time and hope, what
strange things they were. She'd once *hoped* it was only
time needed to heal the void between Stewart and
Malcolm. That hadn't happened. Now she hoped this same
indefinite, often frustrating, progress of existence humans
defined in terms of minutes, hours and days would heal her
granddaughter. Was she hoping for too much?

Malcolm poured them each a dram and settled into
the chair beside hers. The computer screen stared back at
them both like a big blue eye. Fear of what they were to
discover wove a tapestry of hesitation and angst across her
heart. Was it better left alone? Would it change anything?
It wouldn't bring Stewart, Stephen or Lindsay back.

She looked across at her husband. No, they had to
know. Find closure and move forward.

#

Selwyn sat at his oak desk in his home study, a
cigarette in one hand. The large computer screen shone
bright as he awaited the call. He glanced at his

grandfather's pocket watch. It was eight o'clock at night. South Africa was an hour ahead of Scotland.

His stomach roiled each time he thought back to the phone calls he'd received the previous week.

The first from Sadie. "Nan and Malcolm need to know… but I can't Selwyn. I just can't go back there," she'd pleaded. He couldn't go back to that day either, but he'd do it for her. He owed it to her after he had tried to deceive her, even if he had believed it was for her own good.

The phone call from Stewart's mother came the following day. He'd met her the few times she'd come over to visit. Agnus Munro was a gentle soul. Strong, courageous, and knew what she wanted from life, but what he had to tell her tonight would bring the bravest of souls to their knees.

Closing his eyes, he drew in a mournful of steamy country air and prayed. It was only by the grace of God he'd managed to stay the pain of losing his dearest friends. Their lives had been stolen in the most gruesome of ways. A silent culture of murder, torture, and hatred… birthed out of greed, racism, and propaganda had claimed them. Their deaths were now simply a number, a sad statistic swept under the carpet of a corrupt government.

"Adonai…."

Now he had to relive that day; the scene of fire, blood, and Sadie screaming as they loaded her mangled, beaten body onto a stretcher and into the ambulance.

"Elohei Avraham, Yitzchak v'Ya'acov," he called to the God of Abraham, God of Isaac, God of Jacob, in a whisper, barely audible to himself, a prayer he'd recited a thousand times over the last year from a small book, *'Prayers for healing.'* God bless his beautiful wife.

"God, make me brave for life: much braver than this.
As the blown grass lifts, let me rise from sorrow with quiet eyes,
Knowing Thy way is wise."

The computer pinged and ponged, signaling a call was coming through. Selwyn took a last, deep breath and clicked on the green camera.

"Good evening. Are you there Mr. Goldstein? Oh, blasted all Agnus, where's the man's face…"

"Will you just be patient, Malcolm? You heard what Annie said about the connection and… oh, there he is. Good evening, Selwyn."

It took Selwyn a few moments to reply. He rubbed the back of his hand across his eyes – the resemblance was uncanny! Staring back at him from the screen was a face so like the good friend he'd lost, only aged.

"Ah good evening, Mr. Munro, Agnus." He stubbed the cigarette into his ashtray as he greeted them.

"Ah, there he is Agnus."

Clearly neither had ever been on a live call before.

"He can hear and see you *mo ghaol*, no need to shout," smiled Agnus.

"Ah yes, sorry, how are ye Mr. Goldstein?"

Selwyn smiled. Malcolm was just as Stewart had described him, only more vulnerable, older, perhaps gentler?

"Good evening sir. I am well. I take it you are as well? And please call me Selwyn."

Malcolm nodded. "Yes, thank you. Noo, Agnus and I have contacted ye aboot Sadie."

"Is she settling in okay?"

"Oh yes, yes of course." Agnus said before Malcolm continued. "It's just we … well… look heer man, we only know what we have read and the lass, weel,"

Malcolm stumbled so Agnus picked up.

"We don't think it's right to force her, but we need to know…"

Selwyn swallowed hard. "You need to know more than what the news reported of what happened to your son and his family that day."

"Aye, and tae Sadie, if ye dinna mind," Malcolm added.

"Has she shared her... told you of her," Why was it so hard?

"Aye Selwyn. We ken the extent of her physical damage." Agnus replied when he could not.

"I think first we all need a stiff drink." Selwyn leaned forward and took a hold of the crystal tumbler, quarter filled with brandy.

"In hand, man," Malcom lifted his to the screen, and Agnus clasped hers in both hands.

"To one of the strongest men I knew, his son and his wife... and to Sadie his daughter, a survivor, a rose among the thorns," Selwyn lifted the glass toward the screen then downed the liquid.

"Sláinte," echoed the Munro's and followed suit.

#

Agnus watched as Selwyn's hands came together beneath his chin as though in prayer. Her heart raced and the muscles in her throat spasmed. The pallor of his skin greyed and his chocolate eyes darkened allowing anyone who considered them to see his pain. She knew the story he was to tell would shred their hearts.

"The farm beside Stewart's went broke," Selwyn began, "and was bought on auction by a stranger. At first, he came across very ... um... friendly. But soon it became evident he was up to no good."

Selwyn leaned to the left, his face disappeared from the screen. When he returned, it was with another tumbler in hand, this time, half filled. He sipped then looked up.

"The local farmers and breeders all approached law enforcement, but it was evident they were in this man's pocket. That was around the time, Sadie..." His voice cracked. "Sadie discovered the man was using his horses to transport drugs."

"Selwyn, who was this stranger?" Agnus interrupted.

"A powerful player in the Nigerian drug world — a Leonard Obaje."

Malcolm leaned toward the screen. "How was it such a dastardly person came to live in South Africa then?"

Selwyn took another long sip of his brandy. "Our borders here are so porous and corruption rife. It is easy enough for anyone from a neighboring country to simply live here without any kind of visa."

"How is that possible?" Agnus leaned toward the screen.

"This is Africa, Agnus. Some money put in the right hands can buy you half the government."

Agnus nodded, then stood and refilled Malcolm's glass and her own with whiskey as Selwyn continued.

"I have a good friend in the force in a neighboring town, Detective Mahlanghu. He is an honest, and good man, one who has not bowed to the temptation of riches and lies. Stewart and I approached him and so evidence was collected against Obaje, but…" Selwyn turned ashen and Agnus downed her drink.

"What happened?!" Tension got the best of Malcolm.

"Give the man a chance to breathe. Ye can see it's not easy," Agnus whispered patting her husband's knee.

Malcolm didn't look at her, but his hand sought hers out and gripped it like an iron vice.

"A month or so later a raid was attempted on his farm. Some drugs and so forth were confiscated, but all the horses were missing and so too was the king pin. The police managed to round up most of his accomplices and confiscated his list of suppliers, clientele, and corrupt government officials."

Selwyn took another sip. "The man made a bee line for Stewart's farm. He… he and handful of his men who managed to evade the cops. One of them was his brother. They attacked Stewart while the police were raiding Obaje's place."

They all sat a few moments in silence. Apprehension, fear and grief drifted above all their heads like ghosts haunting the living. Agnus found herself wishing, praying, begging Selwyn would tell them it was all a bad dream and her son, her grandchildren and Lindsey were all safe and well. Instead…

Selwyn, now as grey as cigarette ash continued. "They burned the stables with all their breeding stock and farm hands inside. Then…"

Fear wrapped itself around Agnus' throat as tears of devastation clouded her sight.

"Stewart, Lindsay, and Stephen put up a good fight, but in the end, they were outgunned and outnumbered."

Malcolm's hands shook in hers. She shifted closer to her husband as Selwyn went on to explain that Stewart and Lindsay were first tortured, then shot at point blank range.

"And Stephen?" Agnus was almost too afraid to ask.

"Give me a moment," Selwyn asked and disappeared from the screen. A door was closed but it did not help to stay the sound of his retching.

Agnus' body began to shake.

"Aye lass, come sit closer. Weel get thru this," Malcolm wrapped his arm around her as Selwyn returned to the screen, wiping his mouth.

"Ste…Stephen was tortured and …" Tears streamed down his face. "Sorry," he said as he dug out a handkerchief and wiped them away. "Stephen was decapitated with a panga."

Agnus clasped a hand to her mouth to stifle her scream and Malcolm cursed, slamming his fist onto the desk. Silence ensued as the three calmed themselves.

"S-Sadie?" Agnus voice came out in a whisper.

"Sadie was out riding. She returned near the end of the aftermath, but not in time to escape Obaje's wrath. He would have killed her if the Farmwatch had not arrived when they had."

"Did the police not see or hear any of the commotion from next door then?" Agnus leaned into the screen.

"The farms are vast. It was only because one of the stable hands had escaped and managed to alert the Farmwatch that anyone knew the Munros were under attack. That and the black smoke covering the sky."

Selwyn downed another drink before telling them of the extent of Sadie's injuries. "I take it you have seen Sadie's injuries?"

"Aye," Agnus answered between her sobs.

"What did he do to her?" Malcolm's voice, was a mere whisper beside her.

"That would be her story to tell you, when she is ready." Selwyn said as he sank back into his chair.

"I had one of the best vascular surgeons in the country flown in from the Cape, but in the end, her leg simply could not be saved."

The conversation lulled.

Moments stretched into minutes of painful silence as Malcolm and Agnus digested the horror ending of their son and his family.

"Why…" Malcolm broke the silence. "Why did the papers say she had also perished?"

Selwyn rubbed his tired eyes with the thumb and forefinger of his right hand. "Because Sadie… she killed Obaje's brother. She'd managed to shoot and kill the man as he ran toward her. The Farmwatch arrived in time and saved her from a death blow. It must be said, Sadie didn't go down without a fight either. Your son taught her well. But this is the reason he'll come back for her, if he discovers… she survived."

Selwyn's words echoed through the hollow of her grief.

"We… I, pulled some strings and had it leaked the entire family perished to protect her. God knows the police wouldn't. That was why, or one of the reasons it was best for her to… to go to Scotland. It was a risk, but it was better than hiding here."

"A risk?" Malcolm leaned toward the screen squinting.

Selwyn nodded. "Yes, because of the history…"

Malcolm sighed and nodded. "Aye, because o' me. Is that why ye didn't call back after that first time?"

Agnus watched as Selwyn's eyes dimmed in shame and he bowed his head. "Yes."

"I thank ye for protecting her as a father wuld." Malcolm's words of forgiveness warmed the air a little.

Agnus interrupted, "So Selwyn, our Sadie is still in danger?"

"No… yes, well… that depends. We made sure any trace of her as a South African led to a death certificate. That and the fact she is now seen as a Scottish citizen should keep her safe. Also, I had her name added to the grave stone on the family mausoleum. As far as we know, Obaje is hiding out somewhere in central Africa, none the wiser."

"Ye bloody better be sure!" Malcolm said sternly.

Silence.

"Has she cried?" Selwyn asked quietly.

Agnus frowned then shook her head. "Why?"

"Because she never cried here, not a single tear. The doctors were worried she might snap if she didn't let it all out. When I asked her, she said she didn't deserve absolution."

"Why does she think it's her fault?" Agnus asked.

"I don't know. Survivor's guilt?" he shrugged.

"No Selwyn, it's more than that. That's also why we're calling. Sadie blames herself and it's not solely because she survived. Is there anything else you can tell us?" Agnus asked.

Selwyn leaned back in his chair and rubbed his forehead. "It could have something to do with those missing horses. She had been arguing terribly with Stewart in the weeks before about the poor animals. She wanted him to help her steal them from Obaje. Stewart tried to explain how dangerous it would be."

"Have ye found the beasties?" Malcolm interrupted.

"No, but I'll fish around and see what I can find. You don't think…"

"That she herded the horses off by herself, the same day of the raid?" Agnus gasped. "That could be why… did she know about the raid?"

Selwyn shook his head. "Nobody did."

The penny dropped, and three astonished faces stared at their screens.

"It wasn't her fault. Obaje would have attacked either way. He'd threatened Stewart a week or so earlier about meeting with the police," Selwyn defended.

"We dinnae blame Sadie. The problem is, Sadie blames herself. I see the guilt and terror of that night devouring my granddaughter from the inside oot," Agnus explained.

Selwyn nodded and wiped away a tear. "Time and love are the only advice I can give, Agnus."

The trio sat in silence, digesting and re-digesting all the horror. It was Malcolm who spoke first.

"Selwyn, would yew mind chatting a few more minutes?" he asked sheepishly.

"Certainly. What is it I can help you with?"

"Weel, I wondered if ye wouldna mind telling us… telling me more aboot oor grandson, Stephen?"

Selwyn smiled and nodded. "It would be both my pleasure and my honor."

#

Malcolm switched off his computer screen. It had been a long day and a longer night. The witching hour had come and gone. The world outside the manor lay silent beneath the cold blanket of night.

Malcolm dug into his pant pocket for a clean hanky and when he couldn't find one, Agnus offered a tissue from the lavender scented box on the tea table. Malcolm wiped his face, blew his nose, and then looked up at Agnus.

"There is noo way I could ever right the wrong I did both Stewart and ye, *mo ghaol.*"

Agnus took his hand in hers and placed it to her heart. "It wasn't only you. Stewart had a part to play in it also. He didn't have to be so stubborn. Yes, you were stubborn too and perhaps that was the problem. You were both too proud. A trait I think your granddaughter has inherited, and one she believes she has paid the ultimate price for?"

Malcolm nodded. "We're blessed she lived." He pulled his Aggie into him and squeezed her tight.

God what a price they had all paid for their self-righteous bullheadedness. He'd never meet his grandson now. A man who, by the sounds of it, was brilliant in engineering, and design, filled with dreams and an intelligence that would have taken him very far in life.

It was bittersweet, this see-saw of life. Funny how it never granted you your wish and always took what it wanted.

Chapter 26

Standing beside Ghillie, arms folded, Sadie admired their hard work. The week had flown by. She'd used the excuse to help Ghillie with the stables in order to avoid too much contact with her grandparents. She worried what Selwyn had told them and didn't have the strength to discuss it with them either.

"You've outdone yourself, Ghillie," she said, smiling.

"Nae lass, couldna have dunnit without ye." He patted her shoulder.

"Weel noo, when you two braw builders are dun spyin yer fine work, would ye come in and have a dish o tea?" Mrs. Perkins voice traveled across the court yard from the back door.

"Aye, we'll be there in a tick woman," he called back over his shoulder.

"When do ye think ye'd get that beastie in here?"

He looked down at her. Sadie was tall, but Ghillie was something out of the history books. Nan had said he'd inherited every drop of Norse blood there was running through his family's gene pool.

"Give it time, Ghillie. We can't rush her."

He nodded. "Aye, but the two of ye have a bond. I've seen it. I reckon if ye brought her tae take a look, and she smelled the fresh hay and sweet water, ye'd have nae trouble convincing her."

He turned and started walking to where Mrs. Perkins stood, balled fists on her hips, waiting at the back door.

Sadie decided on one last look at the revamped stable and tack she wasn't ready to go indoors just yet.

Sadie opened the door and stepped inside.

Ghillie had done a fine job with the rendering and the floor.

Her eye caught on something. A silver wrapped box with a red bow on top. She walked over to the wooden stool in the corner of the room and picked it up. Her name was scribed on the side in a bold, black calligraphy.

Her fingers pulled the sticky tape off the corner and, careful not to tear the paper, she opened one end of the wrapping. A box, like one would receive from a jewelry store, slid out, a card on top.

Thank you for saving her.

BB

Sadie's heart caught in her throat. Her fingers shook as she removed the lid to find a cameo brooch. It was the size of her palm, round, and molded in gold. A woman's head... not just any woman, it was the Goddess. It was the same brooch Blane had worn, pinned to his tartan, the night of the town meet.

Sadie sat down on the small wooden chair. Her heart pounded in her chest like a Zulu war drum. She glanced at the card. *Calm yourself, Sadie.* Her memories skipped back to the afternoon after Malcolm had surprised her with the tack. Blane had rushed over half expecting to see the mare already tamed, and ready to take back to Saorsa, but Sadie had sat him down and explained the horse needed time. She'd asked if she could keep the horse at the manor and train her.

Blane's eyes had shone like newly polished amber gems. Her body had burned when he placed a hand on her shoulder and said, "Yes, I would be most grateful if you did."

For a moment, she was sure he wanted to embrace her, but he'd wavered, stepped back, and left.

He'd been over to see her and ask about the mare a dozen times since.

While that traitorous part of her thrilled at his presence, Sadie reminded herself that to get too close was to court disappointment and a broken heart. She'd tried acting polite, yet indifferent towards him, but it was so hard to remain unaffected. Especially when his spicy cologne tantalized her senses or the brush of his arm against hers caused her emotions to tumble around like a troop of cheeky monkeys looking for mischief.

According to Annie, Cybil was still residing at
Saorsa.

She should go indoors and thank him. He was there
now with the town council discussing the tender.

Finally, her life here at Munro Manor had meaning.
No longer was she moping around with naught to do but
stare at the loch or fight away demons and fire whenever
her thoughts drifted. Now she had a horse to heal and train.
A chance at love? She doubted it, but the idea wasn't as
frightening as it had been a few months back. Excitement
gurgled up her throat. Like bubbles in a champagne flute
they popped and fizzled in her head. But her happiness felt
hollow. Dad, Mom, and Stephen would have been so
proud.

She pushed their faces back into the dark room
they'd escaped from. She couldn't think on them now.
She'd found some modicum of peace and she was not
about to let it slip from her exhausted grip. The odd
nightmare still plagued, but they were less frequent now,
especially when she'd spent the entire day working and
training Blue. For the last few weeks, everything was filled
with goodness. Except for her leg, which chose this
moment to remind her nothing was perfect, and all that was
good could vanish in the blink of an eye.

Sadie rubbed her thigh.

How was she to ride? She inspected the all-purpose
saddle. She would ride again, but she needed a saddle that
would work with her half leg. She would train Blue by
using her shifting body weight. All she needed was a
stirrup to keep her fake limb in place. Dare she ride without
the prosthesis? No, while she hated thinking of her fake
limb, to look down and see it gone as she sat in the saddle
would be worse.

It had taken a lot of coaxing and tough love to get
her through the three months of grueling occupational
therapy. While the limb was crafted from the latest
technology it took her mind and nervous system a while
longer to adjust to the fake appendage. Not only that, it
physically sickened her in the beginning to even touch the

prosthesis or her amputated stump. But here she was. Semi-whole, and ready to jump back on a horse.

Another thought struck Sadie. She remembered Blane telling her how he'd found Blue tied to a pole and abused. If this were the case, the mare could have problems adjusting to a halter and even a bridle. She rubbed her chin, then grabbed a thick blue rope hanging from a hook beside the bridles. She wouldn't need a bridle or a halter. If she succeeded in gaining Blue's trust, a loose rope around the mare's neck would work just fine. She'd only used this method once before but, was confident it would be the right choice for Blue.

As for the saddle, she fidgeted with the stirrup. Stephen would have known how to solve this. Stephen with his incredible knack of seeing a problem and managing to solve it in a tick, Stephen... No. He was no longer around. This was her problem and she would solve it.

She looked back over her shoulder to where Ghillie stood just outside the backdoor of the manor sipping tea from a tin mug while chomping on a sandwich. Mrs. Perkins chattered on about something. Unless Nan had mentioned it, no-one knew about her leg. Could she tell Ghillie? She trusted the man but, telling people about her missing limb stretched beyond trust. It was personal, so very personal. Perhaps she'd design it on paper and ask him to make it? He was great at building and fixing, and she was sure if she could figure out a design, he could make it. He didn't have to know why.

Sadie closed and bolted the tack room door then walked toward the housekeeper and Ghillie. Thanking Mrs. Perkins, she took her tea and sandwich, and walked around to her and Malcolm's bench on the shores of the Loch.

Oupa wouldn't make it for their tea today. They, that was Malcolm, Blane, and the town council, had received good news from the university and were all gathered in Malcolm's study discussing the matter. Sadie placed her tea and sandwich on the bench beside her then dug the brooch out of her jacket pocket before fixing it to her scarf.

Chapter 27

Blane followed Cybil's gaze out through the library window of Munro Manor to where Sadie sat on the bench at the shores of the Loch.

He'd hoped to spare a few moments alone with Sadie after the meet, but that plan had turned to ash when his passenger door was flung open and Cybil hopped inside.

"I'd love to see Mrs. Munro, again. She promised to show me her roses the next time I popped over."

Her excuse was tepid at best. But Cybil had not gone to look at the roses. Instead, she'd remained glued to Blane's side, eavesdropping on all that was discussed.

He only hoped she wouldn't notice Mrs. Learie was not in attendance. Cybil and the old crone had formed an uncanny friendship since meeting at the inn.

It had been decided by all the members, the woman was a liability and the less she knew about their plans the better. They'd have enough sway with the town to vote her off the council once the tender was successful. Until then, they'd tread lightly.

Cybil turned and caught his eyes. He'd been avoiding her as much as he could of late. Blane feigned a smile and turned his attention back to the meeting. He watched from the corner of his eye as she placed her cold full cup of tea down on the table and strode out. What was she up to?

"Blane, man are ye with us?" Malcolm drew his attention back to the meeting.

#

Sadie bit into her sandwich. The whole-wheat bread was freshly baked this morning. The tomato was sweet and the lettuce crisp, with a dash of Mrs. Perkin's homemade mustard. Her food jammed in her throat when a shadow fell over her and looked up to see Cybil standing beside the bench. She swallowed hard.

Oh, great! What in the hell was she doing here? So much for a peaceful lunch.

"Beautiful day," Cybil smiled. The ice spread across her face and settled in her eyes as she sat down beside Sadie.

Sadie turned her attention out over the water and took another deep bite of her sandwich instead.

Cybil sat down beside Sadie. "This could be a lonely life."

Sadie chewed and fastened her gaze on the water. It was a little choppy today. The wind had picked up.

"It could be," Sadie replied. Nan had said she should practice being polite to people she didn't like. Sadie took another bite of her sandwich, the corner of her vision catching Cybil's nose scrunching. She chomped harder.

"Yes, well. For a young lady such as yourself, a good man could be hard to come by around here."

"Who said I was looking for a man?" Sadie said with a mouth full of food, then swallowed.

"Mmm, well I do suppose a woman with your history would find it difficult, none the less, and perhaps send you looking in the wrong places?"

Was this woman for real? And what past was she talking about? What did she know and how had she found out? An uneasy feeling settled in Sadie's stomach and staunched her hunger. Keeping her face neutral, which was hard, Sadie shoved the last of her sandwich into her mouth, knowing it would gross out the prissy Londoner, chomped, swallowed then slowly, she gathered every drop of her conviction and strength, and turned to look at Cybil.

"Why would you care where I looked for a man? And what does my *history* have to do with any of it?"

A slow, oily, pink lipstick smirk spread across Cybil's face, the likes of which made Sadie's stomach push the sandwich back up her throat. Nan was right. This woman was trouble with a capital B!

Cybil's hard blue gaze considered her. She watched as they roamed her face and landed on her left leg and back up to her neck and froze. Cybil's skin turned white beneath her make-up, her hands trembled as she clutched them together. Sadie looked down - the brooch!

"Men of means have no need for broken little birds. It would be best if you simply kept to yourself." Cybil's voice strained with anger and hatred. She stood and looked down her nose at Sadie. "Best to keep out of harm's way." And walked off.

A tremor of anger rolled up Sadie's back and over her head. It burned hot and heavy and it took all of Sadie's will power not to go stomping after the short blonde snip and demand an explanation from her, or better still, smack her upside her perfectly blow-dried head!

Had Blane said or done something to make her believe there could possibly be anything between him and Sadie?

Sadie's hand instinctively rested on her left thigh.

No man would touch her once he'd discovered how broken she was… Cybil's words returned with a gut-wrenching blow. 'Men of means have no need for broken little birds.'

What did this woman know and how had she found out?

Chapter 28

"What are you so busy with this time of night?" Nan asked as she entered the study. Dressed in a plush turquoise dressing gown and sheepskin slippers, she carried a steaming mug of Horlicks in each hand. Horlicks warmed the places the fire and heaters couldn't. It was nearing the end of October, and the chill of winter had truly begun to settle in.

Sadie looked up and smiled. She loved Horlicks. "I'm trying to design a stirrup that will hold m-my…" she pointed to her leg.

She'd made a lot of progress with Blue, and she hoped that soon she'd be able to get the mare settled in the stable before the weather turned really nasty, and perhaps one day even ride her. Nan came to stand behind her as she sat at her grandfather's desk. She smiled and placed Sadie's mug on a coaster on the table.

"Hmmm, I see. Have yew asked Ghillie fur help?"

"Yes." It hadn't been easy explaining to the Scot what she needed without telling him why.

"He'll no be the type to treat ye differently lass." Nan said matter of factly, sitting down in the chair opposite Sadie.

"I know." By now he must have an idea, but he'd not so much as looked at her in a way which told her he felt sorry for her. She appreciated and respected that.

She and Ghillie had tried several variations this last week. They'd strapped the all-purpose saddle to a barrel and Sadie, with the help of a step, had managed to climb onto it. Even though it wasn't Blue beneath the saddle, the fact she was sitting in one, had re-awoken what it meant to be alive and hungry for life.

Sadie had tried to imitate the movements of a rider in sitting trot, but the foot kept slipping from the stirrup and throwing her off balance. She fell off twice, leaving her fake foot to slip through the stirrup. Had she been on a horse, she'd have been dragged along the ground.

It was painful and embarrassing, but Sadie was not about to give up. Ghillie had not rushed to her side to help her, nor did he flutter around her like an over protective hen, but left her to help herself, as though he understood.

"Lass…"

Sadie's head jerked up. She knew that tone in her nan's voice. She'd been dreading this moment since the day she arrived.

"You've spoken to Selwyn. He's told you all there is to tell Nan." Sadie tried to suppress the quiver in her voice.

"Aye, he did. It was … hard. But he wouldna tell us aboot yew, said it was yer story tae tell, and I agree." Nan sipped her Horlicks.

Sadie turned her gaze back to the sketch in front of her.

"Lass, there's no shame in any of it," Nan whispered.

Sadie didn't answer.

"Sadie?" Nan pushed.

"What?" Sadie cringed inside, her tone was crisper than she'd intended. It was hard to talk to anyone about that day. Why couldn't her Nan simply accept things as they were? She'd had her little chit chat with Selwyn. Could she just not let it all go?

"You were not responsible, lass."

Screams echoed across the room and flames licked the ceiling….

"Lass?"

Guilt burned the back of her throat as she tried to fight the encroaching nightmare. Sweat trickled down her forehead as the flames drew closer. Bile scoured her mouth as their screams grew louder.

She wanted to scream and bawl her eyes out, but that would mean she deserved forgiveness, and she did not deserve anything. *Just let it all out?* Impossible!

The agony, the guilt, the anger, the utter desolation left by their deaths, pushed against the wall she'd erected inside her soul as imaginary flames threatened to burn their way across the library. Sadie took a deep breath and reached for her mug. "Mom used to say Horlicks solved anything."

Go away, you're not real!

"And she was right."

"But it won't help for this."

"For the hurt in yer heart?"

Sadie glanced up to where her Nan sat. Behind her, a shadow began to form. Tall, menacing, with a grin so wicked, so…

Sadie shook her head. It was her guilty conscience playing tricks with her head.

Agnus stood and walked over to Sadie. "Look at me, lass."

Sadie faced her grandmother. The love in those soft violet eyes was much, much more than she deserved.

"It was not yer fault. Da ye heer me?"

The wall broke. A tsunami of emotions, she couldn't put a name to, washed over her.

Sadie pushed herself upright.

"You don't know the whole story Nan. You would never forgive me if you did!"

"Aye, but I do, and I will say it again. It was not yer fault."

No longer able to bite back the bitter hurt, Sadie turned around. "You know nothing Nan. I was the reason that monster went to our farm. I was the reason he slaughtered Mom, Dad, Stephen, our workers, and our animals. I deserved what I got. Every lash of his whip, every cut from that blade, and so much more!"

Tears streamed down Agnus's face. Sadie felt nothing but rage and disgust. Not for Agnus, but for her own sins, for the fact she'd survived, and they had not.

"We know you went to save those horses. Selwyn found them, peaceful, grazing by the stream of that old farm. It wasna yer fault lass! That murderer was going to go after Stew… Stewart no matter what yew did or didn't do. What yew did by saving those horses saved yer life!"

Wh-what?

Flames crept up the edges of the curtains and screams echoed off the walls.

"Get out!" Sadie screamed as she ran around and pushed Nan out of the way. "It's me you want. Leave them alone!"

A guttural laughter floated across the soot-ridden air toward Sadie who turned and ran out of the library with Agnus short on her heels.

Obaje! He'd found her!

"Lass, calm doon. There's nothing to be afraid of."

But her Nan's words were lost in the memory of that day when hell had descended and destroyed her home and devoured her people.

She had to lure him away. It was her he wanted, and it was she who had to pay the ultimate price.

She was back on the farm. The house, the stalls, everything was on fire!

Her vision blurred, and all sense fled her mind as she headed outside into the bitter cold night. Drizzling clouds blotted out the moon and stars, but it did not stop Sadie. She didn't deserve their love, or their forgiveness. She deserved nothing!

"Sadie, dearie, wait!" Nan called after her, but like a runaway horse, Sadie couldn't stop. She had to draw the danger away from her family. It was her he wanted.

\#

Her leg ached, and her insides thrummed. How long had she run? How did she get here? Sadie stopped and leaned forward with her hands on her shivering thighs. A sharp sour tang like fermenting limes filled her nostrils and burned her lungs. Fear. It was her fear she smelled. The confrontation with her nan flashed back between gasps of ice cold air. Oh no! What had she done?

Sadie stood up and looked around her. Nothing but pitch black surrounded her beneath the thick canopy of trees. She could just make out the shape of the tall trunks and bushes. A breeze had picked up, blowing cold against her wet shirt. In her panic, she'd forgotten to grab her jacket. She reached up and instinctively grabbed the woolen scarf pulling it closer around her. A sharp metal object stuck into her palm — her brooch, the one Blane had given her.

Sadie closed her eyes and curled her fingers around the keepsake.

Please, could she just find her way home?

A chill settled in her bones. She had to keep moving. It was getting harder to figure out where she was. She should turn around, go back, and apologize. Yes, and if Malcolm and Agnus couldn't live with the fact she was responsible for their son's death, she'd leave.

But Nan had said she wasn't... her arrogant behavior had saved her life... but it had delivered her family right into the palms of evil.

She would always be responsible for their deaths.

Sadie stopped and turned, took a few steps, and froze. Where was she? Was she heading back in the direction she'd come? She turned again. Perhaps this way? Nothing but black, cold, and the fidgeting whispers of a not-so-asleep forest.

Sadie trudged on, tripping over roots, sticks and small boulders. Falling, she cut her hand on a sharp rock.

"Ouch!"

She sat up and sucked the stinging wound. Mom had always said spit was good *muti* for a graze, but the amount of copper stinging her taste buds suggested this was possibly a bit more than a graze. Using the tree trunk beside her she stood and carried on. The fidgety, scratchy rustling of the midnight forest grew louder, and the cold colder. A strange grating sound stocked the panic re-emerging in her center. A shot of adrenaline flooded her exhausted frozen body and Sadie tried to run. Her left foot caught on a root or log. Her leg twisted. A snap and crunch echoed through the frigid dark as she fell. Her body landed on the lumpy uneven forest floor with a thud. God, it hurt! Once she'd caught her breath, Sadie sat up and prodded her stump and prosthesis. Damn! She'd gone and snapped the socket. Her prosthesis wouldn't fit, and now she was stranded in the middle of nowhere.

"Mom!" Her voice sounded foreign and shrill. She clutched the brooch on her scarf.

Fingers squeezed her heart. She missed them all so much. Mom always had a solution, her voice soothing, and her demeanor calm. Neither would ever comfort her again.

"Dad."

The words tasted strange coming out of her mouth after so long. It hurt, grated the inside of her chest, and prickled her lips.

"St-Stephen."

Her breath caught in her throat.

God, she longed for them. Her very being yearned to see them once more. To beg their forgiveness. To give her life for theirs.

The cold intensified and settled inside her muscles and bone. Her loss and grief broke through the walls she had built around, beneath, and over the unwanted emotions. Its brick and mortar buckled beneath the pressure.

Sadie gulped a mouthful of frigid night air, to stay the urge to let go. But she knew, tonight, nothing could stop the inevitable. Like a mud slide, all the sour darkness tumbled out, and over every barricade she'd erected. Walls she'd spent months building within herself crumbled and splintered as the goo of guilt and the burn of loss oozed like lava from her soul.

"You should have taken me! Do you hear me? It was me he wanted!"

Her wail echoed through the stillness of the wood. She clenched fists full of damp forest earth and threw it indiscriminately. Why wouldn't he answer. Death, the elusive, selfish bastard! Birds fluttered, and owls hooted. Small feet scrambled away. Sadie curled up into a ball and cried. She cried for her horses. She screamed in outrage for Nomvula, Grace, and the grooms who had burned alive in the stables. She wept for her parents and she ached for her brother.

Images of her mother's mangled, bloodied body curled around Stephen's severed head seared the inside of her eyelids. The memory of her father's limp, bludgeoned body pushed what little was in her stomach out thorough her mouth.

The memory of her own punishment followed. Obaje had tied her to the bull bar of the truck, stripped her clothes, and decimated the skin on her torso with a whip. His laughter echoed through the trees. Sadie curled up tighter as the day of horrors replayed in her mind.

Her bonds were weak, and when he walked off to find his men, she'd managed to untie them. She'd dragged her bloodied, half naked self across the dirt to the front of their house where she found her father's .22 bolt action rifle laying on the grass.

Thudding footsteps behind her caused her to roll onto her back and come face to face with one of Obaje's lackeys. She didn't think, her only reaction — to pull the trigger. The man's eyes stretched wide as a rose bloomed across his abdomen and he fell to the ground.

Having heard the shot, a second man came sprinting around the corner. Again, Sadie pulled the trigger.

Bam! Bam!

She scrambled to her feet and turned to run.

Obaje's body hit hers like a concrete wall. She ricocheted off his chest. The rifle flung from her hands. The look of hatred on his face burned forever into her memory.

"You killed my brother, you white whore!"

Sadie peddled backward. Frozen screams shredded the inside of her throat. She turned to run, but she'd forgotten about the man she'd shot lying at her feet. She fell and rolled off his dead, smelly body. Her arms shot out, her fingers digging into the earth as she tried to get away.

"You will pay!" Obaje shrieked like a demon.

He fulfilled his promise as his machete hacked her leg. Her neck would have been next but for the arrival of the farm guard. Sadie couldn't remember much after that.

The stench of fire, blood, and feaces hovered around her nostrils as the memories of that terrible day receded and gave way to the cold, dank, dark of the woods.

Until this night, she'd forgotten she'd killed two men. They were evil. They had murdered her family and friends, but it still hurt to know she'd also taken life. Her heart fractured, and her soul splintered. She cried, raged, and roared, and when there were no more tears left, when the hurt had numbed, and the anger had diminished, Sadie lay on the damp forest floor waiting for death to return her to them all.

But it was not death who came for her.

'*Sadie!*' The voice, like a dozen chiming bells, rang across the dark and engulfed her in warmth.

Slowly, painfully, Sadie pushed up with her hands and winced. The cut in her hand burned as soil and mulch pushed into it.

'*Sadie,*' it chimed again.

There in the distance, stood a woman, hugged in soft yellow light. Her long blonde hair flowed over her shoulders and down her back. She turned to smile at Sadie.

Her face… dear God, "Mom!"

Using her good leg, Sadie stood. "Mom?" she called again.

'*Sadie,*' like the sigh of a thousand angels the voice drifted toward her.

The woman turned and walked away, and as she did, so her appearance morphed, like ripples on a pond. The blond hair turned to flames and her white dress to an emerald green.

"Mom, wait!" Sadie called and hopped after the apparition.

She struggled to keep her balance on one leg in the dark. She fell over and knocked her head on a stump. Stars flittered past her eyes. She blinked. A bright light shone overhead. It evened out, then dimmed, blended, and twisted and, "Mom!"

Sadie reached out to touch the face but grasped at air.

"Mom. Please…" her voice whimpered.

She sat up straight and found herself in the back garden of her home on the farm in Pietermaritzburg. Her body was whole, the grass the brightest green she'd ever seen it. The Poinciana were in full bloom, coloring the sky in their bold reds and bright oranges.

Mom, Dad, and Stephen stood just across from her. "Let it go, my girl. Let us go."

"Mom, Dad," she reached forward unable to move. "Please, Stephen, I am so sorry," she pleaded as she fell to her knees. "Don't leave me, I can't do this without you… I miss you…"

"It's okay, Epona, my Nunu, we're okay. You are strong, my girl, be brave. We love you and we will always be with you," their voices were strangely one.

Her father walked up to her. "My brave, brave girl." His misty fingers stroked her cheek. "Forgive yourself."

Stephen smiled and waved as the garden faded into darkness. "Noo!" Sadie cried. She didn't want to let go. She reached out toward them groping at nothing but an empty cold night.

A slim hand touched her forehead sending a warmth into her skull and down her body. Before Sadie could utter another word, a comforting darkness wrapped itself around her.

#

Eyes closed, Sadie's mind awoke. Hmmm, her bed felt a little hard this morning and her room smelled like…

She sat up with a snap. Not a good idea. The world around her spun. It toppled her empty stomach upside down, then came to rest.

A soft snort drew her attention. Lying curled up beside her, was Blue.

The mare turned her dark, loving eyes to Sadie. "Hey girl. Thanks for the heat. How'd you find me?"

The mare snorted, her eyes saying, *Can't you remember?*

Sadie shut her eyes. The memories of last night trickled back into her mind. She leaned her head into her hands. Ooh, that was a big bump. Her fingers prodded the front of her left temple.

She looked down at her hand. The cut had a scab and her palm was a delicate shade of purple. She inspected her legless limb. It was unharmed.

Blue whinnied and stood. She stomped and scraped her front hoof, nodding her head impatiently. Sadie regarded the mare a moment. Apparently, the roan had a quirky sense of humor and a unique way of communicating.

"Okay, let me just get up, will you?" Sadie rolled onto her stomach, placed her weight on her good leg, and stood, leaning against Blue for support.

Not relinquishing her touch, she looked at the horse. "Over your skittishness eh?"

The horse blew hot air out of her nose. Her ears wiggled, but her eyes remained glued to Sadie's face.

"Okay then. Do you know the way home?"

Blue snorted, sidled up to Sadie, then knelt. Sadie froze. Although honored and humbled by the mare's offer, she was too scared to take it. Blue whinnied and shook her head.

Sadie knew she wouldn't make the walk back to the manor, not without her prosthesis.

Grabbing Blue's mane for stability, she lifted her useless leg over the mare's back. Blue rose to her feet as Sadie clung to her mane. The horse's movements almost jolted her off the mare's back.

Sadie wiggled a little and when she was satisfied with her seat, clicked her tongue, and leaned forward slightly. "Let's go home girl."

The thrill of once again sitting astride a horse almost outweighed the astonishment at the mare's offer. Sadie had thought it would be at least another month before the mare would be tame enough to accept being put into a stable, let alone ridden.

A faint memory, like a dream, floated into her mind.

"Mom." She whispered and looked back over her shoulder. A subtle knowing settled into her belly.

"Thank you, Mom. Thank you for sending Epona."

She touched her brooch then looked ahead. It was time to let go and move forward.

Chapter 29

"Dear God, what if..."

"Wot if nothing, woman. She'll be just fine."

"How do you know that?" Agnus rounded on Malcolm, shooting him a lightning bolt glare. "That's wot ye said the day Stewart rushed out heer. 'Leave him woman he'll be back afor long' and he never came back!" Agnus all but spat the words at Malcolm. "And you stopped me from going after her last night!"

"It was tae cold and the Search and Rescue wouldna help until light. Did ye want us tae freeze also?" Malcolm replied sternly.

A knock at the open door alerted the pair to the group who had congregated in the foyer.

"Sir," Ghillie stood, wringing his faded, brown flat cap in his large hands. "Mr. Buchan has just arrived, and the Search and Rescue are ready tae begin."

Malcolm nodded and walked toward his wife. "I'll not break another promise tae ye wife. I will find her. I swear it on my life."

"I'll leave ye to it then," Agnus watched him walk out behind Ghillie.

It was a wet, cold day, but she would not be left behind. This was her granddaughter, her only living blood. She couldn't sit on her hands and do nothing.

Agnus hurried to the scullery, shoving her stockinged feet into her wellies and donning her water-resistant coat. She pulled on her rain hat as she walked around to the far side of the house, past all the parked cars.

Blane and Malcolm were in deep discussion with the CO of the search and rescue when Prionnsa and Donn yapped sharply and danced around Malcolm's legs in excitement. Agnus watched as they ran to the edge of the wood.

"Malcolm!" She pointed her shaking hand.

\#

Blane rubbed his eyes. Lack of sleep and the deep longing to find Sadie alive and well was messing around with his brain.

He squinted at the sight of the tall red head sitting astride the blue roan. For a moment he was sure it was a vision: a goddess and her Stead. Adrenaline surged through his body as he ran, only slowing as he came to stand beside the horse and its rider.

"Sadie! Dear God. Are you all right?"

He ran his eyes over the length of her body. Her hair was full of twigs and heather. The brooch he'd gifted her. Her cheeks flushed red with streaks of dirt. His eyes travelled down further until… that was why she limped. Was she ashamed? Afraid people might… he might…?

"It's nothing." Sadie said as she pulled down hard on the loose pant leg.

Blane shifted his attention back to her face, keeping his expression calm and neutral.

"Are you okay?" He reached up and gripped his hands around her waist as she slid off the mare's back.

"I'm fine."

His arm slid around her to help her balance. Electric pulses ran up his arm, down his spine and back up his spine again to explode at the base of his skull. The scent of earth, horse and heather filled his nostrils.

Her green gaze met his. The dirt smearing her cheeks only served to accentuate her beauty. Her lips parted in that soft sensuous way a woman's mouth readied for another's, and for an instance, the hustle and bustle of the world vanished. Fire lit up his insides and Blane had to fight the urge to touch his lips to hers.

"Sadie!"

The spell broke.

Malcolm and Agnus Munro's voices called in unison as they jogged up to them. The roan whinnied and shook her head.

"Calm now, girl. It's all right." She spoke to the horse, but her gaze did not leave Blane's. "Leave her be. She is safe in the woods for now. I'll explain it all later."

He nodded, at a loss for words, then handed her over to the paramedics who lay her down on a stretcher before covering her with a space blanket and carrying her off to the ambulance. Agnus and Malcolm followed.

He turned and watched as the mare trotted into the forest. Should he call Mac? No, he trusted Sadie. She'd formed a bond with the mare. Her missing leg came back to him. So much about her made sense now. Her fierce grasp on her independence. Her cold demeanor whenever he'd come too close. He glanced to where the paramedics and the Munros fussed over Sadie. It was the hardest thing ever, not to wrap his arms around her and kiss her when he'd held her.

He was unsure as to how much longer he would be able to ignore his feelings for her. Would she allow him to get closer now that he knew about her leg, or push him farther away?

"I take it this is the missing woman?" The search and rescue coordinator said as he came to stand beside Blane.

"Ah - yes. Yes, it is."

"Lucky lady. It's rare we find them so soon, an' rarer still they find their oon wey oot. That beastie musta saved her life. Whose is it anyway and what is it doing oot in the woods?"

"That's a long story, sir," Blane combed an impatient hand through his mussed-up hair.

"Och weel she's a lucky lass. No way anyone walks oota those woods looking like that after the cold snap we had last night," he said and walked away.

Chapter 30

Blane was no longer able to deny what he felt for Sadie Munro. He slammed shut the door of his car and started the engine. The Munros were settled, but he was determined to return tomorrow and do something about the volcano of emotions Sadie Munro had conjured within him. But he had to take it slow. Like the Roan, Sadie would bolt if he came on too strong. Perhaps he could ask if they could go out for lunch?

Blane skidded the car into its dilapidated garage. He really should get it renovated and soon.

He hopped out and strode toward the back door of the manor house. The kitchen was empty without the wee lamb in it. He'd decided it was time for her to move to the shed after he'd found her munching on one of his shoes in the scullery two mornings ago.

Blane made his way to his library. For the first time in months his soul felt light, happy. He crossed the entrance of his second favorite place in his home, the first was his bedroom, to find Cybil sulking in the corner, and all his plans turned to dust.

"Good morning Cybil."

His ex-fiancé sighed and slid off the window bench onto her stiletto shod feet.

"Really, people will think you have a thing for the poor orphan next door."

No, *good morning.* No, *did they find her?* No, *how are you...* No, Cybil cut right to the heart of her cold hatred. She'd well overstayed her week. But how could he simply throw her out? That was against everything he'd been taught on how to treat a woman, even one he loathed.

"Count your words Cybil," he warned.

Her face paled and her lips pulled tight as she thrust her balled fists on to her hips. "You give her jewelry – your grandmother's brooch, and you run to her side when she purposely gets lost in the stupid forest. Why? *Why her?* What does she have I couldn't offer you?"

And there it was....

He'd wanted to say, *A soul*. But opted for, "I no longer care, Cybil. We're done. You promised to stay only a week longer…it's been several."

Cybil's bottom lip trembled as she paced the length of the library then came to stand in front of him. She placed her small frozen hands on his shoulders. "Blane, please."

Blane rubbed a hand over his face as he shrugged her off. "I can't watch you try so hard anymore," his voice croaked. "You're not happy here, and I am not happy with you here. It's best you leave. You don't have to go back to London right away. I am sure Michael can arrange for you to use the cottage in Nice."

When she stepped closer to him, Blane gently pushed her aside and strolled across to the fire place. He leaned one arm on the mantle, the other rubbing his bearded chin.

"Will you never return?" Her voice, soft and innocent as a child's, floated across to where he stood.

"I sold my controlling shares to Michael. Buchan Consolidated is no longer mine. The board met, they voted, and he is the new CEO."

Cybil gasped, her eyes wide, dark, and angry. Her skinny cashmere clad arms fell at her side. "When!"

"The day I left London." He knew his tone would cut, but honestly, he no longer gave a damn.

"What have you done?!"

It was hard to miss the contempt and horror in her tone.

"I'm not the man you fell in love with Cybil. All this time you've not once faced the truth. I won't be returning to London, at least not to live. And you and I were never meant to be."

Her skin paled to a sickly grey. Cybil crumpled to the floor.

#

The doctor had driven to Saorsa twice over the last forty-eight hours. He'd prescribed some strong medication and Cybil had finally calmed. Mrs. Daily, his house keeper had kept a close eye on her each time he'd left the house.

She was pushing the line now. He knew half of her 'weakness' was faux, and that she was simply playing for time. But what would it say to the town he was trying so hard to win over, if he kicked out the sickly weak ex?

Blane jumped in the rover, reversed out of the shed, and raced down the drive just as a small, dilapidated car passed him. Was that Mrs. Learie? What was she doing here? He slammed his foot down on the brakes and reversed.

"Good morning Mrs. Learie. I didn't know we had an appointment?" He jumped from his front seat to help the old matron from her nineteen-sixties Morris Minor.

"Och no Mr. Buchan. I am heer at the invitation of yer fiancé," she said as she closed her car door.

"Oh, well… "

"I am sure ye have better things tae do than accompany me tae ye door?"

"Ah yes, well have a good morning."

Something akin to a block of ice stuck in his throat and spread its chill through his body. He'd known Cybil and Mrs. Learie had shared some afternoons over tea and cake, but he hadn't realized just how close the two had become. This was not a good thing, but he did not have time for it now. He would question Cybil tonight.

Chapter 31

What a week. Nan and Oupa had not let her out of their sight, even though she'd promised not to wander anywhere near the forest again. Not to mention the fact Oupa had taken it upon his self to teach her to dance. "It's fur the ball lass. We cannae ave ye totterin roond the dance floor like an illiterate."

Sadie had merely shaken her head and obliged. They both ended up in fits of laughter more than they did actual dancing. But, things were coming together, and Sadie and Malcolm had found a way to dance which suited her left leg too.

Blue, more confident now, had taken instantly to her stable. She wasn't sure if it was the food and fresh water, or because she'd allowed Sadie to ride her? Either way, the mare was safe in her stable and happy.

A specialist was flown up and repaired Sadie's socket so her prosthesis, which Ghillie had found, could be refitted. Apparently, Blane was to thank for that.

Blane…

She wasn't sure how she felt about him knowing, or his lack of reaction when he'd noticed her missing limb. Was the storm still to hit? Was he just good at hiding his horror? But the memory of his lips so close to hers, the smell of his skin, his tender touch as he laid her down on the paramedic's pallet… he wouldn't have acted that way if he was appalled… Then again, one never really knew.

As for everyone else, Mrs. Perkins, Ghillie, and Annie had not let on in any way that, either they knew, or were grossed out by the fact she was an amputee, and life was returning to normal. Now she had to assert her space and get her grandparents to back off a wee bit.

"I promise I will be with Blue until tea," she told them after breakfast.

Riding boots on, Sadie walked over to the stable. "Morning girl." She rubbed the mare's nose. Blue whinnied, stuck her head out over the half-door, and softly nuzzled her snout beneath Sadie's arm. She and Ghillie, with the help of extra work men, had put together an outdoor lunging arena. Today would be the day to see what Blue thought of it.

Just behind the buildings and the stable, which formed the northern border of the court yard, preparations were being made for an indoor arena. Blane had insisted on being a part of the construction. It was his mare after all. That soft warm spot in her chest ached. She couldn't deny she had feelings for her English neighbor, nor could she accept it.

Sadie's eyes rolled at the thought. He had come over twice since her adventure in the forest, minus Cybil. The moment she and Blane had shared when he'd helped her off Blue's back that morning invaded her mind every chance it got. How do you ignore something like that? The connection transcended mere attraction. But she had to. He might know of her leg, but what if things went too far… what if he saw all of her scared, broken body…? The thought flipped her insides. She pushed it away and opened the half door and stepped into the stable.

"All right then, it's time my girl. We need to get you used to that arena." Sadie rubbed the mare's neck.

Blue nodded, her ears twitched as Sadie moved around.

To soothe the mare, Sadie sang, and the mare relaxed. When Sadie was happy and the mare calm, she turned and unbolted the stable door. Blue snorted and butted Sadie with her head.

"Ompf! No girl, that's not nice. You can't stand here all day just feeding and getting pampered." She stepped up to Blue and rubbed her nose. "No need to be a bully."

Sadie led Blue out the stable without a halter. She trusted Blue enough not to use one. The mare wouldn't have gotten used to one in any case, not after her abusive past.

They made their way to the west side of the court yard. The roan stopped a few paces away from the strange looking palings, which stood to attention in a circle. Sadie knew she'd been tied up in a similar arena when Blane had first found her.

She turned and rubbed Blue's face and neck, singing softly. When Blue calmed, she left the mare where she was standing and walked to the arena. She opened the gate all the way and walked inside. The mixture of river sand, sawdust, and rubber felt soft beneath her foot. She knew Blue would love this.

Sadie walked across the circumference and leaned against a paling at the furthest side. Blue stood watching, her ears twitching, her head nodding.

Sadie sang.

Blue stood.

Sadie sang.

Blue whinnied and turned her back on Sadie.

Sadie sang.

It was almost tea time when Blue took her first step into the arena. She didn't walk all the way in, but stood front feet in, and back feet out.

Sadie sang.

Malcolm would simply have to make peace with her not joining him for tea today.

Her left leg ached, but she refused to move or stop singing. Blue stood. The lazy sun stroked her cheeks, and on the horizon, dark cold clouds sat like huddled spectators watching the horse and her trainer. Neither budged.

Sadie wasn't sure how much longer her leg would hold. Her knee throbbed and toes which no longer existed, ached.

She sang.

Blue snorted and made her way into the arena and up to where Sadie stood.

"Good girl," Sadie wrapped one arm around Blue as she pulled a carrot out of her jacket pocket with the other. She held it up to the roan's mouth who chomped and munched enthusiastically on the sweet vegetable.

It was after lunch when Sadie put Blue back into her refreshed stable. They had hired a stable hand, a youngish bloke who would apprentice with Ghillie on the estate, as well as help with mucking the stables and keeping the arenas tidy.

Sadie made her way to the back door of the manor and sat exhausted on the step.

"Long day lass," Mrs. Perkins voice called from the scullery.

"Yup."

"Aye, but it were a gud one."

Sadie sighed. This time it was one of relief and joy.

"Yup."

She smiled to herself. She'd done it. She'd managed to save the mare, and quite possibly been saved by the mare herself. Perhaps, once she had Blue rehabilitated and returned to her rightful owner, she'd think of taking on another sorry equine case? But would she be able to give Blue back to Blane?

For the first time in a year, Sadie was content. She wanted to say she'd found peace, and perhaps she had when it came to letting go of her family. But a gnawing sense that a storm brewed just below the calm surface of life, tumbled around inside her belly.

She'd not had any nightmares, but Epona had visited her on a few occasions in her dreams since the night she'd spent in the forest. This time, not beckoning but pointing up to the darkening sky.

She shook her head.

"Enough!" she whispered.

\#

"I'll be away for a few days." Cybil poured each of them a whiskey and handed Blane his.

"Going back to London?" He nodded his thanks as relief eased the knot in his diaphragm.

"No, I'll just drive down to Edinburgh. I'm in need of a gown." She sipped her drink all the while pinning him to the spot with her steely gaze.

"For what? And isn't your cupboard full of courtier already?"

"Mrs. Learie was so kind as to ask me to stay long enough to attend the Munro Winter Ball. Besides, all my good clothing is still in London and much too …," She waved a hand in the air as she pretended to search for the appropriate word. "Opulent for Lairg, don't you think?"

He managed to suppress his astonishment the Munro's had personally invited her, but she mentioned Mrs. Learie had given her the invitation. The Munro Winter ball was an open event. People came from far and wide, and from all walks of life to celebrate the turning of the season.

"Will that be a problem?"

"You're leaving after the ball?"

A deep sigh escaped her thin, pink glossed lips. "Yes Blane. But perhaps the question you should ask is, would you still want me to leave after the ball?"

Blane felt his forehead crease as he considered her. What was she up to? Before he could ask, his cell phone rang.

"I'll be back before you know it," Cybil whispered in his ear then left him to answer his phone.

Chapter 32

Malcolm stood staring out of his study window. His thoughts adrift, sailing the waters of happy musings and bliss filled gratefulness.

"Penny fur ye thoughts."

His wife's words drew him out of his inner meanderings and to her. Agnus sat where she always sat, on the bay window seat, book in hand. God, she was a sight. That day he'd laid eyes on her at the Edinburgh Tattoo all those many years ago, he'd known instantly she was the one.

"Aye just pondering our blessings mo ghaol."

Her smile sprinkled starlight across her blue eyes. She slipped off the seat and came to stand by him, her arms wrapped around his waist. They stood and stared out the window to where their granddaughter sat on the bench, dogs on her lap.

"Oh aye, a blessing she truly is."

"I cannae believe life would bring her heer, no' after the way… me and Stewart… I was a terrible father," Malcolm swallowed back the urge to cry.

"Not a one of us are perfect, husband. Not yer parents, not mine, nor theirs before them. We do what we do out of love. We try to protect them from the dragons and the witches not realizing we might be hindering them all the while."

Malcolm thought back on the night Sadie had gone running off in to the forest. He'd thought it was over. It was the coldest autumn night they'd had in over two decades and she'd run off into it with no care or proper wear.

But the gods or God himself had seen fit to return her to them, and for that he would be eternally grateful. Also, whatever had happened to her that night had changed her for the better, not to mention the arrival of the mare. She'd not shared her story with them, but he no longer cared as long as she was here, happy and safe.

"What is this then? Did MacMillan not do as you asked?" Agnus peered over her shoulder to the paper on his desk.

"Aye, he did. Wrote a fine report on the lost woman and that she was found in and around Lairg, no names mentioned." Malcolm turned and picked up the newspaper.

He'd used some large favors to pull it off too. Apparently, it wasn't only the papers that were to be worried about, but those infernal phones, which acted like a mobile broadcasting station. They simply could not afford the news of Sadie living in the highlands spreading and being discovered by whoever meant her harm.

"Then what is the matter?" Agnus asked.

"Keep yer ear to the groond next ye go play bridge," he asked as he placed the paper down on his desk.

Agnus let go of him. She squinted her eyes and frowned.

"It's Ann Learie. She's been nosing aroond oor private stuff," he huffed.

Agnus nodded. "Will do. Perhaps ye should use the prayer ye taught Sadie the other day? Rhiannon cares for more than the mare." She leaned forward and kissed his forehead.

Such a wise woman. He was blessed twice over.

"Shall we wash up fur dinner?" she asked.

"Aye, but first," he pulled Agnus into him and pressed his lips against hers. "Mmm as sweet as the day I met ye," he smiled as smudges of red spread across his wife's cheeks and neck.

"Och, ye cheeky ol bugger." She softly slapped his shoulder before returning the kiss.

Chapter 33

Three months. A mere twelve weeks since she'd
stepped off the plane and made her way here.
Sadie wondered at how fast time had passed since
she'd walked up to the front door of Munro Manor. How
much had changed. She'd changed, Oupa had changed, and
all for the better.

The wimpy winter sunshine warmed the top of her
head while a crisp breeze blew off the loch and cut right
through her jodhpurs. She uttered a silent prayer of thanks
as she motioned to the mare to move from a brisk walk into
a trot.

Training was going well. Blue was responding
beautifully, and she'd soon be strong enough to be
returned. Sadie's heart sank a little.

Another gust of wind curled its way around her
body and Sadie tugged on her new waterproof coat. Nan
had taken her down to Edinburgh last weekend for some
shopping. Sadie had bought warmer outfits for winter,
including riding gear which disguised the awkwardness of
her leg. Just because the household had seen her limbless
left stump didn't mean she was in any way comfortable
showing off her prosthesis.

They had also, much to Sadie's discomfort, paid a
visit to the dressmaker Nan had mentioned. The woman
was everything Nan had described and more. An amputee
just like Sadie, she understood exactly what Sadie would
need. Large swaths of cloths and fabric were pulled out,
measurements taken, and soon, a darling green satin and
velvet gown, with sleeves of chiffon and silk was brought
to life on Maeb's sketch pad.

The Munros held their Winter Ball the last Friday
of every November. It was the social event of the year, on
all Lairg's calendars. Even the few tourists who ventured
up that way were welcomed. It was a traditional Scottish
gathering with good food, great wine, and much joy –

according to Mrs. Perkins. It was the one time in the year Malcolm brought in outsiders to take care of the catering and cleaning so that even Mr. Foggart, Annie, and Mrs. Perkins could join in the merry making.

It was hard to acknowledge the wisp of excitement brewing within her for the ball. Was she allowed to let go and enjoy life for once?

A glance at her watch told her it was time for tea.

She and Blue had spent at least an hour training this morning. Sadie looked up to where trade men hammered and worked on the almost completed indoor arena. She'd wanted to help pay, but both her grandfather and Blane had refused.

Blue whinnied and pulled Sadie back to the moment.

"Take it easy girl." Sadie lifted her hand to slow the mare's trotting.

Blue slowed to a walk and blew heavily out through her nose. "Head up girl. No slouching."

"Don't think I've ever heard a person speak to a horse the way you do..."

Sadie jumped and Blue darted to the side then trotted straight up behind her.

"Blane!" She grasped at her chest.

The tall bearded Englishman took a step back, palms up, eyes wide. "Sorry, I didn't mean to upset you."

Sadie smiled. "It's all good. I just didn't hear you walk up to us." Blue nudged Sadie's shoulder. "All right, all right. No need to be cheeky now," she said, reaching back and rubbing the mare's face.

"Blane, I don't think I've introduced you."

Sadie leaned forward and took Blane's hand in her own.

A warmth spread from her hand to his and sent tingles up her spine.

"Slowly now." She placed his hand on Blue's nose. "Blue, this is the man who saved you, remember?"

Blue snorted and Blane smiled. "Well that was…um different," he said, reaching for a handkerchief to wipe his snotty palm.

Sadie smiled and turned her back on the mare. Their eyes met, and the world stood still once more. Apparently Blue would have none of that and promptly stuck her nose into Sadie's neck, tickling her with snotty lips.

#

It was like the chime of a thousand tiny bells; something he could only imagine an angel's laughter would sound like. The most beautiful, joyful burst of happiness he had ever heard had burst from Sadie's lips as the mare nibbled her neck and she giggled.

He'd come here to discuss an issue with Malcolm. He had the horrid feeling Cybil sat behind some of the problems heading for their beautiful town.

He'd parked down the side of the manor and couldn't help being drawn to the arena. Her hair like a bonfire on a spring night, the way she moved her arms like a ballerina as she guided the mare he'd believed lost for good around the edges of the arena. And now here he stood, swallowing his words. She simply knocked all common sense from his mind.

"You come to check on their progress?" She motioned toward the builders and the almost complete indoor arena. All he could do was nod. What in the seven heavens was going on with him?

"I've come to see Malcolm but thought…" he began.

Her long black lashes batted as she tilted her head to the side, and the tip of her strawberry red tongue stroked her lips.

Blane's hand acted of its own accord as it rose and stroked her cheek. Desire, hunger, and adoration, the likes of which he'd never experienced washed over him as he stepped closer and lowered his head and touched his lips to hers.

A wet nose and loud snort interrupted the moment as Blue jealously pushed her head in between the pair. "Blue!" Sadie admonished. "I need to rub her down and water her."

She stepped away leaving Blane to swallow his hungry intent and grieve the loss of her lips on his.

Sadie opened the arena gate and walked out with Blue short on her heels.

He found his gaze glued to her. It slid from her neck and down her back. He drank in every curve, bump, and hollow in a way he wished his hands could. She was slim, but not skinny. Her shoulders strong, but not hard and, her arse… His breath snagged in his throat.

He looked away and rubbed his hot cheeks. What was he doing? He glanced back and squinted. Her left leg looked almost normal in her riding pants. He'd wanted to ask, but instinct told him it wasn't a good idea.

"Ah, Blane, heer ye are lad. Come tae see the mare have ye?" Malcolm waddled over.

Blane turned to greet the old man, accompanied by the foreman of the team building the indoor arena. "Good day sir. Yes, and to chat with you about a serious matter."

#

Sweet holy crap!

Sadie thought as she ran her fingers across her lips.

Her skin tingled and the same scary feeling that had filled her belly from the day of their first meeting filled her belly. Only it wasn't so scary anymore, it was exhilarating!

So close, "But you had to get your green on girl. That was terrible behavior," Sadie said as she patted Blue's rump.

She walked into the stable with Blue right behind her. "Okay, time to rub you down and put on your blanket."

It was hard to focus on the job at hand. It was becoming even harder to ignore her feelings for their debonair Englishman. She had to ignore them though. He was out of her reach, even if he hadn't run for the hills that day she'd ridden out of the forest and saw her amputated leg, Sadie still wasn't willing to risk being humiliated and rejected, again. And even if her leg wasn't the problem, the cloying Lady Cybil Acton was definitely a barrier, one which Sadie was not in the mood to overcome.

According to Annie, who heard it from the maid at Saorsa, Cybil had returned to Saorsa after her short sojourn to Edinburgh. Why didn't Blane just make her leave?

Annie also let slip how Mrs. Learie and Lady Cybil often shared morning tea together. This, Sadie hoped, was only gossip, but a chill around the back of her neck told her otherwise.

Chapter 34

"I tell ye it's that damnable crone, Learie!"
Malcolm slapped his hand on the desk.

"Weel it dinnae help tae give yer self a heart attack
Malcolm." Agnus stood up from her window seat and
walked out of the study. "I'll be in my solarium."

"Look, I can probably drive down to Edinburgh this
afternoon and figure out who can give us any information
and how we work around this issue?" Blane rubbed a hand
through his hair.

He hadn't mentioned the heads up from the bank
manager in town about the forth coming foreclosures.
Many of the locals were battling financially, hence his
desire to invigorate the local economy. He didn't think the
town deserved to worry, not before he'd tried to do
something to stall it. Where was this sudden onslaught on
Lairg coming from? Was Learie that determined and
connected... Cybil had just been to Edinburgh. No, surely,
she wasn't capable of such things? Was she?

Yes, Cybil most certainly was capable. Was she so
desperate to think he'd run back to her if she ruined things
for Lairg?

He'd called some friends, pull some strings, and
hopefully, stop whatever tidal wave was ready to wash
over and crush his new home.

Then there was the tender. They were unofficially
notified of their successful application to host the research
teams, and then without warning or explanation it was
withdrawn. Why?

"Who'd ye say was in charge doon there?"
Malcolm asked, his eyes sparkling.

"Dermot McIntyre is the head of the Agriculture
and Environmental Department." Blane answered.

"Ha! Problem solved, if it's the Dermot I think it
is."

Blane gave the old man a quizzical look. "How's
that?"

"Because the Dermot I ken, I kenned verra weel back in the day."

"You're talking in circles Malcolm. What do you mean?" Blane frowned at the old Laird. The man often got carried away, leaving those around him lost and confused.

Malcolm huffed as his forehead creased. "What I mean, young man, is I was his father's commanding officer back when we were both serving in Her Majesty's army. Did his family some great favors back then."

"There are probably a thousand Dermot Mac's in Scotland, Malcolm."

Malcolm raised his hand. "Aye, but I remember noo, ol Dermot was rather chuffed his son had a position at the university a while ago. Wrote and told me. Loves to brag the wee blighter does. Ye leave it tae me. Either way young man, we will get this tender back on track and then the both o us will grab that meddling ole crone by the ears. The world's smaller than ye ken, laddie."

#

Well now...

Blane hopped down the red stone steps of Munro Manor. It seemed Old Munro still had some fire in his bones. He was glad it was not him having to go off to Edinburgh. A thought tickled the back of his mind. Things pointed increasingly to Cybil and Learie sitting behind the wheel of the calamity truck heading their way. Though he'd have to be certain before he approached her.

A movement on the shores of the Loch caught his eye.

Hot air snagged in his lungs.

He should leave, walk straight to his car, not look back, not even steal a glimpse. If Cybil was behind all this, chances were, she had her sights set on Sadie. It was safer to keep his distance. Blane tried to convince himself, but instead found his feet leading him right where he had no business being.

Sadie stood, hands on hips, head leaned backward, eyes shut. She was a sight. Words like fire, passion, and desire flew like brightly colored kites in his mind as he watched her. He cleared his throat as he drew closer, not wanting to startle her again.

"Hmm."

Not straightening her neck, she rolled her head to the side and opened an eye.

"Oh." She stumbled, caught her balance. "Thought it was Malcolm."

"Sorry to disappoint."

"Not at all." Her cheeks flushed, and she returned her gaze to the loch.

"The indoor arena should be up and ready before the worst of the cold and wet arrives. Well that's what Malcolm reckons anyhow." He rattled out the words like an automatic rifle.

Shite! Why was it so hard to say anything coherent when he was around her? He'd regressed to a school boy with stupid-head syndrome.

"I hope so. Somedays these clouds look as though they're ready to wash us away in their winter sludge."

The sun was still out, but there on the far horizon loomed a bank of thunderous clouds. Like an angry bruise, they were slowly spreading themselves across the sky.

"How is Cybil?"

"Huh? Fine." He didn't want to speak of her.

"Going to go back for Christmas then?" Sadie eyed him, head cocked.

"Back?"

"To London?"

Blane cringed. "Me? Ah, no."

Her head snapped in his direction, her deep green gaze searched his face. Why was she asking these questions?

A splash on the shores of the loch drew both their attention.

"Oh my, look at that!" Sadie pointed excitedly. A fish as long as his leg jumped right out the water, landing on the sandy shore before them.

"A brown trout?"

Jogging up to the fluttering fish, Blane edged closer. What a strange thing. He'd never heard or seen anything so bizarre before. It wriggled and bounced as though it had second thoughts and wanted back into the icy waters.

"How do you know what it is?" Blane asked

"I read a lot," she shrugged.

"Should we grab it? It would make…"

Blane hadn't realized how close they'd come to stand to one another. They straightened, nose-to-nose. He allowed his gaze to dip down to her lips. Plump and sweet as strawberries. This was it. All resistance, pretenses, and walls crumbled. And there was no mare to push between them. Blane slipped a hand into the nape of her neck. He thrilled at the touch of her warm, silky skin.

Her lips parted. Her breath, warm and sweet, her eyes aglow.

He leaned in and placed his lips on hers. A zing of electricity shot down into his toes. So, this was how it felt to be struck by lightning? His world flipped on its head.

Sadie responded, opening her mouth.

She tasted like oolong and spring. She smelled of horse and jasmine. In that moment, every atom that made up every cell of his body, mind, and soul, knew beyond all knowing – Sadie Munro was created for him.

#

Sadie's world tilted on its axis. Everything she felt for the suave Englishmen was wrong. So. Damn. Wrong. Her skin on the back of her neck was on fire. Her heart galloped, and desire pooled in her center. Could a kiss elicit such intense sensations?

This was a dream, a wondrous dream, but it couldn't be real. In real life, Blane was untouchable. And she, a damaged, broken woman. But his lips like velvet and his taste, pure unadulterated ambrosia pulled her beneath the surface and in to a world of … Oh, sweet heavens, this felt so right. More right, than anything was allowed to feel. More than….

This was wrong!

Sadie placed both hands on his chest and pushed. "No Blane. I'm… Broken and Cybil…" Her words battled to form in her mouth, still hungry for his.

His gaze swirled in a mixture of amber and honey, his lips red, swollen from the touch of hers… no!

"You're what?" the skin between his eyes creased as the amber of his eyes darkened dangerously.

Sadie couldn't form the words to explain and found she could only shrug and step away. It hurt, but she had to.

Blane cocked his head then ran his hands through his hair pulling it free from its binding, causing his dark curls to fall around his face, "Cybil… blast it all. There is nothing between me and that woman!"

Sadie shook her head. "Then why is she here, living in your home, making sure the entire town thinks she's returning home for Christmas with you on her arm?" Annie had let that convenient piece of gossip drop this afternoon as Sadie had passed through the kitchen.

"It's complicated."

"Life is complicated," the words fell from her lips like boulders.

She shivered as Blane stepped away. Every muscle in her body begged her to pull him back. But she couldn't. He was right. It was complicated. And complication was the last thing she wanted in her life right now. Especially if it harbored the threat of a broken heart.

"It's best if you leave." She turned to face the loch.

"I…I'm sorry, there is no…" He stepped toward her.

"Just…I want to… never mind."

And just like that he turned and left.

Sadie plonked down on the bench. The fish splashed its way back into the frigid lake waters. Her fingers trailed the path of heat he'd left on her mouth. Tears rolled down her cheeks. She was such a cliché.

#

Sparks and white lightning buzzed through his body and singed the tips of his ears. A single word, one he'd last

heard his grandmother use, tumbled around inside his head
— smitten.
Why this word? He didn't care. All he knew was he
was smitten, head over heels, smitten. Then why had he
left? Why didn't he just tell her the truth? Cybil was a
conniving wench and meant nothing to him. But she had a
point. Why had he permitted her to stay so long? Because
he was a decent man. Because he'd hoped that time would
prove to Cybil they were incompatible and hopefully give
him the absolution he sought for dumping her two weeks
before the wedding, leaving her to fend off the callous
backstabbing, the upper echelon of London society so
easily doled out.
Blane pulled open the car door and sat behind the
wheel. "Shite!"
He slammed his hand on the dash. Emotions
tumbled and roiled, each one fighting for first place. The
hand of God had grabbed the orderly cabinet he'd filed his
thoughts, feelings, and plans in, flung it open, and toppled
it over.
Blane found himself pulling to a stop at the front
door to Saorsa. He didn't remember driving back. Too lost
in his inner turmoil, only one thought made sense. Why
had he listened to her and leave? But that would have made
no difference.
Cybil had dug her feet in at Saorsa, and he was a
spineless ass. It might very well taint Sadie's reputation if
he was seen with her while his ex-fiancé still resided with
him. It might not be the 1800's, but it was the highlands
and a small town none the less. It was time Cybil left Lairg.

Chapter 35

Sadie limped toward the stables, her leg, like her heart, ached, but for different reasons. Life was complicated.

She ran her fingers over her lips for the thousandth time. It'd been a week since their kiss and she could still feel his lips on hers, taste his spiciness, feel the soft tickle of his beard against her face. She shook her head. No more thoughts about him. He'd not shown his face since the day she'd asked him to leave.

She turned her head toward the heavens.

The weather mimicked her bruised heart. The sun hadn't shown her golden face in over a week. Everything was wet and mushy and cold. Why had she allowed him in? She'd known it would only lead to ... this!

Enough! She stomped her foot then continued to the stable.

She was determined not to let her feelings and confusion over Blane overshadow her new life. She lived to spend every day with Blue and her grandparents. They were her coat and shield against the unsettling flicker of anxiety, which fought its way to the surface every so often.

When her leg ached from a day standing in the arena, it was a good ache, and no longer a reminder of her brokenness.

The only obstacle left for her to traverse - the winter ball. Nan and Oupa were so excited at the prospect of showing off their beloved granddaughter and she couldn't help but revel in their joy.

Blane Buchan. Her heart teased again.

The memory of his hand cupping her neck as he leaned in to kiss her, sent butterflies flapping around her insides. Best to just forget it.

Swatting Blane and the butterflies from her thoughts she opened the stable door.

"Alright girl, you ready?" She stepped inside.

A bright red blanket was draped over the roan's body. The mare had gotten used to the straps holding it in place. This was a good sign. Sadie stood face to face with the horse, placed her head against Blue's, and closed her eyes. The mare reciprocated in kind.

"What if I can never forget. What if I can never unfeel what I feel for him?" She asked quietly.

A warmth she'd never get used to spread through her soul and into her body as the mare connected with her on a plane few humans travelled to. Total, unconditional love, and acceptance from one of God's grandest creatures was an exceptional honor.

With effort Sadie shifted her emotions and thoughts to the here and now.

Not moving her head or opening her eyes, she said, "you going to let me ride you today? I haven't been on your back since you brought me home."

It had taken time and patience, but she'd gotten Blue to accept the saddle and neck rope. Today it was time to see if the roan would allow her on her back. She'd introduced the mare to the indoor arena a few days ago, and like the outdoor one, Blue had taken to it without too much ado.

Blue's ears tipped forward, then upright. She blew out through her nose and stomped her hoof.

"Gonna take that for a yebo, yes!"

The mare had been fed two hours earlier, which meant Blue would feel comfortable enough when saddled up. Ghillie stood at the door of the tack room with the modified saddle over one arm and the neck rope hooked over the shoulder of the other.

"Ye bring her on through tae the arena lass, I'll take these."

Sadie nodded a little too hard and Ghillie threw his head back in laughter.

"Aye, yer like a wee lassie aboot tae ride her ponie for the first time ye are."

Sadie smiled. "Thank you, Ghillie. Thank you so much for everything."

The man's cheeks reddened. "Och tis nothing." He
turned and headed for the indoor arena.
Sadie stood a moment longer and slowed her
breathing. Her excitement was hard to contain. Crossing
her fingers and toes she repeated the small prayer Malcolm
had taught her. "*Epona, dìon màthair coiseachd còmhla
rium,*" the words evoking the Goddess to walk by her side.
#
Blue hesitated, not following Sadie.
"What's the matter girl?" Blue stuck her head out
and whinnied at the forest. "Ah… nope, we're not going
back there."
Sadie rubbed the mare's neck.
"It's okay, come now," and led the way. She didn't
miss the wide-eyed glare the horse aimed toward the edge
of the forest. Her stomach flipped, but she put it down to
nerves. She repeated the Gaelic prayer as they made their
way to the arena.
It was gorgeous. The domed roof rose high above
their heads. It was the same size as any normal lunging
arena found outdoors, except for the small pavilion
included on the right-hand side.
Oupa had maintained he'd, "need a place tae rest
my weary ole arse when I drink me tea an watch ye ride,
lass."
Sadie stood just inside the entrance. Blue behind
her. It had been finished a week ago, and Blue had been
trained inside twice since.
Sadie walked inside and across to where Ghillie
stood sorting the saddle and numnah. Blue didn't move.
"Come on girl." Blue stood fast, her ears flat
against her head.
"Seriously? It's your space. Out of the cold and
wet. Look at that fresh sawdust, especially brought in for
you. You know this space, it's yours."
Blue would have none of it. She swung her head up
and down, stomped her hoof, and turned around.
Oh, bother, what was up? Sadie walked the outer
edges and through the center, eyes glued to the ground as

she looked for anything which might be out of place –
nothing.
Deciding the horse might be in a bad mood, she
went to sit on a wood bench off to the side. Ghillie stood at
the far end fidgeting with something on the saddle. He
looked back over his shoulder and frowned. Sadie gestured
with her hand for him to stay where he was.
She considered the mare. It couldn't be the saddle;
she was acquainted with it and Ghillie. Blue hadn't gone
far. Whinnying and huffing, she was watching Sadie.
Was she trying to tell Sadie something? Sadie
closed her eyes and listened. Blue felt unnerved, but why,
she couldn't say. Perhaps just an off day? Perhaps the mare
felt her apprehension at riding again?
Sadie inhaled deeply and began to sing.
The melody trickled from her lips and out the door.
Thula thul, thula baba thula sana....
The last note drifted from Sadie's mouth. Blue was
standing inside the arena. She snorted and twitched her
ears.
Sadie laughed and stood up. "Ha-ha. All right, I'm
coming. Pleased you decided to join us."
The pair strolled over to where Ghillie stood gob
smacked.
"I'd heard ye was gud wi the beasties, but that…
what ye did just there… amazing lass."
Sadie smiled. "Thank you, Ghillie. Now let's see if
our hard work with this saddle pays off?" She removed
Blue's blanket and placed it on the wood beams beside the
saddle.
Blue stood easy as Sadie placed first the numnah,
then the saddle on the roan's back. She tightened the girth,
then reached for the neck rope. They'd not be using a
bridle. Sadie had given it a go, but Blue refused. The rope
was just that, a thick looped rope, which would hang
loosely around Blue's neck, used only for minor effect and
nothing else.
She wasn't worried though. She'd never relied on
one anyway. It was about trust and body weight, and on the

rare occasions a horse had bolted with her, to pull on the reins was futile anyway. But she wasn't worried about Blue. The mare might shy, at worst buck, but never bolt, not with her.

Ghillie stepped up. "Ready lass?"

Sadie shook her head. She needed a moment. She reached inside and pushed her nerves down into the dark corner where they belonged. What if her balance was all off? What if she fell? What if she could never ride again?

Blue nuzzled Sadie's shoulder and the memory of the morning she'd come riding home bare back, re-surfaced. She rubbed the horse's neck.

"Yes girl, I remember, thank you."

Sadie would have to mount from the wrong side using her good leg.

Ghillie gave her a hand up and she threw her fake limb over the saddle and sat a moment, catching her breath. Her head swirled a little and her insides trembled. Blue stood firm.

"Ye right up there, lass?" he patted her leg.

Sadie nodded. "Fine, just … just settling in, thank you."

With Ghillie's help, she slid the foot of her fake leg into the stirrup. Ghillie had designed one especially for her fake foot, so that should she fall, it prevented the foot from slipping in and getting caught. Ghillie pulled the Velcro strap loosely across her ankle and the one looping up and under her knee. They'd tested the tension before today. It was tight enough to hold her leg in place but loose enough to rip open should she fall.

Sadie nodded and Ghillie backed off.

Muscle memory kicked in. Sadie felt her bum and thighs tighten. Her shoulders relaxed, and her hands, wrists, and elbows softened. She squeezed with her thighs, unable to use her fake leg as she would have and leaned forward ever so slightly.

"Walk on."

Blue nodded her head. Sadie took hold of the thick neck rope hanging loosely around the mare's neck. Blue lifted her head and walked. Sadie allowed the rhythm of the mare's gait to vibrate through her own body. Her elbows bent and straightened, allowing her hands to follow the motion of Blue's neck, keeping pressure on Blue with her thighs.

Her legs were positioned directly beneath her body. The Velcro strap holding the left knee would prevent her leg from swinging back or forward causing her to lose balance, her right leg had to compensate for her left leg's stupidity. Sadie urged Blue in to a snappy walk and distributed her weight while gently maneuvering the neck rope to coax the mare's head up and under, thereby bringing her onto the non-existent bit.

The mare must have had training before her abusive master had gotten his filthy hands on her. Sadie felt Blue react to her voice and body placements in the saddle with ease.

A single click of her tongue and more pressure from her thighs.

"Trot."

Blue snapped into a trot. It wasn't a fast trot, but nice and relaxed. Her weight shifted, and she fell onto Blue's neck.

"Whoa girl."

Blue slowed to a walk. Sadie righted herself and found Ghillie standing, ready to run to her.

"I'll be okay" she smiled.

Heart pounding in her throat, Sadie readied her herself to try again. She clicked her tongue and leaned slightly forward. Blue slipped into an easy trot. Sadie found her balance as she saddle-hopped for half a lap then placed pressure onto the stirrups. She found her rhythm in a sitting trot by the time they'd started a second lap.

She didn't need Ghillie to show her with his hand gestures. She felt it. Her smile, right across her face.

Sadie sat and dug her bum into the saddle and squeezed... Blue slipped from a trot in to a gentle canter.

Sadie let go of the rope and raised her arms out beside her body, like the wings of an airplane. The breeze tugged the loose tendrils of hair which had come loose from her ponytail and her body moved to the rhythm it was born to move. Her heart soared, and her soul flew thousands of meters above the earth. She was free once more, free to be... *Epona*... the name drifted between her and reality.

After a few laps around the arena, her cheeks and legs ached. "Slow now girl, aaaand let's walk."

Sadie sat into her saddle as Blue slowed to a walk. She rubbed the mare's neck. "Excellent girl, absolutely excellent!"

Chapter 36

Bone weary did not begin to describe the extent of
Blane's exhaustion. If it were at all possible, he was sure
the marrow of his bones ached as much as the muscles
holding his skeleton together. It had been a long day and
he'd avoided the house like one would a stinking corpse.
"Thanks Mac. I'll see you tomorrow?" Blane parked the
four-wheeler in the shed and shook his foreman's hand.
"Aye Mr. Buchan. If ye feel the need, the boys and
I are meetin doon at the pub. Ye look like ye could do with
a pint or two."
Blane nodded then made his way toward the house.
Perhaps he should take Mac up on his offer? Perhaps, after
he'd had a shower.
He'd confronted Cybil yesterday afternoon after
Sadie had asked him to leave.
"Are you kicking me out?" her words cut.
While every inch of him had wanted to reply, "Yes,
and I'm onto you and your attempts to sideline our tender."
Blane had instead replied, "No. But it is time you returned
to London."
"You promised I could stay for the ball!"
"Why, Cybil? This is not your scene. You hate it
here, you hate the people, you hate the fresh air! So why
are you so adamant to attend the bloody winter ball? Or is
it because you've some devious plan up you sleeve?"
She'd left Saorsa in a taxi, only for him to find out
via Mac she was now residing at the Sheep Heid Inn.
Well, if having her stay at Saorsa hadn't stirred up
the local gossips, the fact his ex-fiancé was now hold up in
the local Inn surely had!
Blane kicked his wellies off at the scullery door,
washed his hands, removed his jacket, scarf, beanie, and
jumper. He was making his way up the back staircase to his
room when he stopped dead, ears pitched. Was that? No...
He found Michael, his brother, and Cybil enjoying
drinks in the conservatory.

"What are you doing here?"

"No hello little brother? Nice to see you?"

Blane smiled and walked up to Michael. "I'd hug you, but I smell." Blane stretched out a hand as his gaze floated toward Cybil. Damn the woman!

"Taken to the farm life I see," Michael's grip was firm. "Suits you."

"Running the family company suits you also. Let me shower and we'll have a drink and a catch up in the library."

He turned a questioning gaze toward Cybil who promptly painted a smile as innocent as a child's, across her face.

"Sounds great," Michael replied and sat back down.

Blane climbed the stairs lost in thought. Why was Michael here? He'd just taken over the company. He should be in the office, not flying up to the highlands. Cybil was behind this. What was she planning?

\#

"Where's Cybil?" Blane asked as he poured whiskey into two crystal tumblers, then handed one to Michael.

"Returned to the hole you call an Inn. Really Blane, was it so awful allowing her to stay here a few nights longer?"

Blane ignored his brother's question.

Michael raised his glass. "Cheers, big brother."

"It's you who must be congratulated," Blane smiled tipping his glass, so the edge clinked against Michael's.

"Well, yes, I guess you're right."

Blane shook his head. They were as different as summer was to winter. One would never say they were brothers. Where Blane was tall, dark, and owned a blatant presence, Michael was shorter, and took after his father's light features. He was also manipulative. Blane had always looked out for his younger brother, but Michael always seemed to harbor resentment toward him. It was subtle, present in his remarks, actions, and his never-ending drive to do better than Blane.

"So, what are you doing here?"

"Oh, come now, brother, I'm sure you've figured it out." The corner of his mouth pulled up.

"Cybil."

Michael nodded. "Got it in her head you've fallen for some common redhead."

A wave of anger washed over Blane, "You will mind your tongue, brother. That has nothing to do with…"

"Hang on now, I'm not here to berate you." Michael held out his glass for a refill. "You don't deserve Cybbie, you know."

"I don't want Cybbie," Blane took the glass and poured them each another dram, "but you do."

A thin smiled crossed Michael's face as he reached for his glass. He nodded his thanks and sipped, then held the tumbler with its amber liquid up to the light.

"This is probably the only good thing to come out of this sodden no man's land."

"Are you here to insult me and my new home or to collect Cybil?"

Michael's head snapped toward Blane. "I'm here because Cybil hopes I can talk some sense into you."

Blane nodded. "But that's not what you want to do, is it?"

"Look I'm not here to argue. Fact is, Mamma and Papa haven't seen either of us this happy in… well, in forever, and you know as well as I, when the parental units are happy, all is well in our worlds. Why would I do anything to upset the natural order?" He took another deep glug then eyed Blane. "Just know, I won't relinquish my spot should you ever tire of playing farm boy."

Blane downed his drink.

"I don't plan on returning, and nothing or no one will change my mind, but it'll be good if you could stay until after the Ball."

"Ball? They have social gatherings up here?" Michael's eyebrow arched.

"Yes, Michael. You'd be surprised at how civilized highlanders are. More so than the hollow shadows crowding the halls of London. And it's an annual 'Do' the local Laird throws."

"Laird? My, my, Blane you sure travel in enlightened circles," Michael scoffed and finished his drink. "Well I think I'll go unpack and check in with the office. Will you show me around the place later?"

Blane nodded. "Yeah, why not."

Blane poured another whiskey and sat in the high back leather chair behind his desk. Cybil would not let go easily. That was as plain as the day was cold. He wondered if she realized he'd managed to stay the banks proceedings and foiled her plans at derailing the tender handed in to the universities? He'd wanted to use it as the excuse to throw her out, but had decided not to play his hand, yet.

Where Cybil created allies using fear and blackmail, Blane's connections were forged through strong friendships and honesty. The moment he'd put his feelers out to try and get behind the sudden bank foreclosures on the towns people, the person pressured by Cybil had wasted no time in contacting Blane.

Poor old Riley Reddington was convinced Cybil had photos of him in a delicate situation. It had cost Blane another favor to make certain that she was lying.

Leaving Riley rather embarrassed to find himself at the butt of her conniving scheme.

This was more reason to keep an eye on her and send her back home with Michael after the ball. It wasn't strange that she wanted to stay, and Blane knew beyond a doubt she was up to something. It was a last-ditch attempt to get him back, but what was her plan? He'd need Michael to help him keep her reigned in. While he'd love to send her packing, there was no way he could physically force her to go back to London.

Michael, on the other hand, clearly had his own agenda. He wouldn't have left his newly claimed throne to visit his brother if he wasn't convinced he would gain something. Blane had known from the first that Michael was in love with Cybil. Michael loved most things that were Blane's but thinking back at how his younger brother

doted on her, it seemed he truly had fallen hard for the
woman.

He'd so wanted to leave all these games and power
plays in London. Perhaps it was a good thing? Had it been
anyone else, he would have given them a small warning,
but Michael could hold his own. Now he thought on it, they
suited one another far better.

Blane stood and poured a last dram. The loch
looked calm as dusk settled over the land.

His thoughts drifted further, to the mare and Sadie
Munro. She would be at the ball. Should he hint that Cybil
would attend? He'd wanted to drive over and speak with
her so often in this last week, but the memory of her fear
and pushing him away had stayed his yearning.

He truly was a coward. Any other man would have
gone back, told her how he felt, forced Cybil back to
London….

Chapter 37

"I think I need one of those tumblers of whiskey you and Oupa enjoy drinking." Sadie huffed.
"Och lass, it's going to be grand. Relax." Agnus smiled at her then slipped the black silk cover off the hanger to reveal Sadie's dress.
"Och will ye look at that," Mrs. Perkins gasped, slapping her hands to her mouth. "This lass o yers will steal the show."
Sadie cocked her head and stared at the stunning emerald green ball gown hanging against the cupboard door. "The dress is beautiful, but I could never do it justice."
"Now that's enough of that. You're a beauty in your own right lass, and it's only you who will complement that gown. Come sit. Let Mrs. Perkins do your hair while I get myself finished. The guests will be arriving soon."
Agnus kissed her on the crown of her head and left.
Sadie sat down on the stool by the mirror. She pulled her robe tight across her lacy underwear and knotted the belt.
Sadie considered Mrs. Perkins' reflection in the mirror. The outspoken, chirpy housekeeper had readied herself a while ago. She looked very handsome in a velvet maroon evening gown with her dark, silver flecked hair beautifully braided and pinned on her head.
"I think we'll leave some curls dangling doon yer back fur effect," Mrs. Perkins explained as she began to comb and twist Sadie's red tresses.
"Hmmhmmm." Sadie closed her eyes and enjoyed the relaxing tug and pull on her scalp as Mrs. Perkins wove her magic.
"Take a look lass. Ye'll no be disappointed," Mrs. Perkins instructed, tears glistened in her eyes.
Sadie took a deep breath and opened her eyes. Staring back from the mirror was not the broken woman from a farm in South Africa, but a Goddess, tall and proud.

Mrs. Perkins had done a magnificent job with her hair. the curls held in place with Swarovski crystal and emerald, ivy-leaf shaped pins.

"Right," Mrs. Perkins turned her around on the chair to face her. "Time for a wee bit o color and then the dress.

"You're such a fundi. Where did you learn to do hair and make-up like this?" Sadie asked.

"Och, just because I spend my days cleaning an cooking dinnae mean I have no other passions ye ken. But tell me lass, what's a fundy?"

Sadie giggled. "A f-oo-n-di. It means a skilled and clever person."

"Och noo, dinnae be daft lass. It's just a little paint and pooder. Besides, ye have a natural beauty and ave nae need fur any o this." She winked.

Mrs. Perkins used very little make up as promised, but it made the world of difference. Her eyes stared back as bright and green as the pins in her hair. A touch of rouge on her cheeks, mascara, and a deep mauve lipstick had transformed her into a movie star.

She helped Sadie onto her feet and began to help her dress.

The gown, made from five different fabrics, hugged all her good parts, and hid all the bad ones. Each fabric was a different shade of green, one complementing the other. It was straight out of a fairy tale.

The design was unique and made it easy for Sadie to walk without her prosthesis getting in the way. The bottom part of the dress was made of broad legged pants, and a half skirt, which ran from hip bone to hip bone around her bottom leaving the front to split open and give her freedom of movement, while the trouser part hid the prosthesis.

The bodice sat firm, but not too tight, with a V - neck which pushed her bosom up, but not out. The collar was notched, and the sleeves three quarters. Every scar was classically hidden, and when anyone looked, all they would see was a most magnificent beauty. A pair of closed-heel and toe shoes shaded a similar green to the pants hem, completed her gown.

"Thank you, Mrs. Perkins." Sadie hugged the housekeeper.

"Och noo lass, we'll both be crying soon and streaked in mascara." She smiled, dabbing first beneath Sadie's eyes, then her own.

#

Mrs. Perkins left her and headed down to assist Agnus with receiving the guests.

Blane and Cybil were attending, so was Mrs. Learie, according to Nan. She'd need every ounce of inner strength she owned.

Sadie stood in the passage and leaned with her back against her closed bedroom door. The house carried sound well and she could make out most of what was said by the excited arrivals downstairs. Her stomach summersaulted when she heard Mr. Foggart announce Blane, Cybil, and another man's arrival.

From the landing, she could see the entire foyer had been cleared of furniture. Strings of holly and ivy with bright red berries decorated the walls and tables. On one side stood a carved wooden woman with long hair. On her head, a freshly woven crown of pine, berries, and mistletoe. Behind her was a horse, and at her feet fresh fruit and loaves of bread.

"Epona," Sadie whispered.

Nan and Oupa had felt the need to show their thanks.

Opposite the statue stood a tall pine cut from the forest. Large crimson orbs drizzled in smatterings of gold filigree dangled from its branches, their warm glow accentuated by the exquisite hand-crafted crystal ornaments spread out between the branches. And on the floor at the base of the tree was a hand carved and painted nativity scene.

To the left as one stepped in through the front entrance, four large wooden doors had been pulled back, like a concertina, to open into a large ball room with a

crystal chandelier dangling from the center of the
elaborately carved ceiling.
The dark wood floors had been polished and the
curtains drawn back to show off the grandeur of the six,
ten-feet-tall windows. The intimate and fascinating notes
played by a string quartet danced through the house. The
angelic shrill of a cello brought the jovial notes of "God
Rest Ye Merry Gentlemen," to life.
Sadie stepped back. She couldn't do this. Too many
people, too much fuss…
The closed door to her left caught her eye. Leaving
the rowdiness of arriving guests and clinking glasses
behind, she walked up to the door. She dared not, but…
like a child reaching for something they're not allowed,
Sadie clutched the door handle and twisted it. This time it
did not fight back and opened easily.
The room was dark. She felt with her left hand
against the wall and found the light switch. No flames or
screaming this time; only trophies, photos, and dust greeted
her.
A frame, one she hadn't spotted before, stood on a
table in the far corner of the room. Sadie picked it up. Her
breath caught in her throat. It was a family photo; the one
Agnus had taken on her last visit. Mom, Dad, Stephen and
her. All their happy faces smiled up at her.
"Such a beautiful family."
Sadie jumped nearly dropping the frame. Malcolm
walked in and stood beside her, leaning comfortably on his
cane.
"Aren't you meant to be greeting the guests?" Sadie
placed the photo back on the table.
"Agnus was worried. I said I'd come look fer ye."
He smiled then looked down to where the photo stood.
"I'm that sorry aboot my thick heid and hot temper lass. I
ken it's too late, I blame myself every day. Wot if…"
Sadie tore her gaze from the handsome family
portrait to look at her Oupa. "It was no one's fault Oupa.
These things happen. But I do know Dad loved you. I heard
him and Mom talking one night. It was just before…" She

took a deep breath. It was still painful to remember. She missed them so much, especially tonight. "He wanted to come back, to see you, to make peace, but…"

A single tear rolled down Malcolm's face. "Aye, Selwyn, his friend told me."

The pair stood in silence a little longer. "Och weel, we'd better get tae the ball or yer Nan'll ave both oor hides." He wiped his face with a handkerchief, which he shoved back into his pant pocket and held out his arm for her. "Come lass there's naught tae fear."

Chapter 38

Sadie ruffled the skirt, so it would trail behind her as they made their way down the stairs. She placed her left hand on the balustrade and slipped her right into the crook of Malcolm's elbow.

People were still arriving. Nan stood at the entrance of the Manor, greeting the guests. Agnus looked up and her face split into the broadest smile as she nodded to Sadie, her grey hair done up in a classic coif and decorated in the finest, prettiest tiara. Her dark blue gown showed off a figure toned and shapely for a woman her age. Tear drop sapphires dangled from her ears and around her neck. She was the epitome of regality.

A tall tuxedo clad figure drew her attention to the right, Blane. His eyes were the brightest she'd ever seen them, and his face dressed in the broadest smile. Their eyes met. It was only a split second, but it lasted an eternity. The world around them fell away and for a moment it was only him and her.

Sadie returned a small smile then looked away when Cybil came to stand beside him.

"Let's go," she whispered to Malcolm.

A deafening silence followed by a gasp echoed through the large entrance as Sadie and Malcolm descended. People turned their heads and stared. Most smiled approvingly. Sadie's muscles threatened to freeze, but it was Agnus who kept her going. Her Nan hadn't taken her eyes off Sadie, her blue gaze coaching Sadie down the stairs to meet the throng of eager arrivals congregating in the entrance.

"Och lass, look at ye," one lady Sadie recognized from Agnus' bridge group, leaned forward and pecked each of Sadie's cheeks in greeting.

After greeting half the town, Malcolm nodded to Agnus. "Come, let's go find a drink. Me throats as parched as leather," and led them to the ballroom.

It was hard not to look at him, standing there, beard trimmed, fitted tuxedo, Cybil standing right beside him. He was chatting with a younger man; one Sadie didn't recognize. The man gestured with his head toward her and Blane turned to look.

"Good evening Malcolm, Sadie," a cold voice interrupted, and Sadie found a neatly dressed Mrs. Learie standing beside her.

"My, don't ye look the belle o the ball? Almost as dashing as oor Mr. Buchan's lady?" Sadie's eyes flicked from Mrs. Learie to where Cybil stood, dressed in a pale pink satin gown. Sadie could handle her stormy glare, which told of all kinds of nasty she wished upon her. But, what cut, was the fact Blane had brought Cybil to the ball. She was suddenly glad she'd pushed him away that day at the lake.

"Ye'll no ruin my granddaughter's evening, Learie!" Malcom piped up.

"Och, I wouldna dream of it. That honor is left to her alone."

An icy finger trailed its way up Sadie's neck and around her throat. Mrs. Learie's smile was calculating as her gaze ran over Sadie.

"I see ye dared tae place a heathen symbol right by oor good Lord's side," the bitter old crone motioned toward the foyer with a nod.

Malcolm opened his mouth to shoot another warning at Mrs. Learie when Agnus came to stand beside them.

"Well I'm sure there's somebody who'll enjoy yer company this evening dear, but I cannae say it would be any of us." Her dead pan stare cut straight through any retort the old crone had to offer.

"Come Sadie, there's someone I'd like yew to meet." Agnus led Sadie off into the crowd.

Crystal flute in hand, Sadie was introduced and re-introduced to Lairg's fair population. There were even some well to do folk from Inverness and further north. She knew her nan was making sure to keep her distracted from Blane, but she could feel the chill of Cybil's ice-cold glare scrape down her neck and back as she moved around the ballroom.

Malcolm and Agnus, as per the tradition, opened the dance floor with a most exquisite waltz to an old Scottish folk song. People cheered, and dainty nibbles floated around on brightly polished silver trays. Sadie was certain she'd stepped right into a fairy tale movie, evil witch, and all.

Blane had walked over to her at one stage and introduced the younger man as his brother.

"Just up here for a quick visit from London," Michael explained and shook her hand. Sadie couldn't believe the two were related. Their demeanors clearly differed, like night and day. There were few physical similarities, and something about Michael reminded her too much of Cybil.

Michael strolled off and left her and Blane alone.

"It's…not what you think," he stumbled over his words.

"Why does it matter what I think?" Sadie tried for a soft tone, but the edges of her words cut through the air between them.

"Because…"

"Because, you like to have your bread buttered and soaked in honey, Blane. Enjoy the evening."

Blane's face greyed. She'd not meant for her words to cut so deep, but she was tired of pretending not to hurt.

After that, Blane mingled with the town folk, while Michael and Cybil kept to themselves in the far corner. Blane didn't come near her again.

Sadie's heart sank. Of all people, she had to fall for the man she could never have. Best that way. She had nothing to offer. While the dress hid all the damage, once taken off, she'd turn back into a pumpkin.

Sadie declined a dance or two until Malcolm coaxed her onto the dance floor. "Come noo lass, we practiced. Ye'll see it'll be fine."

It was a slow anthem and Malcolm guided Sadie gently through the steps as they twirled and glided around the dance floor. Sadie tried to relax, but so many eyes were on her, one wrong move... Cybil was dancing with Blane's brother. The same foreboding she'd felt around Mrs. Learie returned.

She looked back to her smiling grandfather. His soft blue eyes were the brightest she'd ever seen them. He had smiled more this evening than the last few months since her arrival.

The song was almost over when Malcolm winked at Sadie and swung her out with one arm, just as they had practiced. She used her right leg to balance. Her left hand stretched out and curled back in as she prepared to swing back to him.

Her left leg caught. She stumbled. An unexpected hand pushed into the small of her back and there was the shrill sound of tearing fabric. Sadie lost her balance and fell forward. It all happened in a painful slow motion.

She landed hard on her chest and hands. A sharp jab told her that her prosthesis had twisted. Her head lunged forward from the force of the fall and her right cheek hit the floor. The jolt reverberated through her skull and down her neck. Bright white dots inhibited her sight before a fuzzy sensation cupped the back of her neck and her vision cleared.

Sadie twisted her head and watched as Michael and Cybil danced past; a glint of dark determination swam in Cybil's ice blue eyes.

Gasps and murmurs echoed as the quartet came to a stumbling halt.

Sadie looked down. Her prosthesis had become exposed in the fall, the leg of her pants torn somehow, and the shoe had slipped off.

Agnus trotted up to Sadie, knelt, and pulled the split material together. Blane was right behind.

"Are you okay?" He bent down, ignoring her protestations, and swept her up into his arms.

Sadie tried to push him away. Anger, humiliation, and fear overrode all logic.

"Get away from me! All of you just get away!"

But Blane ignored her and wrapped his arms tightly around her before he followed Agnus up to her room. He lay her down on her bed.

"Leave."

"Sadie, I am sorry. If I'd known-."

"Just take your sympathy and go, Blane," she cried.

Chapter 39

She could've tolerated the gasps and murmurs, even the sideway glances, and Mrs. Learie who stood to the side sniggering, but it had been Blane's reaction which caught her off guard. She didn't need saving! She didn't need a knight in shining armor to show all and sundry how weak she was.

A knock and the door opened. "Lass…" Agnus stepped inside but didn't close the door and Sadie cringed when Blane followed her.

"What do you want? Come to make sure the invalid's okay?"

Blane stood stiff, a frown creasing his brow. "No, I came to apologize for Cybil and see if…'

"See if what? You're not the one who just showed the entire Lairg what a freak the Laird's granddaughter is. You only pointed out to them how weak I am."

Blane flinched, and Agnus stepped forward, her cheeks flushed. "Now Sadie, that's no way to repay the kindness this man has shown you!"

"Kindness would be to put down the wounded animal, not parade it about for all to see!"

Sadie shifted in her seat so her back turned to them. She was acting like a two-year-old, but heaven only knew she no longer gave a damn. She pulled her legs tight up against her body where she sat at the bay window and stared out onto the forest. *World swallow me now, open your mouth and swallow me.*

"If I'd known for a second what Cybil was up to… Sadie, I don't see you as broken, you're anything but that. It's you who won't let go of your brokenness." Blane's final words were like a bucket of ice water thrown in her face.

No longer able to control the hurt and humiliation, Sadie rounded on Blane. "Go back to London. Go back to the empty shallow people who would stop at nothing to get what they want, and never come back, Blane Buchan."

"Perhaps ye should leave. She's too raw now. She'll not hear a word." Agnus spoke softly to Blane and then, as the door closed behind him, "Lass I'm that sorry for what has happened, but you can't treat me or Blane that way, no matter hoo much it hurts."

"I told you I didn't want to attend. Now the whole town knows I'm a freak. I'm half a person… and that I can't take care of myself."

Heaving sobs escaped her mouth as months of fear, hurt, and pain she'd thought she'd left behind that night in the forest rose to the surface.

"Och, lass. I'm that sorry, but I promise not a soul thinks that of you." Agnus came to sit beside her, wrapping comforting arms around her.

Sadie looked up from her Nan's shoulder.

"I didn't want him to know."

"But he's known since your return from the forest, lass. If he'd wanted to reject you he'd not have kept returning, using the smallest of excuses to come over and see ye? I can never understand the pain of losing a limb or surviving what ye have, but I ken that ye have a strength unlike any. Ye owe that man an apology, lass."

"I owe you one as well. Nan, what I said… there's no…"

"Hush noo lass, it's all good. I love ye more than the air I breathe." Nan said as she pulled Sadie back in to her warm embrace.

Her mouth opened as months of suppressed anguish tumbled out in chocked sobs. Her body shook as she allowed every dark thought, every painful memory, and the knowledge she would always be broken, to engulf her and pull her back beneath its icy surface. Would it never heal? Ever become easier?

Nan hugged her tighter. "That man does not think ye weak lass. If anything, all I saw in those big brown eyes was admiration for your courage and…"

"A-and?" Sadie hiccupped and wiped her nose on her sleeve.

"Och, look now ye'll ruin yer dress. Here, wipe that nose and then I'll help you out of it, aye." Agnus handed Sadie a pink embroidered handkerchief as she cleverly escaped a question she did not want to answer.

Chapter 40

"She's barely said a word since last night."
Malcolm pulled a hand through his thinning hair. "Have we
lost oor wee lass, *Mo Ghaol*?"
Agnus stood beside him as they both stared out the
window in silence. Sadie sat with the dogs on the bench.
She'd barely eaten or said a word. Like Malcolm, Agnus
was worried that the incident at the Winter Ball had pushed
her away for good.
"I dinnae ken husband, but I'll tell ye this, I am that
grateful for the mare."
Earlier that morning Malcolm and Agnus had
driven first to Mrs. Learie, who rather conveniently was not
home, and then to the owner of the Sheep and Heide who
said Cybil had left with Mr. Buchan's brother, only a few
short minutes earlier, for Saorsa.
Once Malcolm had stomped in through the front
door and summarily laid into the petite blonde as he would
a drunken sailor.
"Noo ye look here, ye wee little vixen. Yer greet
and sorrow wilnae soften my ire. Ye had nae right tae walk
in tae my hoos and treat me oon blood the way ye did."
Cybil had tried to plead her case only to have
Malcolm declare, "Haud yer wheesht." The words having
the desired effect and shutting her quivering little mouth up
good and tight.
"I have a gud mind tae gie ye a skulpit lug!"
Cybil shrank away. The words were foreign to her,
but their meaning very clear.
Agnus stepped forward and placed a calming hand
on her husband's shoulder. "Noo husband. It'll help nae
one but the Sassenach if ye warmed her ears with a slap."
"Och, it nae matter either wa. The harm is dun.
Ye'd better pack yer bags and run. Dinnae let me ever
catch ye anywhere near my kith and kin, as there'd no be
an Agnus tae hold me back!" He pointed the end of his
cane at her to enforce his promise.

Blane had stood back and not defended the woman. His brother however, had stood, white as a lily, behind her, one hand on her shoulder.

"I take much of the blame too Malcolm. I should have known she was up to no good." Blane had tried to explain.

Too little too late.

Malcolm sighed. He hated having to dole out any form of discipline it always left him feeling as though he'd swallowed mud.

"What are we tae do with that ole crone?" Malcolm asked.

"Well, husband, as you so keenly pointed out this morning when I offered tae drag her by her hair and proffer her to the Lady of the Lake, it is not my style. So, me dear, it is up to yew. I ken for certain ye'll have the toon's backing no matter yer decision. We've had naught but support from them all, since last night."

"Aye, I think I might have the solution," he said making his way over to his large desk and pulled open a drawer. He slipped out an old weathered folder.

"What de ye have there?" Agnus arched her head.

"A paper clipping. It's old, but it'll do the job. Found it in a magazine one year I was over in Dublin."

Agnus eyebrow arched. "And?"

"It's from one of them naughty books ye ken," he flipped open the folder and pulled out a yellowed page.

Agnus gasped and giggled, 'I'll nae ask why ye ave this then."

Malcolm grinned at his wife.

"Seems oor sweet and innocent cousin is not so sweet and innocent after all," he said squinting at the picture of a half-naked, much younger and slimmer Mrs. Learie.

"Och, ye cheeky old man. Under any other circumstances, I'd clout ye upside yer heid, but today…" She placed a hand on his shoulder. "I'll just kiss ye." She stood on her toes and placed her lips on his.

Malcolm slipped the photo back into the folder and placed it on his table. "Aye, noo she'll ken her place or leave fur gud."

While he wanted nothing more than to rid himself of the woman for good, and get on with the tender, a feeling that all was not well in his small town slithered around the inside of his belly like an eel.

Anne Learie was not the type to have only one plan of action. There was more to her being involved in his granddaughter's humiliation than he'd wanted to realize. Agnus had been right. They'd underestimated the crone. It irked him that he could not figure out her next move.

Chapter 41

Cybil paused and turned as she stepped out the front door, her eyes swollen and red "There's one more thing." Blane sighed.

"You should know Mrs. Learie is up to something."

"Worse than what you have already told me?"

"Yes."

Blane stepped forward. Michael slipped a protective arm across Cybil's shoulders.

"What do you gain by telling me?" Blane wasn't sure he could stomach Cybil or her excuses, a moment longer.

"Because… It's to do with Sadie. Learie knows something, has something from that woman's past that I fear may put you… the town… her in danger."

"How do you know? Were you a part of it?" Blane accused.

"Hey back off." Michael held up a hand.

"It's okay." Cybil took Michael's hand away and held it in hers as she spoke to Blane. "I asked her for damaging information, something like her…leg. The day Michael arrived, I went past her home on the way to the Inn." Cybil dabbed a tissue beneath her eyes. "I didn't have time to look at it properly, nor did I think it relevant at the time…"

"What is it?"

"I don't know, but I think it might have something to do with that farm attack. She'd scribbled a strange name on a piece of paper. Obane? Obji? And a paper clipping from a South African newspaper containing an article about the attack on Sadie and her parents. Sadie's name was circled in red pen. I'm not sure, but it had a flight number next to it. I just thought you should know. I don't like Sadie or her family, but neither do I want anyone…you… to get hurt."

She raised a hand as if to touch Blane's cheek then withdrew and walked out, Michael in tow. Blane didn't wait to see the helicopter off, but ran back through the house, grabbed his keys, and rushed off to Munro Manor. Was that irksome old woman capable of causing the Munros any more hurt? His gut churned in affirmation. He hoped the Munros could clarify.

Until the night of the ball, he'd known nothing more about Sadie's past than what he'd read in the papers or heard gossiped in the pub. Hadn't needed to, nor wanted to. None of it mattered. Sadie was Sadie, and no past or damaged limbs would change the fact he'd fallen in love with her. But when they'd returned to Saorsa after Cybil's horror stunt at the ball, Blane had made Cybil tell all. He'd used a tactic he hated, blackmail. London society would turn their backs on her for good if they, for one moment, thought her responsible for the racist social media attack on the Queen's granddaughter's fiancé. He'd made her sing, giving up all information she had on her dealings with Learie and how it involved the Munros.

It'd became clear Mrs. Learie was a woman with a vendetta. Cybil handed him a folder, which explained the woman's unhappy marriage and how she blamed Malcolm. It also mentioned a time when she'd taken the head of the Munro clan to court to sue for her birthright, and the terrible failure it was.

It still irked him that he'd once been so shallow in his life. It had led people like Cybil to believe injuries such as Sadie's would put him off. What was worse was they were right about the old Blane. But now, after his time in the highlands spent with decent folk and meeting Sadie, things had changed. His perspective had changed, and so too, had his heart.

He'd been shocked when he'd seen her leg the morning she'd returned from the forest, but not for a moment had he felt revulsion. In fact, all he'd wanted to do since that day was drive over to Munro Manor and pull her in to his arms. Not because he thought her weak, that she would never be, but because he loved her. For the first time in his life, he knew what it meant to love, and above all, respect a woman for her strength and courage.

Unfortunately, Malcolm had made it very clear he was not to go anywhere near her ever again. Well, that would not do. Something was up, and it threatened the woman he loved and her family. And all because he couldn't face up to Cybil from the start.

Blane brought his Landrover to a skidding halt at the manor's front entrance. He did not wait to for Mr. Foggart to answer the door but simply pushed it open and strode in to the library where he found Malcolm and Agnus drinking tea and reading.

"Och Blane, look man I told ye…"

Blane raised his hands. "Is Sadie around?"

Agnus stood up from her chair. "No, she's sitting down by the loch. Poor lass hasna been near a saddle since the ball. Blane, under the circumstances…"

Blane silenced her. "Good. I need to speak with both of you. It seems Sadie might be in a world of trouble."

Agnus' lips pulled tight and her cheeks paled. Malcolm rushed to her side and grabbed her hand. "Dear Lord man, tell us."

"Before Cybil left, she told me Mrs. Learie was behind all of this mess with the town and..."

Malcolm cursed. "I knew that old… but what has her interfering wi toon business have tae do wi Sadie?"

Blane pushed on. "Something about her past. About an attack that took place back home. Cybil said she'd seen a note scribbled on a pad in Learie's home with a strange name, Obane? And a flight number on it and some or other South African newspaper article on the attack."

"Obaje!" Agnus fell into her chair and Malcolm rubbed a shaking hand through his thinning grey hair.

"Look, you must tell me. I don't care what it is, but I need to know so we can keep her safe. I know people, have resources."

"We'll take care o' this," Malcolm took a step toward Blane, chin thrust pugnaciously forward, hooking his thumbs into his pants belt as he did so.

But Agnus reached up from her chair and grabbed his arm. "Noo Husband. I dinnae think we can, not this…"

Malcolm took a long steady breath, blew it out and gently extricated his arm from his wife's grip. He considered Blane.

"Aye, but I think first we all need a wee dram?" Malcolm turned to the side table and poured a stiff whiskey for each of them.

After two wee drams, all three were seated and Malcolm told Blane everything.

"But I dinnae ken if that fat nosey crone has the wherewithal to find a man like Obaje?" Malcolm finished.

"Oh, aye," Agnus spoke up for the first time. "That's what's been the problem all along. We've all underestimated Mrs. Learie. I always had a wee suspicion there was more to that poisonous witch than meets the eye. Best we make sure."

"We need to alert the police." Malcolm insisted.

"I think, for now, it's best this problem remains between the three of us. If we alert Mrs. Learie, we waste our chances of remaining one step ahead. I'll get my people onto it. Track this Obaje's whereabouts, see where he's at and make sure you are all safe. I have contacts with private security."

"Och laddie, we dinnae need men wi guns traipsen aboot aye?"

"No, they'll be inconspicuous."

"Do you think it's best to keep Sadie in the dark?" Agnus asked.

"Until we know for sure what hornets' nest Mrs. Learie's kicked, yes I think its best. I've never spoken to Sadie about the trauma she's endured, but the fact she's withdrawn to the extreme of not even riding Blue tells me this could serve her a greater psychological blow. It's pertinent we know exactly what's going on, so we can sit her down with all the facts in hand," Blane explained as he paced back and forth.

"She'll no forgive us from keepin it from her," Malcolm said.

"I'm not suggesting we lie to her. But Sadie is the sort of woman who wants all the facts, Malcolm. Give me a day or two to gather them, please?" Blane requested.

"Aye, two days. What do we do in the meantime?"

"Stay close to home and try to act as though nothing is out of place." Blane suggested.

Chapter 42

Sadie lounged in a chair opposite her grandparents. It was raining, had been for the last three days, which made it impossible to enjoy her usual spot on the shores of the loch.

She hugged her mug of Oolong to her chest. This was from her favorite batch. Its rich malt and roasted nut aroma comforted the hollow that had re-opened in the center of her heart. She sipped and allowed the steaming liquid to warm her mouth, throat, and insides.

Nan and Malcolm seemed restless.

"What's the matter? You two have been pacing past that window like kids wishing away the rain, all morning."

Agnus smiled, about to say something when a knock at the library door drew Sadie's attention from her grandparents. She started at the sight of the visitor. "Why are you here?"

"We need to talk." Blane made his way to where she sat. "Good morning Malcolm, Agnus."

"Is there truly more to say?" She looked over to where Malcolm and Agnus sat. She'd made no attempt to contact Blane since the ball and apologize. She knew she'd been a bitch, but she simply could not bear to look into his eyes and see sympathy.

Her grandparents came to sit down. Nan had paled and her Oupa couldn't look her in the eye.

She motioned for Blane to take a seat.

She tried to avoid his face, but his gaze caught hers like a deer in headlights. Her stomach clenched, and her heart thudded. His eyes were warm, like the day he'd kissed her, in stark contrast to his creased forehead and pale lips of today. His hair was tied back. A look of worry clung to his cheeks and mouth.

"Dear, we've had some troubling news." Agnus leaned forward. "Tea, Blane?"

Blane leaned with his elbows on his knees. "No, thank you Agnus." Then he addressed Sadie. "First, I need you to know, if I knew or suspected at any point what

Cybil was up to I would have put a stop to it. What she did to you at the ball is unforgivable and believe me, she will never hurt another person again."

Words hit the back of Sadie's throat at a hundred miles an hour. Angry, bitter, vengeful things that stabbed at the inside of her mouth, but Sadie kept her lips sealed. It wasn't his fault, and cutting him to bits, with a pain that was hers to bear, would not be fair.

"I know. I'm sorry for treating you so badly. I-it's-Sorry." It'd never been easy for her to apologize.

Blane reached across and took her hand in his.

"I'd have done the same."

Sadie smiled nervously as she felt a wave of warmth travel up her neck and over her cheeks.

Blane let go of her hand and sat back.

"Look, before Cybil left she warned me that Mrs. Learie had been planning something dangerous."

Anger dissolved into fear as Sadie's vision blurred and her diaphragm knotted.

"I didn't want to tell you, not until I was sure." He rubbed a hand over his face, stood and walked to the window and back.

"Sure? About what?" The sense of foreboding, which had circled her like a wake of vultures for weeks now, landed in the pit of her stomach and pecked at her innards.

"Mrs. Learie dug into your past. She had a friend send her all the police files and information concerning the attack on your family in South Africa. We think she might have found and contacted Obaje."

Sadie's world crashed around her. She tried to listen as Blane explained he'd had people investigate the Nigerian's whereabouts and discovered Interpol had lost track of him more than a month ago, but it all faded into the background.

"Look, we don't know for sure, but for now there's no evidence pointing to him being here, or anywhere in Scotland."

She rubbed a hand across her face and tried to swallow the rising tide of bile pushing up her throat. Tried to stand. Tried to breathe, but her lungs refused, and her brain shutdown. All she could do was stare down at the bloodied bodies of her family.

#

Blane swooped Sadie up in his arms and made his way to her bedroom with Agnus short on his heels. This was not how he'd imagined he'd hold her in his arms again. The shock of Mrs. Learie's treachery had been too much for Sadie. She'd simply shed a tear and fallen limp to the floor.

Malcolm had remained in the study to ring the town physician. Blane had offered to fly one in, but they'd refused.

He helped Agnus remove her shoes and her prosthesis. Blane pulled the covers over his sleeping beauty and sat beside Agnus on the couch at the foot of the bed until the doctor arrived.

He would do everything in his power to make sure no harm came to her, or her grandparents.

"Do either of you mind if I stay the night? I know it's presumptuous but..." There was no way he was leaving Sadie now.

"I'll have Mrs. Perkins fix up a room doon the hall." Agnus patted his shoulder.

"Thank you. I'll be in the library. May I use your computer please?"

"Aye anything ye need." Malcolm said over his shoulder from where he stood at the foot of Sadie's bed.

"Thank you. I want to get onto the security detail and make sure there is no way any stranger comes near you or anyone in this town."

"Keep it discreet, Buchan. We don't need Mrs. Learie warned."

Chapter 43

Sadie sat, elbows digging into her thighs and fists clenched beneath her chin. She chewed on her bottom lip, drawing blood. The taste of copper spread across her tongue sending a shiver of foreboding down her spine as she stared out over the loch. The dogs had not left her side, and Blue stood chomping the lawn close by. Ghillie thought the mare needed some time out of the stables. Sadie hadn't ridden since receiving the winter ball. Her nightmares had returned, and her lust for life had simply faded away.

Every sound, and every shadow had Sadie ready to pounce, ready to throw herself in the path of the destructive evil headed their way. It was time she made peace with the fact her life was over. She would have no one else harmed because of her.

The handful of new faces all around Munro Manor did naught to stem her anxiety. One pretended to tend the gardens beside her. Everyone moved about their day in a false sense of safety with the new 'help' pottering around, providing 'protection'.

What no one realized was that Obaje was a force unto himself. If he wanted her dead, no army could stop him. But it would not be her he would take aim at.

So, she sat every day, out here, alone, waiting for him.

"Hi." Blane greeted as he came to sit beside her.

He'd spent the last two nights at the manor only returning to Saorsa in the mornings. While their friendship had grown somewhat, she'd found it incredibly frustrating he would not heed her warnings.

"Hi." Sadie kept her gaze glued to the loch. If Obaje was watching, he'd figure out the man meant something to her. It was bad enough her presence had painted a target on both Nan and Oupa's backs.

"You're a ball of nerves Sadie. Please, we're safe and there is no sign of the man anywhere."

"Agh! Why won't you listen to me? You won't know he's here until he's standing right behind you, machete slicing your neck. He'll come after my grandparents and y- anyone he thinks I care about, Blane. You think you have it all sorted with your secret spies and armed ex-military. Have any of them ever been to Africa? Africa doesn't play by the rules like the rest of the world." She pleaded balancing her forehead on her fists.

"I need you to trust me… us, Sadie. Please."

Fukkit!

"You haven't ridden in a while." He shifted closer to her.

She stared out onto the choppy waters biting back her frustration that this seemingly intelligent man couldn't or wouldn't comprehend the danger they were all in.

"Would it be better if I brought in a new trainer for Blue?"

This caught her attention. "No."

"Shall we saddle her up then, or even just run her around the arena?"

Sadie sat up and turned to face him.

God he was beautiful. He wore his hair loose of late. The dark curls folding into his neck and caressed his well-trimmed beard. It was his eyes she found she lost herself in the most. Dark, deep and molten.

But the strain of the last few days were taking their toll.

His face was drawn, and dark rings hugged the bottoms of his eyes. His clothes were crinkled as though he'd slept in them.

Her resolve melted, and Sadie cupped his cheek.

"I'm sorry, but…"

Blane covered her hand with his. "I'm trying to grasp all this darkness. But I swear I won't let him touch you or your family ever again."

"Why?"

"Because I care."

She stiffened. So, he felt sorry for her was all!

He sucked in a deep breath. "You know, your eyes give away every thought that passes through that stubborn mind of yours."

"Is that how you've beaten me at chess these last two nights?"

Blane threw his head back as a deep bellied laughter burst from him.

Sadie wasn't sure how to react and tried to pull her hand away, but he held it tight to his face. His beard pricked her palm, and the warmth of his skin beneath the beard took the edge off the chill, which had clung to her fingers all morning.

"I don't pity you, Sadie Munro. Never have. But from that first day, when I ran you off the road, you have haunted me. I loved you the moment you pushed me away and battled up that hill on your own terms. I fell deeper the day you scolded me for telling you my mare was a lost cause. I lost myself completely when you rode that mare, bare back, out of the forest. And I knew you were meant for me, that afternoon, when my lips touched yours."

A single tear trickled down her cheek.

"I am not repulsed by your leg, or your past. I do not see you as weak." He rolled his eyes and laughed. "Weak is a word that simply could never describe you."

Words failed her. How did one respond to all of this?

She slid her hand from his cheek, around and up to the back of his head, and pulled him closer.

Spicy cologne drifted up her nose. His breath was warm, with hints of cinnamon and toast. The warmth of his body stretched out and hugged her as he pulled her into him before planting his lips on hers.

They were swimming between the stars, dancing across the ocean, sipping silver trickles of moonlight from goblets made of the Milky Way.

She opened her mouth and allowed him in. He pulled her onto his lap, a hand slipping beneath her shirt and tunic. Her muscles stiffened as his hand stroked the scars across her back and belly, but he did not flinch.

Instead he continued to taste and explore what she had to offer.

She let go. No more barriers, no more pain. She wanted to give him all of who she was.

They came up for air. Sadie pressed her forehead against his. "We have eyes all over the place. Perhaps we should go inside?"

She saw the question in his eyes. "Nan and Oupa are in town, and my bedroom door has a lock... Hey!" she exclaimed when Blue pushed her wet nose into her back. "No need for the cheeky attitude you," she laughed, slipped off Blane's lap and stood.

"We'd better put her to stable first." She patted the mare's rump. Sadie took Blane by the hand. With the dogs at their feet and the horse behind them, they made their way, lost in the sublime bubble which enveloped all lovers, to the stables.

Perhaps life wasn't as bleak as it appeared? Perhaps it would be different this time? They knew what was coming. They were prepared.

The pair rounded the bottom of the manor house closest to the forest. Blue whinnied and shied. Eyes wide, she stepped away to put some distance between her and the trees.

"Hey girl, what's up?" Sadie placed a hand on the horse's neck and a shiver ran up her arm. The horse sensed danger! Sadie squinted into the shadows. Prionnsa and Donn stood at her feet. Prionnsa's ears pitched. Donn growled, the hair on the pup's neck standing to attention. Blane called to two of the security personnel who promptly radioed in to their colleagues, and a search of the forest was conducted.

Chapter 44

Once Blue was settled into her stable, Sadie made
her way to the back door where she met Blane.
"Nothing there. No tracks. Perhaps a deer? Or a
rabbit?"
Sadie let out a sigh. "Perhaps."
She gave the trees one last suspicious glance then
looked back to Blane. "You don't have to stay…"
"I'd like to." He stroked her cheek.
Blane closed and locked the door to Sadie's
bedroom. He took her trembling hands in his. He didn't
want to mess this up. "If you're not ready…"
She turned her starry green gaze onto him.
"Promise me if it's too much… my mangled…"
He placed a finger on her lips. "Trust me. I trust
you."

He took her hand and led her to her bed. He guided her to sit down as he knelt and pulled off her right shoe and then the left. Her right sock and then the left. He heard her suck in her breath. He stood, pulled her into him, and kissed her. He started on her lips and moved across her cheek to her neck. His hands reached up and pulled out the hair pin.

Thick red tresses, infused with jasmine and rose, tumbled down her back. Her hands clutched his shirt as he sprinkled more kisses into her nape and onto her collar bone. He leaned back and thrilled in the flushed desire he'd brought to life in this Goddess — his Goddess.

Not breaking eye contact, he reached down and unbuttoned her shirt. She stiffened again, but he held her gaze as his fingers slipped one button at a time through its hole. He spread the shirt apart and gloried in the sight that was Sadie Munro.

Kneeling, he pressed his lips against her belly, trailing soft kisses across the scars, which wrapped around her torso like the tendrils of a thorn bush.

Her hands cupped his cheeks as she made to push him away.

Blane leaned back. "You are beautiful, and I will love your scars until the day I die. I will love your hurt for the both of us Sadie Munro. You are everything and so much more… you are enough… more than enough." He straightened then wiped a tear from her cheek and continued his loving of the woman he'd waited his entire life to love.

Her groan shot a bolt of heat from his core down between his legs. Trailing his fingers up her back, he unhitched her dark blue lace bra and let it drop to the floor. Her nipples were hard and red and begged for his mouth to love them. Blane placed both hands on her bottom and pulled her toward him as he twisted and sat on the bed. Her legs straddled his. He cupped one of her breasts and placed it in his mouth.

Sadie's hands pulled his hair as her back arched. Her nipple was as hard and sweet as sugar candy. Satisfied, he moved to the other. Sadie's groans of pleasure pushed him further and further toward the edge.

He leaned back and looked up. Her eyes blazed, and her sanguine lips were plump and wet. His fingers found the button to her jeans. Her hands instinctively clasped his. "Trust me," he said. Her eyes glued to his as she nodded, her cheeks losing some of their brilliant flush.

Perhaps if she lay on her back. He grabbed her by the arse and swung her down on the bed.

"Whoop!" she giggled.

Her pants undone, he stood and tugged at the hem, slowly slipping them down over her thighs and legs. Blane straightened. What a sight.

Flaming locks spread out beneath her, skin as pale as milk sprinkled with freckles like her nose, his eyes fell on the crest still covered by her panties. God, he hoped it was as flaming red as her head.

"Do you want me to leave it on?" A flash of uncertainty flickered in her eyes as she reached to touch her faux limb.

"Would it be easier to take it off?"

She shrugged, paled, and tried to sit up, but he put a hand on her shoulder. "Let me, please."

She acquiesced and lay back, biting her lip, and folded her arms across her breasts.

This wouldn't work. He needed her to relax. "How about I first get rid of some of my clothes?"

#

What was she doing? Letting this man see her like this, naked, in full daylight! She watched as he began to remove his shirt. Holy shit! She'd imagined him naked, but this was....

Blane wasn't a bulky man, but he was roped. Every muscle stood taught and toned, bulging against his skin. Muscled flesh ran down his arms, across his shoulders, and across his torso, dipping into... holy cow! Between his legs, his desire bulged, proud and strong.

He gave her the cheekiest smile before kicking off his shoes and untying his buckle. He whipped off his jeans to reveal black silk boxers. If Sadie had any doubt about his attraction for her they were washed away as he dropped his rods and stood naked in all his hard-throbbing glory before her.

"Shall I?" He motioned to her limb.

Shit! She'd forgotten about it till he pointed it out. She bit her lip. This was it. She braced herself for the rejection. With Sadie's assistance, Blane managed to loosen then remove the prosthesis. Not flinching, the desire in his eyes not subsiding even a smidgen, he placed the faux leg on the floor and returned all his attention to her.

#

Sadie turned onto her side and leaned with her head on her arm. Blane was asleep. His face looked far more relaxed than it had this morning.

Nope, this was no dream. Blane Buchan had truly made love to her – all of her! He had brought her body back to life, had reveled in all she was. She stroked a finger down his chest and around his nipple. She leaned forward and flicked her tongue over the small hard bud. It tightened. She leaned in deeper, placed her mouth over it, and tasted him. He groaned as his hand slid down her back, coming to rest on her bare bottom. If she ever saw heaven… she knew it would hold him in its center.

Her heart ached with joy then crashed to her toes. Why was it nothing good in her life lasted? She huffed and fell onto her back. Where was Obaje? Had Mrs. Learie found him and lured him to Lairg?

She turned her head and looked back at Blane half asleep beside her. If he was here, surely, she would already be dead? Perhaps Malcolm and Blane were right and Obaje was nowhere near them. God, she hoped so.

Chapter 45

Icy, fresh morning air washed over Blane as he stepped out of his back door at Saorsa. He'd raced over from Munro Manor to get here in time. He had a meeting with his property manager and then a skype appointment with his father.

The last few days had been something of a dream. A glorious dream. Malcolm and Agnus had not so much as looked sideways at the fact he'd spent every night since in Sadie's bedroom. In fact, according to Sadie, they were over the moon. Although, Malcolm had cornered him that first night.

"While I'm not opposed tae ye spending time with me granddaughter, she's no a part time distraction either!" Blane was shocked at Malcolm's straight forward approach of his and Sadie's relationship, but he respected what the old Laird was getting at and promised he was not out to hurt Sadie.

Today, though, he had to put in some serious work at Saorsa. He'd left Sadie at the stables and told her they'd need to come up with a more suitable arrangement soon. While Malcolm and Agnus seemed comfortable, he didn't like the idea of sleeping with their granddaughter beneath their roof. He hadn't said it in so many words, not sure how Sadie felt, but his ultimate dream was to slip a ring on her gorgeous finger.

But for now, he needed to help Mac check up on the sheep and fences. The sun was out for the first time in days, and while it was cold, it was a good day. Some of the locals had predicted snow, which meant they had little time to finish their final preparations before winter slowed them down.

A chill ran the length of his body, and it was not from the icy wind. He'd had the oddest sensation of being watched these last few days. He shook his head. There were men on constant patrol around Saorsa and Munro Manor, even a few sprinkled randomly through town, disguised as tourists. He shrugged the feeling off. It was the mere idea Obaje could be here. It was getting to them all. He hoped to hear from his contact at Interpol this evening for an update.

Blane made his way across to the shed to fuel the quad bikes.

A face appeared from the office door beside the shed.

"Mr. Buchan!" Mac called as he ran over from the shed, phone in hand. The man's leathery face was all wrinkled and tears streamed down his cheeks.

"Good God Mac, what's wrong?"

"It's…it. There's…" Mac, out of breath, put up his hand and with the other leaned on his knee as he caught his breath. When he straightened, he said, "There's been a murder in toon."

The chill, which had wrapped itself around Blane's body a few moments earlier, turned into a full-on snow blanket. Sadie!

He grabbed Mac by both shoulders. "Who?!"

"Mrs. Learie!"

#

Blane's rover skidded to a halt in a pool of sludge a few houses down from Mrs. Learie's. He'd made sure to double the protection around Munro manor as he made his way in to town. He should be with Sadie, but he also had to find out firsthand what had happened to Learie.

The air hung thick with panic, horror, and emergency lights. A yellow tape ran across her fence and front door, pronouncing it a crime scene. Opposite the road, stood most of Lairg.

Crying! Panicked! Horrified!

Blane walked across to the crowd. Smythe, the owner of the Farmer's Co-op was quick to fill him in on what was for what.

"Tis poer, old Mrs. MacFee who foond her. They'd had to rush her straight tae hospital. Think she mighta had a stroke from the shock."

"And Mrs. Learie?" Blane whispered not wanting to draw attention.

"Dead as a door nail." The man replied then
swallowed hard.
The town didn't have much patience or love for
Mrs. Learie, but none of them ever wished her ill. If only
they'd known.
"Somebody she knew, I heard the copper say. No
sign of a breek in. Boot..." The man's cheeks turned the
shade of the snow caps on Ben Nevis.
"Deep breath, Smythe. You don't have to..."
"Nae, I can. They foond her wi her throat slit, bled
oot like an animal, they did."
In the moment Smythe told of Mrs. Learie's
demise, a bucket of frozen water poured over Blane's body.
His gut twisted, and his bowels turned to water.
"Sadie!" His voice was a mere whisper.
He said nothing further, but simply turned on his
heels and ran for the plain clothed copper interviewing Mr.
Ferguson, the butcher, who also sat on the council.
"Ah, sorry but ye'll havta..."
Blane put up a hand. "No, you need to follow me.
This is much larger than you understand, and more people
are in danger."
The man, around Blane's age, with dirty blond hair
and matching eyes regarded Blane a moment. "You can
drive with me," Blane reinforced his point and turned to
make his way to his rover.
"Hang on now," the Inspector hung back.
"I'll explain along the way. But time, Sir, is of the
essence."
Something in Blane's voice must have stressed to
the man this was no crazy gesture. The copper turned to
one of his constables and gave him orders before trotting
up to Blane. "All right then ah Mr....?"
Blane stuck a hand out as they walked briskly to his
car. "Blane Buchan. My estate neighbors on the Munro's."
"Inspector De Wit."
Blane gave the man a sideways glance.
"Yes, I know, not very Scottish. My father was
Dutch."

\#

"Where is Sadie?" Blane demanded as he stomped in through the front door of Munro Manor, Inspector De Wit on his heels.

"Miss Munro should be ooot side wi the horse, sir." Mr. Foggart explained as Agnus and Malcolm strolled out of the library.

"Oh Mr. Buchan, are ye all right?" his voice carried the strain of worry from the last few days as he peered past him to the detective short on his heels.

The inspector came to stand beside Blane.

"Inspector De Wit, Sir." He held out his hand which Malcolm took wearily in his own.

"Ah, perhaps we should go back to your library?" Blane waved a hand forward then turned to the butler. "Mr. Foggart, please ask Ghillie to fetch Sadie at once, thank you."

"I'll fetch her meself, Sir." The seriousness of the situation showed on the butler's face. He turned and quickly marched out the front door.

Blane watched as both Malcolm's and Agnus' who'd made her way in to the foyer from the library, skin paled.

"Have you not heard?" He ushered the elderly couple back into the library.

"What man? What?" Malcolm demanded.

"Has no one called you this morning?" Blane strode to the window of the library then turned to face the pair.

"Och, Donn chewed the chord of the phone again!" Malcolm gestured towards the bureau.

God! When all this was over, the first thing he would do was buy each one of these two a decent cell phone.

"Oh, dear Lord, Mr. Buchan. Has something happened?" Agnus called back over her shoulder as he ushered her, Malcolm, and the inspector into the library and closed the door behind them.

After both Munros were seated, and all except the inspector had swallowed a decent sized dram of whiskey, Blane told of Mrs. Learie's gruesome end.

"Dear God, what do we do noo?"

"So yer saying that ye ken who the man was who'd kilt Mrs. Learie?" Inspector De Wit said as he scribbled in his note book.

"Aye," Malcolm's voice was heavy as granite.

"Care to tell me?" De Wit scratched his chin.

Malcolm stood, poured another dram, and began with the murders of his son and family in South Africa, ending with Ms. Learie and her need for revenge.

"So ye see detective," he sipped his whiskey. "That scunner seems tae have foond Sadie an is oot fer his revenge." He turned his sharp grey gaze onto De Wit and Blane. "And we know that sly old crone Learie had a hand in it, all the way."

"If you knew she was involved, why not come to us?" the inspector asked.

Blane stepped forward. "We were waiting for conformation from Interpol. And there was no hard evidence. She would have denied it all."

"It was Interpol who informed you of this Obi…"

"Obaje," Malcolm said.

"Not yet. I was waiting for my contact to confirm Obaje had left Africa for Scotland."

De Wit rounded on Blane. "And why is it you were in contact with Interpol, and not local law enforcement?

"I have connections."

"Ah, of course you do."

The doors to the library burst open and Sadie strode in, her jaw line grey as burnt coal and her cheeks flushed.

"Where is he?"

Chapter 46

Obaje was here! She'd known it, but ignored her gut, and now everyone close to her was in danger. Mr. Foggart had said nothing, but only summoned her urgently to the library. She could tell by his ashen color and wide-eyed glances, this was beyond urgent.

"Ah, Ms. Munro?" A man in his early thirties, Sadie judged, notepad at the ready, stood and held out his hand. Sadie took it and shook it hard. "Sadie Munro...You?"

"Inspector De Wit... Dutch father."

She turned to her grandparents. Their eyes were wild, their demeanor calm.

Blane stood at the far side of the library, though his neatly tied back hair and crisp clean outfit belied the storm brewing with in. Jeez they were all good at keeping it together.

"What happened?" she asked no one in particular.

"Perhaps ye'd best sit doon lass." Malcolm waved a hand toward a chair.

"No thanks. Where is he?" she aimed her question at Blane.

"We don't know." He rubbed his chin. "But that's not why... Mrs. Learie's been murdered."

Bile churned like clotted milk in her belly.

"Obaje?"

"Sorry tae interrupt. But is that the man ye was talking aboot in the car Mr. Buchan?"

Detective De Wit stepped toward the shell-shocked quartet.

"Yes." Blane said keeping his gaze on Sadie.

"When?" she asked.

"The coroner put an estimated time o' death at around midday yesterday," The detectives word drifted past Sadie.

Blane took two long strides and came to stand half an arm's length from her.

"I warned you all, but no one would listen!" She'd meant for her words to sound heated. Instead her voice cracked and pitched making her sound like a terrified three-year-old.

\#

"I will not live in fear, cooped up like a sitting duck."

Was this man crazy? Did they honestly expect her to remain locked away in the house until they found the crazy Nigerian?

"Ms. Munro, tis fer yer oon safety that we keep a close eye on both yew and the situation unfolding heer in Lairg." The detective tried on his best authoritarian cloak. But Sadie would have none of it. She'd faced down the devil and his reaper before. No highland copper was going to tell her what to do. She glanced at her grandparents whose eyes pleaded with her to listen, then she turned to Blane. His expression told her he was on both the detectives side as well as hers.

"No! You have all these cammo clad warriors patrolling and following my every move. I'll be fine, but I will not hide!"

With both hands balancing on her hips, she said, "Look if anyone needs extra protection it's you lot." She pointed to her grandparents and Blane. "This man is evil incarnate. He won't kill me. He wants me to suffer. He'll come after you first, so I am begging you, *please,* re-arrange the guards so that you three are more protected."

The inspector held up his hand. "Perhaps the safer thing would be for all four of you to leave Lairg for a while?"

"No!" The man paled as all four of them rounded on him.

Sadie stood in the foyer with Agnus as Malcolm as Blane walked the inspector out.

Why was this happening? She'd come to Lairg to find her family and believing that the evils of Africa would remain there, where they belonged. Now both her life, her only living relatives, and the man she loved were in peril.

"It's all my fault, Nan."

"Och dearie, stop being so daft. It's all that silly woman's fault. She'd allowed her greed and hatred tae get the better of her and look what it got her — a gruesome end." Agnus wrapped her arms around Sadie.

Blane closed the door, turned on his heel and strode toward them.

"I promised you. I will not break it! He'll not lay a hand on any of you!"

The sincerity and conviction with which he spoke gave Sadie a sense of false hope. Nan's arms slipped off Sadie, who stepped forward and pulled Blane to her.

While she wanted to believe him, a part of her knew the devil was one step ahead of them. But she'd cling to it and the love they now shared, for without it none of them would survive the storm which threatened to wash away her new life.

#

"Well an early night is wot we all need," Agnus ordered as Mr. Foggart and Annie removed their half eaten plates of food.

"I suppose. Blue needs exercise. I'll need to be up early." Sadie said as she stood.

"Lass, surely…"

"Nan, I've told you, I will not be kept prisoner," she said as she leaned over the chair and kissed her nan on the forehead.

"Why don't you and Oupa go have a night cap and try for a good night's rest, okay?" she said as she stepped back, walked to where Malcolm sat and bent down to hug him goodnight.

#

Blane sat on the edge of the couch in Sadie's bedroom and pulled off his shoes.

"Can I ask you something without you freaking out?"

Sadie stood starring out of her window of her bedroom at the forest, "Depends?"

"What happened that night?"

He watched as his words settled in her mind. She did not pale, nor did she run, or send him packing. Instead, she sighed deeply then came to sit beside him.

"Has my body not told you the story?"

"But you haven't," he stroked a hand down her wayward sanguine locks.

He expected her to snap. Tell him he was trespassing into an area of her life he was not welcome. But he could no longer go on what he read or the gossips in the pub. The damage to her body told of a horror he hoped never to face in his life, but he'd fallen deeply in love with this strong-willed warrior goddess and a part of him wanted to be able to share every inch of themselves… even their demons.

Again, she surprised him.

"Well, if my leg and my scars haven't scared you away, I guess my story might."

"Nothing you could do could scare me. Surprise, not scare."

The bright green of her eyes darkened to the color of moss in a downpour, her lips pulled tight and her fists clenched.

"Would you still think that if I told you I've taken lives, not a life, but two lives."

"Yes." His hands moved and wrapped themselves over her balled fists.

"Why?"

"Because you are no killer. If you took those lives I am certain it was because you were left with no other choice."

Blane sat quietly as Sadie shared her nightmare.

With every word he wanted to pull her in to him, hold her, promise her that no one would ever harm her like that again. But he also knew that this was her story to tell. If he did that, he would rob her of her power, the very strength he'd fallen in love with, which burned inside her like a bonfire on old hallows.

"I didn't think. I had no time... the rifle was there... my finger curled around the trigger without a second thought..." she wept.
"When the doctors told me about my leg... my first thought was, *I wished I'd rather died.*" She wiped the back of her hand across her face.
"And now?" he had to ask.
"And now ... it's still hard to look at my half a leg but you've reminded me how to love myself again... I want to live every day to the fullest... wi-with you," she smiled.
Her eyes lit up and Blane found he could no longer hold back. His arms moved around her and pulled her on to his lap as her head bent forward and her lips met his. Their kiss became a slow connection of give and take as Blane made a promise to himself.
When all the drama with Obaje was sorted, the first thing he'd do was ask her if she'd would consider him in to her life until the day they died. And hopefully that would be when they were both grey and ratty with a manor house full of grandchildren of their own.
#
Sadie allowed Blane to help her into the steaming bath before he stepped in and sat behind her. They'd both decided a hot bath was in order after the emotional half hour spent on the couch. While it had drained the last of her energy recounting the horrors of that day, she felt strangely free. Unburdened and almost happy.
"You are the bravest person I know," he whispered in her ear.
Sadie merely shrugged as she leaned back into him.
"Brave... is loving someone as broken as me?" she replied. How was it this man, this beautiful human specimen, loved her? She still battled to comprehend.
"You make it so easy to love you Sadie Munro," his lips grazed her shoulder as his words melded together the last piece of her fractured heart.
She twisted around, splashing water on to the floor.
"Oops." She giggled as she settled herself somewhat

uncomfortably astride the man who held her heart and soul, cupping his neck in her hands and rewarded him with her unconditional love.

Sadie wrapped the towel around her body.

"We'll have to mop up this mess before the morning," she warned as Blane wrapped a towel around his torso. God he was simply breath taking. Built like a Michael Angelo sculpture. No wonder most women were drawn to him.

"I'll see to it," he winked cheekily as he reached out a hand toward her.

Sadie took it as her gaze caught the chair on the far side over which she draped her clothes and scarf. The brooch of the goddess reflected the soft golden light shining down from the ceiling. *Epona, dìon màthair coiseachd còmhla rium.* She prayed silently.

A knowing as deep as the marrow in her bones echoed a certainty she would no longer ignore. Come hell or high water, someone would lose their life before Christmas. Sadie prayed it wasn't anyone she loved.

Chapter 48

A memorial was to be held for Mrs. Learie in town
that morning. It had been a weekend filled with fear,
sorrow, and constantly looking over one's shoulder. But
this was Lairg, and a Nigerian would stand out like a
Leopard at a garden party. So where was Obaje hiding?
Sadie knew he was here, somewhere, biding his time. Like
a wounded lion, he'd pounce when she least expected it.

Sadie bolted the stable door and left Blue to enjoy
her breakfast. She needed space to think. Friday's events
had turned everyone's lives inside out. Blane had spent the
weekend with her but had left to finish off work around
Saorsa before the memorial service that morning.

Agnus was busy planning Christmas, determined
the latest events would not ruin any of the joy. And in
between it all, they were preparing to mourn the woman
who was responsible for all the trouble.

Sadie sat down on the bench outside Blue's stable.
Fat angry clouds hid the blue heavens. Everyone except the
weather channel predicted snow. It would be her first white
Christmas if the town's people's predictions came to
fruition. This would be a Christmas filled with a lot of
firsts.

No Mom, Dad, or Stephen. But with snow,
Blane…

Strange popping sounds caught her attention.
Sadie turned. Blue gave a low whinny and backed
into the far corner of her stable.

Mrs. Perkins rushed out the back door screaming,
blood sprayed across her body and face.

Sadie ran. "Ghillie!" She grabbed Mrs. Perkins as
the woman fell into her arms. "They…they…."

Ghillie ran towards them from his workshop.

"Make sure she's okay," Sadie ordered. *Where was
the security?*

Sadie frantically pressed the panic button she
carried around in her jacket pocket.

"Wait lass ye cannae run in there wi no…"

His voice faded into the panic as she stumble-ran as fast as she could into the house, almost falling over a body. In her haste she had enough time to glance down, see a dark sticky liquid ooze from the man's head. Her mouth popped open, but no sound escaped as her throat constricted and black dots swam across her vision. Her muscles froze. Visions of her mum and dad....

Nan! Oupa! She had to get to them before he did.

"Pull yourself together Sadie Munro!" she gritted her teeth.

Grabbing a knife from the carving block, she hurried to the entrance hall, gagging as a familiar smell of copper and feaces drifted through the air. The front door stood wide open. Mr. Foggart and another guard lay sprawled on the floor. Sadie ran into the library where Malcolm's papers lay strewn across the room.

"No!" her voice echoed at the sight of Donn and Prionnsa laying lifeless on the floor.

She ran toward them. Dropping the knife on the ground beside her, she cradled her sweet little prince in her arms. He had a single shot through his head. Anger and fear threatened to devour the adrenaline surging through her veins.

A soft yelp. "Donn?" The pup was wounded but okay. Sadie grabbed the table cloth from the small table beside her, ripped it, and wrapped the pup's wound.

"I promise we'll get you to a vet soon." She kissed the dog, picked up the knife, and stood.

Her legs wobbled. Where were her grandparents? She stumbled back out.

"Nan! Oupa!"

Mr. Foggart's arm moved and a painful groan followed. Sadie rushed to his side.

"I'm okay lass. That man saved my life. Threw himself on tae me and took the bullet."

Sadie glanced back over her shoulder. A head wound — Obaje!

#

"You'll stay at Saorsa tonight." Blane handed her a whiskey where she sat in the kitchen.

Mrs. Perkins had not been harmed. It seemed they were only after the guards and her grandparents. Mr. Foggart had escaped with a large bump to the back of his head. Both now sat at the kitchen table with Sadie and Blane.

Three men were dead. "I told you he was good." She downed the dram. The liquid burned its way down her gullet and she handed Blane the glass. "I need tea."

"I'll make some," Mrs. Perkins made to stand.

"Noo, I ken hoo to boil a kettle an add some tea bags," Ghillie pushed away from the counter waving Mrs. Perkins back to her seat.

The house was crawling with policemen.

"Have they found anything to say where he's taken them?" Sadie asked.

"No, except that they'd used Malcolm's Land Rover to get away, and because of the rain, they can't follow the tracks. Look, why don't you get some clothes and we'll head over to my place?" he asked.

"Blue?"

"Ghillie said he'd stay here. Mrs. Perkins and Mr. Foggart are pretty shaken up. I'll send Mac over too."

"Fine, but I'm telling you, he won't come for anyone else. He wants me."

Why wouldn't they listen to her? Sadie made her excuse to go and pack then trudged up the stairs to her room.

Frustration and terror twisted and churned in her stomach. She'd warned them and now look. Obaje had Nan and Oupa, doing God knows what to them. The horror of his evil buckled her legs. Sadie sat on the top step and wept. *Epona I call on you, please spare them. Fill my blood with your strength, stoke my soul's fire with vengeance and show me the way.*

As she stood, she noted muddy foot prints smudged into the carpet at her bedroom door. Something was out of place. The police had done a quick sweep of the entire manor but were concentrating on the foyer and library. Did they miss this? But she'd been to her room afterwards when she'd looked for Agnus and Malcolm...

Her heart pounded against her rib cage and her limbs turned to ice. Someone had been in the house... her bedroom... since....

Sadie hurried through the door and gasped.

Ripping the paper from the daggered grip of a knife stabbed into her pillow, she read, hands shaking.

You know what to do.

58.025733-4.409916

Sadie stared at the paper. What were these numbers? She grabbed her phone and typed them into the search engine — co-ordinates.

Chapter 49

"Ah, Mr. Buchan, Sadie said tae come see ye over bringing Blue to Saorsa? I didnae think ye had…" Ghillie made his way up the front steps of the manor and stood at the front door where Blane was deep in conversation with a constable.

"I beg your pardon?" Blane looked up, confused.

"The lass said I need tae chat with ye over the mare going to Saorsa," Ghillie pulled his flat cap off his head and slapped it across his thigh in frustration.

"No, I told you the mare would remain here. Why would she… Did you leave her with the mare?"

"Aye," he gave Blane a puzzled look as though he'd lost his marbles.

"Follow me." To the constable, he said, "I'll be right back."

An uncomfortable sensation filled Blane's belly as he and Ghillie walked through the house and out the back to the stables.

The stable door stood open, with no sign of Sadie or the roan. "I'll check the indoor arena. See if you can find anything out of place in the stable and tack room," Blane ordered.

His heart beat a rapid warning as he ran to the arena. What if Obaje had returned and taken both her and the horse?

Blane returned to the stables and found Ghillie at the door of the empty stable.

"She's gone sir, but I foond this on the stable floor." He handed Blane a crumpled piece of paper. "And there's tracks oot back leading off intae the wuds."

The words sent a chill down his spine. Blane unraveled the crumpled piece of paper. "Shite!"

"The lass is heid strong enough to go after him."

The tall Scotsman voiced Blane's thoughts.

Blane plucked his phone from his pocket and stared at the screen. A message from Sadie. His phone was on

silent and he'd ignored the vibration when he'd followed
Ghillie out to the stables.

I will love you always. I can't let him hurt them or
you.

Blane bit back his anger and fear and instead typed
in the co-ordinates.

Voices and footsteps alerted the two men of the
inspector, followed by a handful of constables. Blane
shoved his phone in his pant pocket.

The inspector held up a see-through plastic bag
with a knife in it. "It seems someone left a warning after
we'd searched the top floor."

"It must have pinned this down." He lifted the
crumpled note, "She and the horse are gone! Do you think
he came back for them?" Blane asked.

"I can't be certain," the detective reached for the
note with a blue latex gloved hand, "These are
coordinates."

He said as he slipped the note into another clear bag
held open by one of his constables.

"I gathered as much. We need to follow them
immediately!" Blane commanded.

"Noo, I cannae send oot a search party until this
weather lifts. Look, I'm heading into town. I need to get
this into evidence. I'll leave two constables to stand watch.
Let me know if you hear anything. I'll have men on the
ready and as soon as the weather permits, we'll begin oor
search." The detective babbled.

Blane nodded as the men walked away.

"We're not goin tae leave the lass oot there
tonight?" Ghillie whispered.

"Absolutely not. Look, do you know where this is?"
Blane turned the screen of his phone to him.

"Aye, that's Himself' old hunting cabin… are
those?"

"SShhh, I think this is where Sadie's headed. How
do we get there without alerting Obaje?"

Ghillie straightened and rubbed his forefinger to his
chin. "It's a long trek ye ken." Then thinking on it some

more. "But I ken a way that's fast. We'll need tae prepare. Do ye have any weapons? Training?"

Blane smiled. "Not military if that's what you're after, but I was captain of the sharp shooting squad at university and I have a safe with three rifles in them back at Saorsa."

Ghillie's eye stretched wide. "Weel then, between ye and my time with the royals of Scotland, I'd say we stand a chance."

"Okay, let's get going then."

"Aye, sir." Ghillie patted him on his back.

#

Sadie slowed Blue to a walk and glanced at her cell phone screen. She'd long ago lost signal but had taken a screen shot of the map. Judging by the time it had taken her, and her phone's compass, she was roughly two miles from the cabin. The sky was dark and the woods darker.

She brought the mare to a stand beside a tall tree around which thick ferns had congregated. Sadie hadn't bothered with a saddle and kept the blanket on Blue after flipping it inside out so that the red was underneath and the black on top. "All right girl. This is as far as you go. You'll be safe here okay? Please stay."

She reached into her rucksack and dropped a few molasses blocks to the ground before she hauled out the empty plastic container and water bottle. "Here, drink some first."

She looked to her phone one last time then switched it off and shoved it into the bag before shoving the bag underneath the ferns. She wanted to run, but dusk was ebbing into night, and the shadows already hid sneaky roots and cheeky rocks from plain sight. Sadie knew that with her stupid leg, she'd make too much noise and risk getting hurt.

She'd dressed in layers. It was bitterly cold. She hoped her dark slacks, and the black woolen beanie and jacket she'd snagged out of Ghillie's shed gave her some camouflage as she made her way through the bush. In her heart, she'd made peace with the fact she'd not make it

home alive. It had been hard not to leave Blane a goodbye.
A piece of her heart cracked. She loved the man and it hurt
to think she'd never see him again. But she would try her
darndest to get her grandparents out safely, if... she
swallowed, Obaje hadn't tortured and killed them already.

The sun dropped below the horizon by the time she
reached the edge of the clearing. A small fire burned
making it easy to spot the three men who sat around it.
There was a dim light inside the old cabin. Sadie hoped
Nan and Oupa were inside and safe.

She lay flat on the ground and pulled a pair of
binoculars from her jacket pocket. She'd grabbed them off
Malcolm's desk where they'd lain collecting dust. They
were old, but still in working order. It was dark, but thanks
to the fire Sadie could make out the men were sitting at the
back end of the cabin, cooking and drinking.

Obaje wasn't expecting resistance. He looked too
relaxed. She lay the binoculars down on the ground,
couldn't drag them along, and patted the hunting knife
hooked to her she'd taken from Ghillie's workroom.

Remaining within the cover of the trees, she circled
her target until she faced the front of the cabin. First, she
had to free her grandparents, then she'd go after Obaje.
She'd been taught in girl scouts how to leopard crawl, but
that was years ago. She hoped she could still do it with her
faux leg.

Before she left the safety of the trees, she closed her
eyes and visualized the Goddess. *Epona I call on you,
please spare them. Fill my blood with your strength, stoke*
my soul's *fire with vengeance and show me the way.*

As if in answer, a breeze stirred through the
branches of the trees and a distant owl hooted.

It was painful, and slow. She was out of breath and
covered in dirt by the time she reached the door. She
twisted and sat with her back against the wall of the
cottage, swallowing her need to gasp for air, and listened.
Obaje and his men gabbled away by the fire on the other
side of the cottage, obviously confident the two old folks
couldn't escape, and that Sadie would simply appear

waving a white flag. Using her good leg, she stood and peered through the window.

Her heart jumped into her throat. Bound together, sitting on the floor with only a small lantern for light, were Nan and Oupa. They looked unharmed for the most part except for a bruise across Malcolm's cheek.

She gripped the door handle and turned it.

Nan's muffled squeals caused her to speed up.

Please don't squeak, please don't squeak.

The door obeyed and opened without so much as a creak.

Agnus squirmed when she saw Sadie, who quickly put a finger to her mouth. She slipped the knife from its sheath, cut through their bonds, and removed their gags. Standing still a moment, Sadie listened to any change in chatter around the fire. She motioned for Agnus and Malcolm to follow her out of the cabin and across the field to the woods.

Oupa was limping without his cane and her leg protested against all the strain she put on it.

"Quickly," she urged the elderly couple as she peered over her shoulder. There was little to see in the dark.

They were halfway across when a voice called out.

"Hey! Hey!"

"Run! Don't stop. Don't look back. Run!" She pushed her grandparents forward.

Malcolm hesitated.

"For the love of the Goddess, just go!"

"Yew need tae come with us lass!" Agnus pleaded as she reached out to grab Sadie.

A bullet ricocheted off a rock at Agnus' feet.

"I'm coming. Go… run!" She pushed them again.

The pair turned and ran, believing Sadie was right behind them.

They vanished into the forest and Sadie skidded to a halt. It ended here, tonight, with her. She slipped the knife into her boot, unhooked its leather sheath off her belt and dropped it to the ground, then raised her hands and turned to find one of Obaje's lackeys running toward her.

He skidded to a stop.

"Where are they?" he shouted.

Sadie shrugged. The man lifted the butt of his rifle and slammed it into the side of her face. A jolt of pain sliced down her neck and into her spine as the world twisted, turned and went black.

Chapter 50

Zulu war drums thrummed against the inside of her skull. Sadie's eyelids fought the heavy lead pulling them closed, and the area where the butt of the rifle had connected with her head felt as though a ten-ton truck had rammed in the side of her face. Her tongue sat fat and parched like leather inside her mouth. Her vision blurred. And her body felt oddly immobile. Ugh, where was she?

Memories rushed back as the dancing flames of the fire in front of her took the shape of a man. He wore a dark colored beanie and matching jacket -- Obaje.

She waited for the paralyzing effects of fear to flood her body. But that did not happen. Instead, a fire like the one which burned before her, ignited within the depths of her soul and a resolve fed the flames until it ragged with vengeance.

The clouds had shifted allowing an ominous orange moon to shine down on them and Sadie was aware of a presence moving around them in the dark.

Obaje came to stand in front of her. Two beady black eyes looked at her. Even in the shadowed light afforded by the fire and devil's moon, it was easy to spot Obaje was on something. He was nervous, uneasy, and even with her vision affected she noticed his skin was clammy. Could he be suffering withdrawals? That made him extra dangerous. Sadie dared a quick glance at his hands. Sure enough, the telltale white track of a powdered line was smudge across the dark skin of his left hand, between thumb and index finger.

His gaze darted to a limp body lying on the ground, then back to her.

"You've been out for some time. I didn't want you dead… yet. He disobeyed me. Only I am allowed the pleasure of causing you pain."

He turned his head from her to the far side of the clearing.

"These woods are treacherous at night. Do you think Maruru has found them? He is well known for his tracking skills in his village. I told him to be quick about it. No more play time."

Sadie kept her face blank. She drew strength from the knowledge the Goddess was close by and would protect her grandparents. She tried to wipe the hair from her face. It was then she realized she was tied up. She hadn't felt the bonds or the cold until that moment. She looked to her sides and followed the large stumps, which stood planted on either side of her. Up, up, up to another running across the top. Her arms stretched to the point Sadie feared they might pop from their sockets.

"Ah, I see you are admiring my handy work. I decided to go with one of my old favorites. It's known by many names, but I like the original term — Strappado."

His fat lips hugged the gruesome torture title. His tongue flicked out as if to taste the thrill of what was to come.

Sadie's hands were tied behind her back, a rope around her wrists, and over the beam above. This had her arms stretched out behind her at a painful and awkward angle. He hadn't pulled it tight yet and she could still stand. But he would, and she would scream when he pulled that rope taut, lifting her, and placing enormous strain on her shoulder joints. She looked down. He'd stripped her of all clothing above her torso. She stood in only her bra, long pants, and boots. She wiggled her good ankle. The knife was still inside her boots.

Obaje made his way over to her. Grabbing her face between index finger and thumb, he lifted her head and squinted. She'd plaited her hair before leaving Munro Manor, but strands had pulled loose and clung to her face.

"I have yearned for my revenge. You killed my brother."

Sadie spat in his eye. "You slaughtered my people and my family!"

He would kill her no matter. Might as well make good use of her time left.

His free arm pulled back like a trigger, landing his fist squarely in her belly.

"Ompf!" Saliva and oxygen flew out of her mouth. He slapped her face to the side as he walked around her. His fingers traced the scars he'd left on her back, neck, and stomach. She bit down on her tongue as revulsion tightened its grip around her throat.

"Mmm, some of my best work. Ahh, and the sweet Mrs. Learie, she told me all about your leg. I shall enjoy taking the other. Balance out the score."

Obaje fidgeted behind her, and before Sadie could wonder what he was doing, the rope tightened.

"Aaah!"

Pain grated through her body as her arms were pulled back and up, lifting her onto her toes.

"That's better. Now I can see more of you."

He stepped back to look at her. She was already taller than him, but on her toes, she could look down at him. Anger took over. Ignoring the splicing pain in her arms, shoulder, neck, and spine. Sadie drew back her head and brought it down hard on his, nailing him on his bottom left eye socket.

Stars blinked in and out of her vision. She was sure her brain shook like jelly. She heard rather than saw Obaje stagger back. "Fucking bi…."

Obaje pulled back and gut punched her, this time with more gusto. All the air in her body was forced out through her mouth and the world went black once again.

It was still dark and freezing when Sadie came to. Her shoulder blades were numb, and her arms had lost all sensation. She looked around but saw no one. She prayed Nan and Oupa had gotten away safely, that they'd survive a winter's night out in the forest. Sadie drew in a painful breath and let it rush out. She prayed to the God of her mother and the Goddess of her father, who'd saved her. She called on death to be swift. But that would not be. A distant whinny pulled her back from the edge. A whisper drifted across the icy breeze. "*It is not your time. You are brave.*"

It was now or never.

Sucking in a deep breath, she used what little strength she had left and wiggled her hand until her right thumb joint leaned against the knot in the rope. She'd seen this done on a survival reality shows a long time ago. Biting her bottom lip, she prayed it worked. She took another deep breath as she bent her knees. Pain shot down her spine and into her neck. She jumped, using what little ground she had beneath her toes and picked up her feet. The force was just great enough for her body to slam down and knock the knot against her thumb and push the joint out of its socket. It jolted her shoulders and elbows. Dear God, she hoped she hadn't broken anything.

Sadie bit back an agonizing groan and slid her hand free of the bond.

Her right arm fell limp beside her body. She wiggled her shoulder and clenched her teeth as the blood rushed to her finger tips, bringing with it the scorching sensation of awakening nerves. She pulled at the bond and freed her other hand, then slumped to the floor. Once she had regained some movement in her arms and repaired her dislocated thumb, she dug out the hunting knife and snuck around to the front of the cabin. There was no light. She hoped Obaje lay sleeping inside.

An icy hand gripped her shoulder. "Leave you for two minutes and you try to escape."

There was no time to second guess or think, only do. Sadie stepped back, aiming the knife toward Obaje's carotid. But he was prepared and dodged her well-aimed blade, though the tip bit keenly into the flesh, slicing a bright red line across his chest.

Before he could recover, she took off. Her left leg battled to move and twice she fell over. A distant whinnying caught her attention as she stood, calmed her breath, and whistled.

Obaje had regained his composure and was in hot pursuit. A river of red staining the front of his shirt. Sadie changed direction and ran for the woods to the back of the cabin. With any luck that was where Blue would find her. A rock bounced off her back between her shoulder blades, sending her careening forward and hitting the wet dirt, face first. Obaje grabbed her legs and flipped her onto her back. He sat on her stomach pinching her arms down beneath his knees.

"Enough! Now you die!"

He reached for the knife she'd dropped and raised it above his head. Sadie tried frantically to wiggle free.

Time slowed, and peace washed over her. Behind Obaje stood her father, her mother, and her brother. They were whole and smiling. *I'm coming.* She reached out with her thoughts.

She watched as Obaje's eyes stretched and fear washed over his face. His body twisted as he flung his arms across his head. A large dark shadow jumped over him, knocking him off her. Time sped up.

Blue! Blue had heard her call.

Sadie rolled onto her side and tried to stand. Her left leg wouldn't work her arms were too exhausted to push her up. She looked around. Where did the mare go? Obaje came screaming toward her, knife in the air. A crack spliced across the frozen night and Obaje dropped to his knees. A hole the size of a two-rand coin opened between his eyes.

His hand fell, and his body followed.

Sadie turned and sat down on her bum. What had just happened? Blue came trotting up to her. "Hey girl."

"Sadie!" a voice called from the darkness.

She looked up to the horse. Nope, horses couldn't talk.

"Saaadie!" Her name echoed out across the open field.

Sadie turned, and from out of the woods ran Blane. Dressed in… Were those army fatigues? He carried a rifle in one hand as he sprinted toward her. It was only when he reached her she saw his face was covered in black oily paint.

"Oh, for the love of God, are you okay?" He slid on his knees and grabbed her shoulders causing her to wince.

"Yes," was all she managed before he leaned down and placed his lips on hers. His kiss soft at first, quickly intensified as his hands roved her body checking for injuries. Sadie delighted in the warmth of his touch.

A sharp whiney and stomping of hooves on frozen dirt pulled them from their frenzied greeting.

"He-he didn't..."

"No. I'm fine." She promised.

Blane grinned as Sadie motioned with a waving hand toward the mare. "Hush you."

Blane stood and pulled Sadie up to stand beside him before he wrapped his arms around her.

"It's time to go home." He pulled his thick cammo jacket off and wrapped her snuggly inside it.

The pair mounted Blue. Blane sat behind her as they rode back to Munro Manor.

\#

"Och, listen heer laddie, I dinnae need any moor of ye fussin," Malcolm ordered as he swotted away the young paramedic trying to disinfect a gash across his forehead.

"The man's only doing his job dear..." Agnus began before looking up top see Sadie and Blane stride into the house.

Ghillie who was standing off to the side of the library, explaining what had happened to a frustrated Inspector De Wit, stopped mid-sentence.

"Thank the Lord!" Agnus pushed past the paramedics and ran over to Sadie, Malcolm short on her heels.

\#

The sun sat like a plump egg yolk above the peaks of Ben More when the police were satisfied with their statements. The clouds had receded, and the day promised to be cold but sunny. A police patrol had radioed in to confirm they'd found three bodies around the old cabin area. "Well then, I think that is all for now." Inspector De Wit bade them a good day.

"Please come down tomorrow, just to confirm yer statements."

Mrs. Perkins and Mr. Foggart brought in a tray of tea and a mountain of sandwiches and cakes.

"Perhaps we can ask Annie to come tomorrow? The danger is over and the two of you could use some time off after this last week?"

"Oh, aye, I'll ring momentarily," Mrs. Perkins nodded as she placed her tray down and turned to go.

"Ye'll join us?" Agnus said, matter of fact.

Mrs. Perkins, Mr. Foggart, Ghillie, Mac, Agnus, Malcolm, Sadie, and Blane sat around the fire in the library sipping whiskey, and tea, staring at the food.

Sadie was first to break the silence. "How is Donn?"

"Och, she'll be right as rain in a few days the vet says." Mr. Foggart answered, a cup of tea in hand.

Malcolm dabbed his eyes with his handkerchief.

"I'm sorry about Prionnsa." Sadie placed a hand on Oupa's who nodded and chugged down his drink.

"How did the third man die?" She turned her gaze to Blane.

But it was Ghillie who knew the answer.

"Yer mare lass. It seems she came across the wee fool and stomped him tae smithereens, just beyond the wood at the back of the cabin."

Sadie nodded, not sure if she was proud or a little freaked out.

"That mare is worth more than her weight in gold," Blane said warmly. "She saved your life twice last night."

"Right, weer no wastin my fine food. Eet up," Mrs. Perkins stood and passed the tray around.

After everyone had nibbled on a sandwich, it was decided they needed their beds.

"I'll wake ye all fur supper," Mrs. Perkins said as she and Mr. Foggart collected the trays.

"Are you …okay?" Sadie asked the housekeeper and Mr. Foggart.

The woman's face was drawn, but her eyes were bright, and the butler looked his normal perfect self.

"Aye lass. T'was a shock, but it'd take moor than that tae turn the two o' us to jelly and tripe." Mrs. Perkins smiled before walking off tray in hand.

Sadie walked over to where her grandparents stood staring out the window.

"Will you be okay? Did he hurt you?" Sadie had to know.

Agnus stroked a hand down Sadie's face. "No sweet child. We were bait. Except for the wallop yer grandsire received for fighting back, he merely tied us up and dumped us on the floor."

Relieved, Sadie hugged them. Blane did the same then followed her up to her room.

"I need a bath," she said as she unzipped his jacket and dumped it on the floor.

Blane gently stroked her shoulder which were less swollen after she'd taken the pain tablets from the paramedics. "Will you be okay?"

"I've been through worse, and unlike most victims, I actually got to slay my demon... with a little help of course. Nice shot by the way."

Blane grinned. "I'll run the water?"

Chapter 52

Chan e seo an deireadh ach an toiseach.

**A woman with strength creates her own world
and attracts a man who will not want to change her.**

Sadie ran her fingers over the photo of her family
on the table beside her bed.
"I know you'll be there in spirit," she said to their
smiling faces before she walked up to the full-length
mirror.
Mrs. Perkins had set her hair in a traditional Celtic
braid. Her nimble fingers had then taken an hour to thread
a hundred small pearls in to the braid. Their soft off white
color bold against the red of her hair.
She picked a long black tube out of the small red
satin bag where she kept a meagre amount of makeup and
screwed open the top before she applied her mascara.
Closing the tube, she replaced it and picked up the 'red as
berries' lip gloss. She puckered her mouth then smacked
her lips together, "There… that'll do," she said as she
glanced down to where Donn lay at her feet.
She'd asked both Nan and Mrs. Perkins to give her
a few minutes alone after all their fussing.
She leaned back and took in the white lace and gold
trim of her bridal gown. No more makeup needed. Her
freckles were what made her.
It was Christmas Day, a little over a year after Mrs.
Learie's murder, and Obaje's attack. As good fortune
would have it, it snowed. The much-predicted white flurry
had proved the townspeople wrong the year before and
saved its best for this Christmas. The world outside was a
winter wonderland. A thick carpet of white covered
everything.
Things hadn't gotten easier after the trauma caused
by Obaje and Mrs. Learie's evil deeds. It had left her
grandparents shaken, not to mention Mrs. Perkins and Mr.

Foggart who'd starred death in the face. But the one thing
they all had and which in the end was their saving grace,
was each other.

It had also taken Blane a few months to let go of his
over protectiveness of her, and though it still tended to rear
its head every now and then, the couple had managed to
find a pleasant balance, one which both knew would serve
to strengthen their bond in years to come.

Sadie reached up and pinched her veil between
thumbs and forefingers to bring the single layer over her
tiara and covered her face.

"Ready?" She glanced down at Donn who jumped
to her feet and barked, tail wagging.

Malcolm waited at the top of the stairs for her. The
balustrades were draped with fresh green ivy and blood red
poinsettias. Her bouquet blushed with the same red flowers
trimmed with green ivy leaves.

"Ready lass?" Malcolm leaned in and kissed her
through her veil.

"As I'll ever be," she said and smiled.

They made their way down the stairs and out
through the front door. With some imagination and a little
help from all the townsfolk, the front of the manor had
been turned into a fairy land. People stood dressed in
gorgeous winter garb along the red-carpeted aisle, which
led straight to where Blane and the priest stood beneath an
arch woven out of wood. The wooden sculpture of the
Goddess was placed beside the priest. Her head adorned in
a crown of red and green. Beside him, his brother, and
behind them, Blane's parents.

Sadie had met his mother a few times over the last
year and loved her. The woman was typical upper-class
English, with a twist, his father, an English version of
Malcolm. Michael had come sans Cybil, now six months
pregnant. That was interesting news.

Donn trotted proudly beside Sadie as Malcolm led
her down the aisle. She rarely left Sadie's side since that
terrible day. Opposite Blane stood Blue and Agnus. Plaited
into her mane and tail were beads and lace to match Sadie's

dress, and hanging from a slim red ribbon around her neck, their rings.

\#

"Welcome home, Mrs. Buchan," Blane swept Sadie off her feet and carried her across the threshold of Saorsa.

His butler and housekeeper waited just inside, ready to welcome them back from their honeymoon in Kwa-Zulu Natal, South Africa. Sadie had wanted to show Blane her homeland. They'd met up with Selwyn. Past grievances were buried, and Sadie thanked him in person for all he had done for her and her family.

Sadie, with Blane's support, had gone back to her farm, closed that chapter of her life, and put it up for sale. Then she'd said good bye at her family's graves. Once all the heavy stuff was dealt with, a glorious three weeks was spent at the Wild Coast Sun.

"Now the hard work really does begin," Blane winked as he put her down and they greeted the staff.

"We have a town meet tomorrow, and the first of the research students arrive within the next week," he snaked an arm around her waist as they made their way toward their study.

"While I don't mean to speak ill of the dead, I can see matters progressing with a lot more ease than when Mrs. Learie was around." Sadie said as she came to stand by the large window behind her desk, which was moved in a few weeks before the wedding.

Now they were back in Scotland. Sadie couldn't believe how much she had longed for the tall purple mountains and the thick green of the forests.

"It's not sunny South Africa," he smiled at her.

"It'll do husband. It'll do."

She smiled and kissed him.

THE END

Author's Note

Epona came to me in a dream. A dark dream. A man with long dark hair, a runaway horse, and a woman who had survived the unspeakable against all odds.

Sadie Munro has a teaspoon of myself and a dollop of true blue South African in her veins.

Like Sadie, my maternal ancestors come from Scotland before farming sugar in Kwa-Zulu Natal South Africa.

And similar to Sadie, I have a passion for horses and have suffered the violence so rampant in the country of my birth; I carry my scars on the inside.

Epona shows the world that no matter the devastating heartache, love will always triumph. That life changes us, molds us, and if we allow it to, improves us.

Epona is my attempt to bring awareness to the farm murders destroying a once beautiful country, at the same time as it's a tale to carry its reader on a journey across continents and into the heart of true romance.

About Michelle Dalton

G'day, howzit, sanibonani, goeie dag.
My readers know me as Michelle Dalton, and my friends, as the call-a-spade-a-spade-South-African.
Originally from Pretoria, South Africa, Michelle Dalton and her family fled the rising

violence taking over her beloved country and
now lives near Brisbane, Australia with her
husband and triplet sons.
While juggling a nursing career and
teenage sons, she loves to escape into her
fictional world. Michelle has a deep love of horses
and enjoys weaving them into dramatic stories
with honourable men and strong women.
Her other hobbies are gardening (usually
trying to save her precious herbs and bulbs from
an overactive miniature Jack Russell), painting,
and reading. She's also a huge Star Trek and
Marvel Comics fan, and as of recently a wee fan of
DC too.

You can connect with Michelle here:

http://michelledaltonauthor.com

michelle@michelledaltonauthor.com

Other Books By Michelle Dalton

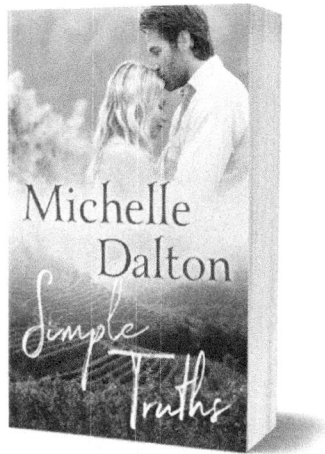

Can broken hearts reclaim their forever love?

A stolen kiss beneath the stars and the gut wrenching heartbreak which follows, rips apart Rochelle Le Roux and Thomas Campbell's young lives.

But when their paths cross over a decade later, they are forced to consider that maybe fate has brought them back together for a reason.

In a country fraught with danger, adversity, and cultural differences, can the long lost lovers face the simple truths for a chance at re-claiming their happy ever after, or will the pain of their past succeed in keeping them apart?

This thrilling, romantic suspense, and ARRA nominated first book in the Lost and Found series, is a must read by bestselling author Michelle Dalton.

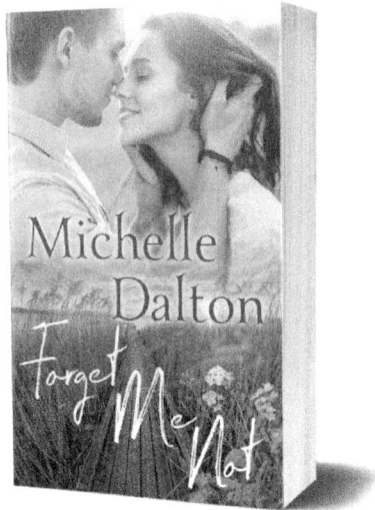

Will her heart remember when her mind cannot?

Isabella Irish has no memory before the day a terrorist bombing left her scarred and damaged.

Issi, having created a new life with a devoted fiancé, still grapples with the hollow darkness of her missing past.

Then a bouquet of Forget Me Nots are left at her front door and Issi begins to experience a strong sense of DeJa'Vu.

Is the stranger telling the truth? Is her fiancé really who he has claimed to be?

Will Issi find her lost past and true love? Or will she be forced to succumb to a life of darkness and terror?

From the bestselling author of Epona comes another epic love story you won't be able to put down.

Made in the USA
Las Vegas, NV
05 August 2021

27647522R00166